# Creatures Like Us?

### A Relational Approach to the Moral Status of Animals

Lynne Sharpe

IMPRINT ACADEMIC

Copyright © Lynne Sharpe, 2005

The moral rights of the author have been asserted
No part of any contribution may be reproduced in any form
without permission, except for the quotation of brief passages
in criticism and discussion.

Published in the UK by Imprint Academic
PO Box 200, Exeter EX5 5YX, UK

Published in the USA by Imprint Academic
Philosophy Documentation Center
PO Box 7147, Charlottesville, VA 22906-7147, USA

ISBN 1 84540 017 8

A CIP catalogue record for this book is available from the
British Library and US Library of Congress

Cover illustration:
The J. Paul Getty Museum, Los Angeles
Detail from *The Entry of the Animals into Noah's Ark*
by Jan Breughel the Elder 1613, Oil on panel 54.6 x 83.8 cm

# Contents

Acknowledgements . . . . . . . . . . . . . . . . . . . . . . vi

Introduction . . . . . . . . . . . . . . . . . . . . . . . . . . . 1

1. Us and Them . . . . . . . . . . . . . . . . . . . . . . . . 7

2. Friends and Neighbours . . . . . . . . . . . . . . . . 55

3. Nearest and Dearest . . . . . . . . . . . . . . . . . . 81

4. Beyond the Pale . . . . . . . . . . . . . . . . . . . . 113

5. Creatures Like Us . . . . . . . . . . . . . . . . . . . 169

Epilogue: Dogs, Frogs and Extraterrestrials . . . . . . 217

References . . . . . . . . . . . . . . . . . . . . . . . . . . . 223

Index . . . . . . . . . . . . . . . . . . . . . . . . . . . . . . . 227

# Acknowledgements

This book owes its existence to more people and animals than I can list here but particular thanks are due to Professor David Cockburn, whose enthusiasm and acuity helped shape an earlier version of it into a PhD thesis, and to Professor Stephen Clark who examined it, offering advice and suggesting publication. I fear that my text does not adequately reflect either my admiration for these two philosophers or the extent of their influence upon my work. I am also indebted to the late and much missed Professor Dick Beardsmore; to Professor Colin Lyas for reading the manuscript and encouraging me to publish it; to the publisher's readers, Mary Midgley and Dr Richard Ryder, and to my publisher, Anthony Freeman and his wife Jacqueline for their advice.

Above all my thanks to my husband Bob (Professor R.A. Sharpe) whose wisdom and humanity tempered the wilder excesses of my pen and without whose encouragement, support and unfailing patience this book would never have been published — not least because he typed the entire hand-written manuscript on to the computer.

*Lynne Sharpe*
*March 2005*

# *Introduction*

Like most children who share their homes with dogs, cats and other animals, my siblings and I never had any doubt that the non-humans in the family were essentially 'creatures like us'. Like us they mostly enjoyed company, games, exploring and fine weather and disliked being alone, enforced baths and wet days. There were differences of course — for one thing the animals enjoyed the privilege of staying at home while we went to school — but the differences seemed, on the whole, less significant than those between ourselves and adults.

It came as a shock, then, to discover that the acceptance of animals as pretty much like ourselves was not universal. For me it was not until I reached junior school that I realised the implications of this as teachers and other well-meaning adults attempted to persuade me that although 'of course' we must 'be kind to animals', we must never forget that they are still 'only animals' and that our 'kindness' must not be allowed to interfere with our acceptance of the fact that only humans *really* matter. Later on, when career choices were discussed, my determination to spend my life with animals was dismissed as frivolous, not suitable for anyone of reasonable intelligence and even as a wicked waste of time, effort and abilities that could only legitimately be devoted to human beings.

Not surprisingly, the attempts to change my attitude were counter-productive. Instead of distancing me from animals they made me feel increasingly alienated from human society. If my views were wicked, then wicked I must be, since I could not change them. Most frustrating of all, since I was never given any *arguments* to support the objections so often put to me, I had no opportunity of challenging them.

Many years later, when, aged forty, I found myself — almost by accident — on a philosophy degree course, I was delighted to learn that 'the animals issue' was increasingly attracting attention from philosophers. But again I was in for a shock, for I soon discovered that among the wide range of opinions held by these philosophers were all of the prejudices that I had met so often before. There was, however, an important difference, in that at least the opinions of the philosophers were supported by arguments and arguments were something I could challenge.

The selection of philosophers that I have chosen to discuss in this book may seem eclectic but it was made because the views they express reflect the range of those that I have heard most often expressed by the general public. What they all have in common is the conviction — often unquestioned — that Homo sapiens is not only 'special' but *superior* to all other species. Many of them also share a residual form of mind/body dualism which regards animals as essentially bodies while human beings (or at least, those of them who are 'like us') are essentially minds.

The advantage of having come late to philosophy is being able to draw on the accumulated experience not only of a lifetime spent in the company of animals as family, friends, neighbours and workmates but also of many different aspects of human life. Particularly influential has been my experience as a teacher, especially of language and languages, to all ages from pre-school to post-retirement and all abilities from 'special needs' to university level. My interest in language and communication has deepened through many years spent as an interpreter and translator. An earlier period of several years as a nurse to the elderly, the senile and the dying also helped to shape my thought.

Although the motivation for this book came from the challenge of those with whose views I disagree, it would never have been written had I not been emboldened by the discovery that I was not alone in holding the views that had been described as 'wicked' by my teachers long ago. The anthropocentric bias of much of my early philosophical reading had seemed only to reinforce that judgement but the work of Mary Midgley revived my confidence with its good sense and humanity and when I read Stephen Clark's books I felt vindicated indeed. I realised how much I had been affected by this support when, addressing a philosophy seminar on a chapter of this book, I was again called 'wicked' — by a professional philosopher — but this time I felt that the wrong was his.

I do not expect that *Creatures Like Us?* will change the views of such people or of the philosophers whose work I challenge but I do hope that it might give confidence to those who, like me, believe that 'we' are just one group of creatures among many, all of which have their own lives to lead on this shared planet which is no more 'ours' than theirs.

Chapter One starts by challenging the view that the moral status of animals can be decided according to whether they are 'like us'. I examine a number of claims that humans or 'persons' or 'we' are more valuable or more important than other creatures and argue that none of the cases made in support of these claims withstands close examination. I also conclude that the very idea of lives as having a measurable or comparable value is misconceived. Further, I suggest that the intellectual and introspective characteristics cited as evidence of 'our' superiority are not those which are most important to or about normal human beings and that these theories give a distorted view of humankind. Equally distorted is the view of animals as being merely concerned with seeking pleasure and avoiding pain; animal lives are therefore trivialized because of a failure to recognise that they — like us — have many interests and concerns which are quite as important to them as ours are to us.

One of the conclusions of Chapter One is that the philosophers discussed, in spite of their professed egalitarianism, are in fact deeply prejudiced in favour of their own kind and in Chapter Two I examine the evidence for this more closely in the context of attitudes to personal relationships. Again I find serious misrepresentation not only of animals but of humans too, especially in a tendency to underestimate the importance of relationships to all social creatures, including, of course, Homo sapiens. After a brief introduction to some social and historical evidence for contrasting theories about attitudes to animals, I discuss the importance of knowledge gained by living with animals in social relationships and the vital role that such understanding must play if discussions of the 'interests' of animals are to be valid.

Having amassed considerable evidence of a deep-rooted anthropocentric bias even among some philosophers who argue for animal rights or equal consideration of animal interests, I move on in Chapter Three to explore the widespread assumption that 'we' are at the top of a natural hierarchy in which all other creatures are ordered according to how closely they resemble 'us'. I challenge the view that language use and the introspective self-consciousness that it makes possible are the most significant features that any animal can have, arguing that they are neither necessary nor sufficient for membership of a mixed-species community. The failure to realise this is responsible for one of the leading advocates of equal consideration for the interests of animals making demands which could not possibly be in the interests of the animals concerned.

Using examples both from my own experience of living with animals and from such publicly observable human/animal partnerships as those with guide dogs and ridden horses, I contrast the mutually beneficial relationships with these language-less animals with the wretched lives of captive language-using great apes. The chapter ends by questioning not only the validity of the 'personhood' theory but also the notions of 'equal consideration of interests' and of 'speciesism' as analogous to racism.

The first half of the book has discussed the views of those who, although retaining the traditional view of humans as occupying the top place in the alleged species hierarchy, present their theories as a radical move towards equal consideration of the interests of all. In Chapter Four the focus switches to a group of philosophers who argue that animals are given too much consideration already and that this is anthropomorphic since any suggestion that they are significantly 'like us' is misguided. Like the first group, they believe that language-use is crucial to human experience and perception but they go further in arguing that even the pain of language-less animals is not comparable with that of humans.

My examination of these views, however, reveals that these thinkers also base their arguments on pre-conceived theories without any useful understanding of animals. In many cases their attempts to illustrate the differences between humans and animals serve only to emphasise similarities. I consider the use of the term 'anthropomorphism' — originally used for the belief that God could be described in human terms — and conclude that it is not an appropriate term to describe the mistakes that we sometimes make in our thought about animals, since, unlike

God, non-human animals really do have many things in common with humans and need not be a mystery to us.

Having dismissed various views that animals are either alien to us or that they are Cartesian automata more akin to machines than to human beings, in Chapter Five I first consider the ways in which we can and do come to know, to understand and to communicate with, our non-human fellows and then go on to explain my claim that at least some animals have an understanding *with* us.

The Epilogue is a short section in which I attempt to crystallise one of the main themes of the book by returning to the views with which I opened the discussion in Chapter One. John Harris is interested in the possibility of there being other 'creatures like us' among non-humans, not on earth but on other planets. Even a brief examination of Harris's suggestion that these alien 'people' would not only be sufficiently 'like us' to allow communication, but would also recognise us as 'creatures like them' and therefore 'valuable', is enough to show that Harris's optimism is ill-founded. There are, however, plenty of non-human 'creatures like us' living all around us on our shared earth.

# Chapter One

# Us and Them

*... weighed in the balance ... (Daniel 5)*

Of those philosophers who ask the questions 'what are our obligations to animals, do they have rights and what is their moral status?', many have chosen to answer by raising another question, 'are they like us?'. But *this* question can only be answered if we know who 'we' are, what are our defining characteristics, and what, if anything, gives us moral status. In this chapter I will first examine the view that the quality that defines 'us' is rational, self-conscious 'personhood'; then that which argues that 'we' are 'normal adult human beings' — which amounts to much the same.

Although it is generally agreed that 'speciesism' — usually defined as a prejudice against creatures not of one's own species — is analogous to racism and sexism and therefore unacceptable, the work of many philosophers who write on the animals issue seems to honour the letter rather than the spirit of the principle of unbiased objectivity. This is especially apparent in discussions of the 'value of life' put forward by such writers as Raymond Frey, Thomas Regan, Peter Singer and David DeGrazia, whose arguments reveal a prejudice which is even more pervasive than speciesism. Although the charge of speciesism is avoided by agreement that the lives of *some* animals are 'more valuable' than those of *some* humans, the criteria for inclusion in the category of 'normal human being' or 'person', taken as the paradigm of the valuable life, are such as to exclude not only animals but such a wide range of humanity that it seems reasonable to interpret this use of 'normal human being' as 'person like us' (the 'we' perhaps referring to the writer and his readers), so that speciesism is replaced by what might be called 'us-ism'.

Such a prejudice is perhaps unsurprising in a writer like Frey, whose book *Interests and Rights: The Case against Animals*, indicates his position, but it is remarkable that it should also be found in the views of Singer and Regan, whose titles include such classics of the animal liberation movement as *Animal Liberation*, *The Case for Animal Rights* and *In Defence of Animals*.

It should be noted that of the four philosophers named above, on whose work I shall concentrate here, only Singer and Frey frequently refer to the 'value of life' as such. Regan avoids talk of values of lives, preferring to speak of 'the magnitude of harm that death is', while DeGrazia writes of some lives being 'more sacrificeable' than others. In spite of these varied locutions, they all assume, not only that life has a measurable value, but that the life of a person like themselves is more valuable than any other. I believe that the views expressed are sufficiently similar to be considered together and, for ease of reference, I will refer to them collectively as 'the value of life view'. But I will start with a philosopher who, although not primarily involved in the animals debate, clearly shares the prejudices of those who are.

# I

John Harris opens the first chapter of his book *The Value of Life* with a statement of what is presented not just as his opinion but as a truth. For Harris, as for Singer, it is crucial that he proves the objective truth of his judgement because his aim is not to persuade us that his views are reasonable but to show us that they are *right* and *must* dictate our decisions and actions if they are to be moral. I shall argue that he fails to prove this. The claim at issue is that

> [t]he ultimate question for medical ethics, indeed for any ethics, is also in a sense the very first question that arises when we begin to grapple with moral problems. The question is simply: what makes human life valuable and, in particular, what makes it more valuable than other forms of life? [1]

But there are two immediate objections to this, which Harris does not even consider. The first is that we do not have to accept

---

[1] Harris 1985

that this question — or any other— is *the* ultimate question for ethics. Other philosophers have had very different priorities and many would deny that there can be an ultimate question at all. Secondly, even if we were to accept Harris's question as an important one, we might well argue that it must be preceded by another. That is, that the *first* question should be not '*what* makes human life valuable?' but 'can we make sense of the claim that human life, or any other life, *is* valuable'?

Harris, however, *starts* from the assumption that there is a 'special value' which 'attaches to human life'[2] and his inquiry is aimed at 'trying to identify those features, whatever they are, which both incline us and entitle us to value ourselves and one another, and which license our belief that we are more valuable (and not just to ourselves) than animals, fish or plants'.[3] The features identified by Harris are those which distinguish 'persons' as defined by the seventeenth-century philosopher John Locke for whom a person is '[a] thinking intelligent being that has reason and reflection and can consider itself as itself, the same thinking being, in different times and places'. For many philosophers currently involved in the animals debate, it is this self-conscious 'personhood', rather than mere membership of the human race, that defines 'us' and gives us moral status.

For Harris, the point of the personhood criterion is to tell us how we should treat the individual. If he is a person we must have concern for his welfare (defined as 'things like happiness, health and living standards')[4] and respect for his wishes. We might agree that persons are certainly entitled to this consideration, as are all creatures with wishes and welfare but Harris's 'personhood' is essentially *exclusive*, which implies that since this is what distinguishes our treatment of persons from our treatment of non-persons, then our treatment of non persons should be characterised by our *not* having concern for their welfare or respect for their wishes. We might object that it clearly is the case that many people *do* have concern for the welfare and respect for the wishes of at least some animals. Fido is taken for a walk in the park because Fido wants to go for a walk in the park. Tiddles is vaccinated against cat flu out of concern for her welfare. So does our treatment of them indicate that they are, in fact,

---

[2] Harris 1985: 8
[3] Harris 1985: 9
[4] Harris 1985: 193

persons? Harris is adamant that this is not so, arguing that 'People are not people because they are accepted, but rather they are accepted because they are people'.[5] The personhood approach is not a matter of deciding which creatures we *do* treat in particular ways but which creatures we *ought* to treat in particular ways. Harris seems to be saying that if we treat 'non-persons' with concern and respect we are mistaken in one of two ways. Either we wrongly take our response of recognition and empathy as an indication that the creature does have the 'requisite inner qualities' that justify our concern for it or we have failed to recognise the need for such justification. Whichever mistake we have made the result is the same; our response to the creature is unjustified because the object of our concern does not possess the only quality which could justify such concern.

For Harris, our concern for non-persons is not only mistaken, it is somehow not *real* concern at all. While allowing that the responses of non-persons to us do sometimes evoke in us feelings of empathy, he asks '[w]hat reason is there to suppose that we feel empathy only in the presence of self-awareness?,'[6] adding that the empathy evoked by non-persons (i.e. in the absence of self-awareness) is 'just the soggy sentimentality classically evoked by proximity to dependent sentient creatures, like puppies'.

We might expect that Harris would disapprove of any concern for animals at all but, on the contrary, 'although like embryos, animals do not have the status and protection that must be accorded to persons . . . we must remember that the very same reasons which make it wrong to inflict pain on persons make it wrong to inflict pain on any other sentient creatures'.[7] Unfortunately we are not told what these 'very same reasons' might be since Harris has not explained why it is wrong to inflict pain on persons. The obvious assumption that inflicting pain on a person is in contravention of both our duty of concern for his welfare and respect for his wishes is of no help in the case of animals because, as non-persons, they are specifically excluded from the group to which these duties are owed.

Can we make any sense of the distinction that Harris makes between pain and welfare ('health, happiness and living stan-

---

[5]  Harris 1985: 14
[6]  Harris 1985: 13
[7]  Harris 1985: 219

dards')? I do not believe that we can because pain is not separable from the other things in our lives; it affects our 'health, happiness and living standards' and the same is true for animals.[8] The tendency to over-emphasise the importance of pain to animals while trivialising their lives and deaths is characteristic of the writing of all the 'value-of-life' philosophers discussed here. Even DeGrazia, who allows that there are things that animals 'want to do', assumes that these things are less 'central and important' than the things that a human might want to do. But that the avoidance of pain is not invariably of paramount importance is obvious from the way in which animals, like humans, will put up with pain in order to do the things that are important to them. Observation of this can give a useful guide to their priorities. When an injured dog goes without his dinner rather than rise from his bed to eat but, seeing his companions going out for a walk, scrambles to his feet to hobble after them, it is reasonable to conclude that, on this occasion at least, avoidance of pain is more important to him than food but that following his companions — or just going for a walk — is more important than either. But if there are things in the dog's life that are more important to him than the avoidance of pain why should Harris's concern be for one but not the other? He seems to make an arbitrary distinction either between 'pain' and 'welfare' or between 'persons' whose happiness, health and living standards matter and 'non-persons' as beings whose happiness, health and living standards do not.

The explanation would seem to be that, according to Harris's theory, *nothing* can be important to the dog because for something to be important to an individual he must 'value' it and 'valuing is a conscious process and to value something is both to know what we value and to be conscious of our attitude to it'.[9] There is something very odd about Harris's use of 'value' here. We might well agree with his definition of valuing as a conscious process — indeed that is how the word is generally used — but object to the word because it has monetary and comparative implications which are not — or should not be — applicable to our attitudes to the things that we find most worthwhile. We do not have consciously to 'value' our friends, children, homes or occupations in order for them to be important to us. Yet the insis-

---

[8] A more detailed discussion of pain appears in Chapter Five.
[9] Harris 1985: 15

tence that we should is crucial to Harris's 'value-of-life' theory which deems the lives of all persons and only persons to be valuable because all and only persons are capable of 'valuing' their lives. Thus '[t]he reasons it is wrong to kill a person is that to do so robs that individual of something they (sic) value, and of the very thing that makes possible valuing anything at all . . . creatures that cannot value their own existence cannot be wronged in this way, for their death robs them of nothing that they can value'.[10] Clearly then, in Harris's view, non-persons are not only incapable of valuing their *lives* — they cannot be said to value anything at all. Harris's argument that animals 'cannot be wronged' by being killed is only one consequence of his view. The logical conclusion is that animals cannot be wronged by any deprivation at all because they cannot value *anything*. The implications of this are far-reaching and horrific. Because the class of non-persons includes not only embryos and puppies but all beings lacking sufficient language to qualify as persons, Harris's claim that animals cannot be wronged by being deprived must apply equally to all pre-linguistic children. We can take from them their teddies or their lives without doing them any wrong. Indeed, since Harris's reservations about medical research are limited to a concern that non-persons should not be caused to suffer *pain*, it seems that neither animals nor young children would be wronged if we were to deprive them (painlessly) of their sight, their legs or anything else that we might find interesting or useful to experiment with.

Even Harris's prohibition on the infliction of pain on animals (and, presumably, any other non-persons) turns out to be far from absolute. Although he argues that ' [s]ince animals cannot consent to pain or distress, the infliction of these upon them is always a case of torture', he continues 'and as such is justifiable only for the strongest of reasons'.[11] That is, it *can* be justified as long as the reasons are strong enough, and for Harris, of course, this does not mean that the reason has to be that the pain or distress is in the long term interests of the sufferer himself, as it might be in the case of veterinary treatment or the rescue of a trapped or injured wild animal, (in which case, pace Harris, we would not call it 'torture') but that it should be in the interests of a *person*. The infliction of pain and distress on animals is, for Har-

---
[10] Harris 1985: 18–19
[11] Harris 1985: 219

ris, in spite of his claim that it always amounts to torture, *justified* if it is 'necessary in order to save a person's life or to prevent *serious* injury or suffering to persons . . .'. That is, the pains of animals are important, but not, after all, as important as the pains of persons. Further, the loophole that this leaves in the prohibition on inflicting pain and distress on animals is a very wide one indeed, since Harris is particularly concerned with the use of animals in medical research and those who are engaged in such work invariably counter objections with the assurance that their use of animals, however horrific, does indeed save human lives and prevent serious human suffering.

These implications of Harris's view illustrate the all-pervasive effect of his belief in the supreme value of 'persons' and the inferior moral status of 'non-persons'. Like the other 'value-of-life' philosophers, Harris pays lip service to the principle that the infliction of pain on 'non-persons' is wrong, while ignoring the impossibility of detaching pain from all other aspects of life. Equally, the belief, again typical of the 'value-of-life' view, that the killing of non-persons is of little significance, is inextricably linked to the view that their lives are of little importance either. While Harris recognises that 'people's lives are made worthwhile by the friends, relatives and familiar things that surround them, as well as by the skills, pastimes and occupations that they have developed,' [12] he does not consider that the same could be said of dogs and indeed of most social mammals, and that self-consciousness is not relevant here.

Harris has offered no explanation as to *why* self-conscious beings should be accorded higher moral status than others. Yet it is by no means obvious that the presence or absence of self-consciousness makes it wrong to deprive one individual of something he 'values' (such as his Rolex watch), but not wrong to deprive another of something that is hugely important to him (such as his mother, friend or freedom). Although he is insistent that '[w]hen we treat any principle as inviolable we turn our backs on morality,'[13] he never questions the one principle on which his own theory depends: 'that it is right to treat people as the equals of one another and as the superiors of other creatures'.[14]

---

[12] Harris 1985: 250
[13] Harris 1985: 235
[14] Harris 1985: 9

As for the objectivity of his view 'that we are more valuable (*and not just to ourselves*) than animals' (my italics), Harris's argument is incoherent. He argues that what makes our lives *valuable* is not the same as 'what makes our lives worth living'. What is crucial is 'the *capacity* to value one's own life' and this is so even if one does not, in fact, value it. For Harris, someone who does not value his life is nonetheless a *person* 'for only someone with the capacity to value their (sic) life could disvalue it '.[15]

Harris is asking us to accept that our self-consciousness renders our lives valuable quite independently of whether we value them. But what sense can we make of our lives being valuable if they have no value to us? Is it that they might be valuable to others? The British philosopher, Ann Maclean argues that this cannot be Harris's answer because:

> As far as a person is concerned, the value of his life in the metaphysical sense is something that should constrain the behaviour of others towards him; it is *because* his life is valuable, according to Harris, that it would not be right — other things being equal — for others to kill him, for example, or allow him to die if they can prevent it. This remains true even if his life is of no value to them in some other sense or senses.
>
> So on Harris's account, just as a person's life can remain valuable in the metaphysical sense even when he himself has ceased to value it, so too it can remain valuable in the metaphysical sense even when others have ceased to value it also. The value, in the metaphysical sense, of a person's life is not — it would seem — its value to anybody at all; in which case I must confess that I do not know what sense to make of it.[16]

I have discussed and rejected Harris's claim that the life of a 'person' has an objective value which is not dependent on whether the individual values his own life or even whether it is of value to anyone else. My objection, however, is not only to the notion of lives having objective value, but also to the claim that persons can value their own lives and want to go on living them whereas animals cannot. I can make no sense of wanting my life to continue as separate from my desire to continue doing and experiencing the things that make up my life. A life with nothing in it would not be a life at all. All we can say is that our lives are made worth living by there being things which are important to

---
[15] Harris 1985: 17
[16] Maclean 1993: 29

us. But this is true of animals — and human 'non-persons' too: deprive them of their friends, relations, pleasures and interests and what is left of their lives? Harris's view suggests that their lives are never worth living anyway, because nothing is important to them. 'When a non-person loses its life, it loses nothing it can desire, it loses nothing it can value and hence nothing of value to itself. On the other hand, when a person loses her life, she loses not only *something* she values and desires, but *everything* she values and *all* her desires.'[17]

Based as it is on the spurious claim of the superior value of 'persons', Harris's position has little to recommend it. But although the 'personhood' theory has few adherents in the world beyond academic philosophy, we need only extend the class of 'beings of superior value' to include all human beings, rather than persons only, to have a position which is not only widely held but actually forms the basis of the legislation which governs the use of animals in scientific experiments in the UK. Since this legislation sanctions the infliction of acute suffering and death on millions of animals in British laboratories every year, its basis is not a matter of merely academic interest and it might be expected that it would have been subjected to the most rigorous examination. Yet as recently as July 2002 an 82-page report by the House of Lords Select Committee on Animals in Scientific Procedures limited its chapter on ethics to just half a page which, after a brief reference to 'people [who] hold that being sentient confers a moral right on animals that they should not be used by human beings for research whose purpose is mainly to benefit humans,'[18] continues: 'More commonly, there are those who hold that the whole institution of morality, society and law is founded on the belief that human beings are unique amongst animals. Humans are therefore morally entitled to use animals, whether in the laboratory, the farmyard or the house, for their own purposes.'[19] The next paragraph expresses '[t]he belief that human beings have the moral right, and in some contexts the moral imperative, to use animals in research'. Although we are offered no arguments to support this extraordinary claim, it appears to be accepted by the committee, since the 'ethics' section of the report ends with the statement that ' the unanimous

---

[17] Harris 1998: 58
[18] Select Committee Report: para 2.2
[19] Ibid: para 2.3

view of the Select Committee is that it is morally acceptable for human beings to use other animals, but that it is morally wrong to cause them unnecessary or avoidable suffering'.[20]

Again, this statement is unsupported and I can only assume that paragraph 2.3 is supposed to explain it, which it clearly cannot do. We are not told what it is that makes human beings unique, nor is it clear whether the uniqueness applies to individual humans or to the species Homo sapiens. It is obvious that, in a trivial way, all individuals are unique, simply by virtue of *being* individuals, and that this is true regardless of species. It is also obvious that although Homo sapiens may be in some ways a unique species, the same could be said of many other species. In any case, the alleged uniqueness of humans invalidates the use of animals as experimental 'models' for human reactions, whether physiological or psychological. If humans are truly unique, only medical research carried out *on humans* will be of relevance: if animal research *is* relevant, the animals used must be significantly *like us* and the uniqueness of humans, claimed as a justification, is anthropocentric nonsense.

Not only is the claim for human uniqueness both vague and unsupported, it is also irrelevant to the case since it cannot be used to claim moral entitlement for one individual, group or species to inflict suffering on another individual, group or species which does not consent and will not benefit. The Committee's conclusion was nonetheless welcomed by the Government which declared that it 'shares the Select Committee's view and believes it to be the view held by the great majority of people in the United Kingdom'.[21]

The claim that this is a generally accepted view is disputed by the British Union for the Abolition of Vivisection, whose submission to the Select Committee[22] quotes a number of independent opinion polls by MORI and others which indicate that public opinion is much more divided than the Government statement suggests. Even if the view was a majority one, however, it would not follow that it is 'morally acceptable'. The report's wording might be taken as implying that the majority view is necessarily the right one and the apparent acceptance of paragraph 2.3 of the

---

[20] Ibid: para 2.5
[21] Government Reply to the Select Committee's Report: p. 2
[22] BUAV's Submission to the Select Committee June 2001 p. 9 'Public Opinion'

Report seems to support this assumption. But it is by no means obvious that this should be so unless 'morally acceptable' is defined as whatever the majority supports. It is very likely that a majority of British voters would support capital punishment but there are no plans to re-instate it on the grounds that it is therefore morally acceptable.

What *is* likely is that many people would take the Select Committee's condemnation of 'unnecessary or avoidable suffering' as an assurance that licensed experiments cause little distress to the animals involved. This would be quite wrong, however, since experiments which do *not* cause suffering do not have to be licensed. Those which are licensed are, by definition, those 'which may have the effect of causing [an] animal pain, suffering, distress or lasting harm'.[23] The Home Office figures for the year 2000 show that 2,714,726 such experiments were carried out in the UK, 60% of them without any anaesthetic at all.[24]

Just as Harris's apparent prohibition on the infliction of pain on animals proved to contain so large a loophole as to offer very little practical protection, so is the condemnation of 'unnecessary or avoidable suffering' obviously no more than a fig-leaf which does nothing to cover the anthropocentrism on which vivisection depends. For the implication that the suffering caused by 'legitimate' experiments is necessary or unavoidable depends upon the prior acceptance of the claim that it is 'morally acceptable' for animals to be used in this way. By parity of argument, a burglar could claim that his torturing a householder was morally acceptable because it was necessary in order to get the keys of the safe. In this case it is obvious that he cannot justify his actions by reference to 'his own purposes' and we have been given no reason to think that the use of animals in laboratory experiments for 'our own purposes' is significantly different. I believe that the only morally acceptable justification for the infliction of suffering on an animal is that it is in the longer term interests of the individual animal itself, in which case the suffering may legitimately be described as the necessary or unavoidable cost of its future well-being. The licensing of animal experiments in the UK is indeed based on what is known as the 'cost/benefit test', but there is a crucial difference, for in this case the costs are all borne

---

[23] 1986 Act section 2 (1)
[24] BUAV Supplementary submission to the Select Committee January 2002

by the animal while any benefit is to others, notably to the business interests of the companies involved.

> In determining whether and on what terms to grant a project licence the Secretary of State shall weigh the likely adverse effects on the animal concerned against the benefit likely to accrue as a result of the programme.[25]

There is considerable evidence that the supposed 'benefits' are frequently far from 'likely'[26] and no legitimate formula could weigh these nebulous gains against the real suffering of the animals but even if such calculations were possible they would not amount to a justification for a practice which involves knowingly inflicting suffering on animals for the benefit of others. (And the implication in 2.2. of the Report, quoted above, that opponents of vivisection would not object if the beneficiaries were other *animals* is surely wrong. That one animal should be made to suffer for the benefit of other animals is no more morally acceptable than that one innocent and unconsenting human should be made to suffer for the benefit of other humans.) The implication of Section 5.4, also quoted above, that even the most extreme suffering inflicted on the animal can be 'morally acceptable' provided that the benefit (which may be only financial) is likely to be substantial, is outrageous.

In the absence of any other explanation, it seems that the Select Committee's view, which is shared by the Government, is based on Para 2.3. of the report, which claims that the alleged uniqueness of humans entails their being 'morally entitled to use animals, whether in the laboratory, the farmyard or the house, for their own purposes'. I have argued that this claim is unwarranted. However, if, as I suspect, the thought behind the claim is that the 'uniqueness' of humans makes them a *superior* species, the attempt to use this as a justification for using other creatures as 'tools' or 'products' is suspect, since a species which treats others in such ways can hardly be regarded as superior to them. Is such 'superiority' any more than the 'might is right' of the schoolyard bully and the vicious dictator? We conceive of our species as typified by its 'humanity' and by its being 'humane'. To be humane is to be kind, tender and merciful, to act with forbearance to those in one's power, which is incompatible with the

---

[25] 1986 Act section 5 (4)
[26] See BUAV documents above

notion that being 'unique' or 'superior' entitles us to 'use animals for our purposes' or that there might even be a 'moral imperative to use animals in research'.

## II

The Australian philosopher Peter Singer is a long-standing opponent of the use of animals both in laboratories and in intensive (or 'factory') farming. His 1976 book, *Animal Liberation*, which gives a detailed account of the practices involved and the objections to them, has won many supporters throughout the world and it is sad to reflect that, nearly thirty years later, the situation he describes has not improved and that the abuses he exposes are now more widespread than ever.

Singer's work in this field is rightly respected for its sincerity and effectiveness and he is widely regarded as a leader of the animal liberation movement.[27] There is, however, another side to Singer's position which is at odds with his fight against what he describes as 'the tyranny of human over non-human animals',[28] for, like Harris, Singer is an adherent of the 'personhood' theory and his views on the value of life are broadly similar to those of Harris. Just as Harris condemned the human empathetic response to 'dependent sentient creatures', so Singer dismisses the protective attitude evoked by 'the helplessness or the innocence of the infant Homo sapiens' [29] as a sentimental susceptibility to the appeal of what he refers to as the 'cute and cuddly'. Urging us to 'put aside these emotionally moving but strictly irrelevant aspects of the killing of a baby', he assures us that if we do so we will recognise that babies, as 'non-persons', are only entitled to protection from suffering, not from being killed and that 'the grounds for not killing persons do not apply to newborn infants'.[30] Singer's suggestion that we have — or need — 'grounds for *not* killing persons' (my italics), with its implication that we can kill babies without having any 'grounds' at all, echoes Harris's demand that we be able to *justify* our concern for others. Harris explains that his 'concept of the person sets out to

---

[27] He was visited in America by the Select Committee who, having heard his case, appear to have dismissed his views with a brief footnote to 2.2 of the Report.
[28] Singer 1976: vii
[29] Singer 1997: 170
[30] Singer 1997: 171

identify which individuals and which forms of life have the sort of value and importance that makes appropriate and justifies our according to them the same concern, respect and protections as we grant to one another'.[31] This view that it is compassion, concern and respect which need to be justified, while neither grounds nor justification are needed for the killing of innocents, is presented as the judgement of rationality over emotion. (Singer and Harris would argue, of course, that they *do* have grounds and justification for the killing of babies and animals; but this hardly represents the rhetoric of the arguments: it is what babies and animals *lack* which makes it permissible to kill them — they are not 'persons'.) And here we see the full force of what Singer deems 'rationality'. It is not just that rationality is an essential component of personhood, it is also that rationality ought to dictate the *actions* of persons. Rationality is normative. But in presenting morality as a matter of rationality versus emotion, Singer is guilty of an ancient error. There is nothing *irrational* in the view that babies are to be protected and cared for. Indeed, I would go further and say that there is nothing irrational in the view that all creatures are to be protected and cared for. Instead of assuming that all lives are at our disposal unless we have 'grounds' to respect them, why should we not assume that *no* lives — except our own, perhaps — are at our disposal? Is there not a very good argument for putting the onus of justification on those who do kill, rather than on those who do not?

Like Harris, Singer presents his view of the value of life as objective, but his method of demonstrating this is different. Having argued that Harris's claim to objectivity failed, I now want to examine Singer's. While Harris sees the personhood criterion as a threshold above which all persons are of equal value, Singer allows that there may be degrees of self-awareness and hence degrees of value. Unlike Harris, he does at least raise the question of 'whether we can accept the idea of ordering the value of different lives at all',[32] but his assurance that we can is based, not on an objective judgement (as he — like Harris — claims), but on assumptions which are both anthropocentric and speciesist. Sensitive to the charge of speciesism against the view that 'the life of a normal adult member of our species is more valuable

---

[31] Harris 1985: 18
[32] Singer 1997: 106

than the life of a normal adult mouse',[33] Singer looks for 'some neutral ground, some impartial stand-point from which we can make the comparison'[34] and 'defend such a judgement' — and believes that he has found it. But far from solving the problem, Singer's solution seems only to convict him of the very charge of bias that he has tried so hard to avoid. He asks us to imagine that he possesses 'the peculiar property of being able to turn myself into an animal'[35] and that, having lived as both human and horse, he 'can enter a third state in which I remember exactly what it was like to be a horse and what it was like to be a human'.[36] In this curiously stateless state, Singer imagines himself choosing which life he would rather live, human or horse, and concludes triumphantly; 'I would then be deciding, in effect, between the value of the life of a horse (to the horse) and the value of the life of a human (to a human)'. 'Fairly confident' that this solves the problem, Singer assures us that, after all, 'it would not necessarily be speciesist to rank the value of different lives in some hierarchical ordering', and that '[i]n general it does seem that the more highly developed the conscious life of the being, the greater the degree of self-awareness and rationality and the broader the range of possible experiences, the more one would prefer that kind of life, if one were choosing between it and a being at a lower level of awareness'.[37] But who is the 'one' who 'would prefer that kind of life' if not Singer himself? Since the point of the exercise was to gauge the 'value of the life of a horse (*to the horse*)' (my italics), rather than from a human point of view, the conclusion as to which life *'one* would prefer' (my italics) is irrelevant and the move from 'this is the kind of life *I* would prefer' to 'this kind of life is more valuable' is illegitimate.

Can we, then, make anything of Singer's suggestion that he can imagine the experience of being a horse? As one who probably spends as much time in the company of horses as of people, I have to admit that I don't even know how to attempt such an exercise. Nor do I believe that the problem is one of species: I have no more success when I try to imagine living the life of my husband. My best efforts seem to amount to no more than imag-

---

[33] Singer 1997: 106
[34] Singer 1997: 106
[35] Singer 1997: 106
[36] Singer 1997: 106
[37] Singer 1997: 107

ining myself doing — and enjoying — the things that my horses and my husband respectively do and enjoy. But even the very simplest attempts — such as imagining that I enjoy eating olives, instead of thinking them revolting, as I do — do not obviously count as the requisite sort of imagining. In any case, the thought that a comprehensive A-to-Z catalogue of such imagining would give me the 'impartial stand-point' from which I could decide whether I would rather live my life, my husband's or a horse's seems absurd.

It is important to distinguish between the difficulty — or impossibility as I believe it to be — of imagining living the life of another and the difficulty of understanding the feelings of others. My total lack of interest in football prevents me from sharing my husband's enthusiasm for it but does not prevent me from understanding its importance to him. That horses are of no interest to him doesn't prevent his appreciating that to me they are an endless source of fascination. When, on a frosty January morning, the dogs hurl themselves into an icy stream with obvious delight, I can imagine all too well how I would feel if I joined them. Delight is not a word I would choose to describe my reaction, but I do know what delight feels like and I recognise it in the dogs. Would I choose to be a creature to whom an icy plunge on a January morning is a delight? That is a question I cannot begin to answer.

Again I want to emphasise that this problem is not peculiar to our thoughts about other species, but applies equally to other humans. Some humans probably love to plunge into icy water, some dogs probably love olives (I once had an Irish Wolfhound with a passion for pickled gherkins) but the best that I can do is to suppose that these pleasures to them are roughly equivalent to the pleasures of hot baths and grapes to me.

Singer's shape-shifting thought experiment was intended to answer the objection raised by those who 'say that it is anthropocentric, even speciesist, to order the value of different lives in a hierarchical manner. If we do so we shall, inevitably, be placing ourselves at the top and other beings closer to us in proportion to the resemblance between them and ourselves'.[38] I believe that he has failed to find the impartial stand-point that he needed to prove the objectivity of his judgement and thus justify his 'hier-

---

[38] Singer 1997: 105

archical ordering', and since, on his own admission, he has
'nothing better to offer than the imaginative reconstruction of
what it would be like to be a different kind of being', [39] his argument fails.

One reason for the confidence with which Singer decided that he
would rather be Singer than a horse might be his tendency to
equate animals with defective human beings. This negative view
of non-humans as deficient rather than different is typical of the
value-of-life philosophers who insist on regarding normal animals as on a par with mentally defective, disabled or senile
human beings — the 'marginal cases', as they are often referred
to. Some animals, like some humans, suffer physical, mental or
psychological defects and it does not seem unreasonably biased
to regard this as a deprivation or handicap, compared to a normal creature of the same species. It *is* unreasonably biased, however, either to treat perfectly normal animals as defective
humans (see further below) or to move from the recognition that
some animals and humans are handicapped, to the conclusion
that their lives are either less worthwhile or less valuable, in the
'value-of-life' sense of 'more sacrificeable'. If I were to lose my
right arm I would consider myself to be both handicapped and
deprived but I certainly wouldn't consider my life to be more
expendable.

Perhaps it is a determination to avoid being labelled 'less valuable' that leads some humans to deny that they are handicapped
at all by the absence of some 'normal' abilities. The philosopher
Martin Milligan, blind from infancy and with no recollection of
visual experience, wrote on this subject in his correspondence
with the philosopher, Bryan Magee. In answer to Magee's query
as to whether such blind people appreciate the extent of their
deprivation, Milligan agreed that 'blindness is a major handicap
and deprivation' but went on

> You would be wrong to imagine, however, that no one could
> possibly say otherwise. There are a substantial number of
> intelligent and competent blind people in the USA who support the views repeatedly propounded by Tom Jerrigan to
> the effect that blindness is not a handicap but just a difference, and that particular differences can be in some circum-

---

[39] Singer 1997: 107

stances handicapping and in others advantageous, and that is true of blindness. I disagree with that because I believe that blindness is a 'difference', which is so disadvantaging in such a wide range of frequently encountered circumstances that those who suffer from it should count themselves, and be counted as, suffering from a serious general handicap.[40]

Since I don't believe that I can experience blindness by closing my eyes or languagelessness by refraining from speaking, I cannot even imagine how life is for many human beings, let alone members of other species. I am fairly sure that if I could experience human life without sight or without language and then choose between that life and my own, I would choose the latter, but that is not to say that such a life is more valuable in the sense that it is less wrong to kill those who do not share the full range of 'normal' abilities.

A serious mistake is made, however, by those who fail to realise that in normal animals, the absence of some human abilities really *is* 'not a handicap but just a difference'. That an animal, of whatever species, does not speak or write books does not make it comparable with a defective human anymore than the human's inability to fly makes him comparable with a defective bird. But, for Singer, life as a horse would be like life as 'a person with an intellectual disability' as is clear when he refers to J.S. Mill's famous assertion that 'It is better to be a human being dissatisfied than a pig satisfied; better to be Socrates dissatisfied than a fool satisfied,' and comments:

> Mill's argument for preferring the life of a human being to that of an animal... is exactly parallelled by his argument for preferring the life of an intelligent human being to that of fool. Given the context and the way in which the term 'fool' was commonly used in his day, it seems likely that by this he means what we now refer to as a person with an intellectual disability... as Mill's argument suggests, it is not easy to embrace the preference for the life of a human over that of a non-human, without at the same time endorsing a preference for the life of a normal human being over that of another human at a similar intellectual level to that of the non-human in the first comparison.[41]

---

[40] Magee & Milligan 1995
[41] Singer 1997: 108

The assumption that the life of an intelligent adult social mammal — a pig in Mill's example, a horse in Singer's — is on a par with that of a human with 'an intellectual disability' is a pervasive influence in the 'value of life' debate and deserves closer attention. The Singer/horse case is not 'exactly parallelled' by the Singer/fool case since an 'intellectually disabled' human has no alternative to living the life of a human being and is likely to be genuinely handicapped as a result, whereas a lack of human abilities is no handicap to a horse, whose particularly equine abilities equip him superbly to live a horse's life. A human who fails to realise that this is 'just a difference' is guilty of anthropocentrism. It is interesting to note that horses do not make the same mistake about human beings. As I describe elsewhere, my horses certainly take account of my relative frailty and lack of physical size and accord me the physical protection appropriate to a foal. They do not, however, assume that I am therefore equivalent to a foal or a defective horse in social status or psychological ability. That they are able to recognise a member of another species as different rather than defective suggests that they have an ability lacking in many philosophers.

In Chapter Five I will discuss the case of Clever Hans as a well-documented example of the acute perceptiveness of horses which enables them to 'read' the behaviour of others, including humans, even when the signs are so slight as to be unnoticed by the most attentive human 'experts'. Singer's reference (quoted above) to the horse as 'a being at a lower level of awareness' is astonishing to anyone who is familiar with horses, but to Singer, of course, the only awareness of interest is *self*-awareness. It is perhaps unsurprising that a being obsessed with the contemplation of his own thoughts and feelings should be less skilled at noticing those of others.

## III

Singer's assertion that 'the broader the range of possible experiences', the more desirable the life suggests a totting up process to produce a score by which we can decide where in the 'value' hierarchy any individual life fits. This is the method favoured by the philosopher David DeGrazia of the George Washington University in support of his claim that human life is more valuable than animal life (De Grazia 1991).

DeGrazia's arguments in support of this claim betray the 'us-ist' prejudices typical of the 'value of life' argument. In speaking of the 'interests different animals have in life',[42] he makes the seemingly uncontroversial statement that; 'a cat has an interest in continuing to live a cat's existence, while a human has an interest in continuing to live a human existence'. DeGrazia continues: 'That is why it makes sense to say (and, I think, is true) that death takes away things of different value when it takes away the lives of cats and of humans.' DeGrazia's claim that this conclusion can be drawn from the preceding premiss is unjustified and, far from 'making sense', it introduces the notion of 'value' which is absent from the premiss. It might well be agreed that the lives of cats and of humans are different without this entailing a difference in *value*: that apples and pears are different is generally taken as evidence of their incomparability. That I might have a preference for apples is not to say that they are necessarily of greater value than pears. An additional problem is the ambiguity of the phrase 'things of different value' which fails to distinguish between type and degree. We frequently distinguish between objects of 'sentimental' value and those of monetary value: some — a wedding ring, for example — might have both. That these are different values does not mean that one is greater than the other: they are different types of value and cannot be compared. By contrast when we speak of coins as being of different value there is usually no such ambiguity: the difference is one of degree. That a twenty pence piece may be more valuable to me than a five pound note in some circumstances, such as when I need to use a public telephone, only serves to illustrate the significance of context when comparing values. Whether the note or the coin is more valuable to *me* depends on what I want it *for*.

I want to suggest that the values of lives can only be commensurable if lives are means to ends, as seems to be suggested by the practice currently under discussion, of weighing the value of one life against that of another as if lives were money bags, the value of which could be reckoned simply enough by the bank teller placing them on the scales. Yet placing the bags on the scales — or perhaps totting up the number of coins that each contains — is pretty much what is advocated by this line of argu-

---

[42] De Grazia 1991: fn 15

ment. DeGrazia summarizes the views of Frey and Regan and adds: 'I make essentially the same point as Frey and Regan by asserting that the death of a human thwarts more interests, and more important or central interests, than the death of an animal, so that the former is the greater harm.'

My own response to this 'totting up', together with the quite unsupported claims about the importance and 'centrality' of human interests is shared by the American philosopher Kathy Squadrito (whose commentary on DeGrazia's article appeared in the same publication). Squadrito writes:

> Since, in general, white males tend to do more various types of important things than blacks and women, we might as well conclude that they have a higher moral status.
>
> We may deem some interests to be more important than other interests, but I doubt that this is based on any objective criterion. To consider our own interests and opportunities more important and central in some cosmic sense is an elitist position that I cannot defend.[43]

DeGrazia applies the same 'number crunching' method to his assessment of the harm caused to individuals of different species by the loss of their freedom. We can measure the harm caused, he tells us, by considering '*the range and nature of things an individual wants to do*' (original italics). In general, DeGrazia believes, humans want to do more things than dogs do, and he adds: 'I ask the sceptical reader to consider all the things she wants to do in the next, say, five days, and where she would have to go to do them.'

Well suppose there is nothing I want to do in the next five days but carry on working on this book, just where I am now. There is nowhere I want to go. Not so the six dogs who share our lives. They want to go to the beach and are trying to lure me to the car. If I ignore them they will eventually lower their sights and agitate instead for a walk in the forest by trying to draw my attention to my hiking boots. No doubt they would also like to play ball, paddle in the stream, have a biscuit and, after all that, to go upstairs and sleep on our bed. There is no denying that 'the range and nature of things' that they want to do greatly exceeds that of my single desire. Yet DeGrazia is confident that his 'sceptical reader', after making the comparison, will agree that it

---

[43] Squadrito 1991

gives 'us' a reason 'for preferring the use of animals over humans in (freedom-restricting) research'.

DeGrazia's 'totting up' method clearly fails, and not only because the sums do not — in my case at least — add up to a justification of his claim that loss of freedom 'does more violence to a human's plans than it would to the totality of things the dog would want to do'.[44] It fails because we cannot compare the wrong that imprisonment is to two individuals by asking each 'to consider all the things she wants to do in the next, say, five days, and where she would have to go to do them'.

This method is as absurd when applied to two humans or two dogs as it is when applied between the species. Suppose that two women are confined to their respective homes. They have free access to all the usual household comforts so they can eat, sleep, wash, read, listen to music etc. as they wish; the only restriction is that they cannot go out. We decide that, after all, we need only one for our research study and we are ready to release whichever can be shown to be suffering the greatest frustration of her interests as a result of confinement. Using DeGrazia's method, we ask each woman to list all the things she wants to do and where she would have to go to do them. Mary has an appointment with the hairdresser, wants to meet a friend for coffee and had been looking forward to a day's shopping in London. Jane has only one desire, which involves no more than stepping outside her front door to reach her three year old daughter who is lying badly injured on the doorstep, screaming for her mother. On DeGrazia's reckoning there is presumably no dispute: we tot up the numbers, which show that Mary has 'greater moral status' where freedom is concerned and is therefore the obvious candidate for release. To substitute two dogs — or two bitches — for the two women in this case would make no difference. If Penny and Patch are confined to the house it does not seem reasonable to judge that Penny suffers a greater thwarting of her 'freedom-interest' because she would like to sit on the lawn, play ball, jump in the fish pond and dig up the flower-bed whereas Patch — a devoted mother — is so frantic to reach her injured puppy crying outside that nothing else concerns her.

My examples are intended to show that DeGrazia's method of assessing and comparing the 'freedom-interest' of different indi-

---

[44] De Grazia 1991: 75

viduals or different species can lead to counter-intuitive conclusions. My objection to his argument, however, is not simply that the sums do not add up as we think they should, but that sums are irrelevant here, because the wrongness of imprisoning or killing an individual, of whatever species, cannot be measured according to his plans for the future. That I intend to spend the day working in my study does not entitle you to sneak up and lock me in, anymore than my deciding to spend the rest of my life doing nothing absolves you of blame if you kill me. The wrong that you do in locking me in cannot be measured in terms of what plans, if any, you might have frustrated. What you have done is to deprive me of control of my situation and this seems to me to be basic. Having control over one's situation is not only important to humans but to animals too. My horses make much use of their stables for shelter and comfort but they prefer to choose whether to be in or out. If shut in or shut out they will knock on the doors until they are opened but what they want is not necessarily to go in or out but to have the choice. The failure to recognise that to be able to control one's environment is not an exclusively human desire is the cause of much animal suffering. Even mice, it seems, like to choose for themselves whether to have lights on or off, as is shown by an extensive study from which the researcher concluded that the mice showed 'a complex interplay of tendencies to modify features of the environment, to avoid conditions imposed compulsorily and to select preferred levels of illumination'.[45]

My horses also like to be able to turn their stable lights on and off and used to be allowed to do so until, faced with an alarming electricity bill, I took to disconnecting the power when I went to bed, only to find that the pull-cords were wrenched out of their fittings by frustrated horses. If this need to be in control is important to species as diverse as horses, mice and men, it may well be far more widespread than is generally believed and suggests that the deprivation that captivity causes is not limited to the frustration of plans for the future. Few would disagree that an imprisoned human being, even in the most luxurious accommodation, suffers from the loss of control over his life. I believe that a serious mistake is made by assuming that an animal in comparable circumstances 'wants for nothing'. De Grazia's belief that

---

[45] Kavanagh 1967: 1638

the wrongness of imprisonment could be measured according to 'the range and nature of things an individual wants to do' takes no account of the possibility that imprisonment is wrong simply because it removes control from the prisoner, regardless of what he does or doesn't want to do. Marian Stamp Dawkins discusses the importance of identifying the preferences of animals and describes 'choice' tests devised to show not only what is preferred but how much it matters to the animal in comparison with other things.

> Animals do not just choose or express a preference. They can be made to put a price on what they choose and to tell us how important something is relative to the other things in their lives.... An animal that tells us by its behaviour [that it] gives something such high priority that it is prepared to give up everything else for it, including the chance to feed, is effectively saying a great deal about the importance it attaches to that particular thing and the extent to which its life is dominated by the need for it.[46]

This is enormously useful and important work but what does not seem to have been considered is that it is not only the 'particular thing' that is important, but the freedom to choose.

DeGrazia concludes that, since the totting-up method yields the result that both the freedom of animals and their lives are 'more sacrificeable' than those of humans, 'there are two prima facie reasons to prefer the use of animals over humans in freedom-restricting research that ends in the subject's death'. I believe that both his method and his conclusion are invalid.

DeGrazia's tally of the 'range and nature of things an individual wants to do' cannot be used to compare wrongs in the way that he wants it to do, but it can tell us something of great importance about the wrongs of confinement and deprivation in general. That my dogs have a very considerable range of things that they want to do is a result of their having a varied range of opportunities, experiences and choices, all of which would be denied them if they were to be confined in a laboratory cage. A purpose-bred laboratory beagle, whose whole life had been spent in a cage, would presumably be incapable of having any but the most basic desires and could not therefore be said to be prevented from

---

[46] Stamp Dawkins 1998: 158–9

doing anything like the range of things that my dogs would be prevented from doing. My concern is that if we conclude that my dogs therefore have higher moral status in what DeGrazia calls the 'interest of freedom', on the grounds that their confinement results in the thwarting of a greater range of 'things they want to do', we underestimate the wrong done to the beagle which has been deprived of even the possibility of 'wanting to do' anything. Again, this is not a species-specific point; it would apply equally to a comparison between a privileged Western child and one confined from birth in a Romanian orphanage. I see no point in trying to decide which one in each pair has suffered the greater deprivation: each has been outrageously wronged and the loss is incalculable.

## IV

In arguing his case for comparative values of human and animal lives and the harm that is done by killing, DeGrazia claimed the support of the American philosopher and leading figure in the Animal Rights movement, Thomas Regan, and he may be justified in this, but Regan would certainly not support DeGrazia's use of the same argument in the case of deprivation of freedom. Regan argues that 'harms' do not necessarily entail either suffering or the victim's awareness of having been harmed or 'knowing what he is missing', and describes such harms as 'deprivations or losses of those benefits that make possible or enlarge the sources of satisfaction in life'.[47] Unlike DeGrazia, Regan is totally opposed to the confinement of animals either for scientific experiments or in commercial farming. This sharp contrast between the views of DeGrazia and Regan is important because it connects with Regan's assertion that 'though death is the ultimate harm, because the ultimate loss, it may not be the worst harm there is'. This suggests that, although Regan's 'harm of death' theory would result in the killing of the deprived but unknowing animal (he gives the example of a caged wolf kept in a drugged and barely conscious state) being a lesser harm than the killing of a free-living one, it might still be the case that the harm done by the deprivation would equal, or even outweigh, the harm of the killing of either.

---

[47] Regan 1983: 97

In this respect I have more sympathy with Regan's view than DeGrazia's, but my objection to DeGrazia's 'totting up' method of calculating moral status or value of life applies equally to Regan's claim that '[t]he magnitude of the harm that death is . . . is a function of the number and variety of opportunities for satisfaction it forecloses for a given individual',[48] which is vulnerable to the same absurd comparisons that arose when I tried to put into practice DeGrazia's suggestion that the sceptic should 'consider all the things she wants to do in the next five days'. If 'number and variety' are what count, we are apparently to suppose that the death of a person who enjoys a great number and variety of minor satisfactions such as finding bargains in the January sales, watching television, gossiping etc., is a greater harm than that of one who dies before he can complete the one great project to which his life has been dedicated — perhaps a great art work, the establishment of a philanthropic organisation or an environmental scheme to secure the future of our planet. To illustrate his point, Regan uses the familiar intuition pump of a lifeboat situation. In this case we are to imagine that it is occupied by 'five survivors, four normal adult human beings and a dog. The boat will support only four.' To Regan it is obvious that the dog must be ejected and he adds 'and it is not speciesist to claim that the death of any of these humans would be a prima facie greater harm in their case than the harm death would be in the case of the dog'.

Remembering the results of my own 'totting up' exercise to test DeGrazia's similar scheme for comparing the moral status of dogs and humans, Regan's confidence that the dog will have the lowest score seems misplaced. But even if we were to replace 'number and varieties' with 'degree' or 'amount' of satisfaction, which would at least allow one great satisfaction to equal or outweigh a dozen minor ones, how could we possibly measure and compare, even between conspecifics? To assume that the human score must necessarily outweigh the canine is blatant 'us-ism', although Regan's assurance that it is not speciesist is supported by his view that 'Death is a comparable harm if the loss of opportunities it marks are equal in any two cases'. This dubious criterion means that, had one of the four humans in the lifeboat been senile, with the result that his 'opportunities for satisfaction' were fewer than those of the dog, it would have been he, and not

---

[48] Regan 1983: 351

the dog, who was heaved overboard. I will return to the morality of this choice later, but I now want to examine the notion of 'opportunities for satisfaction', which, although vital to the 'value of life' argument, is not adequately defined. It is not clear whether my 'opportunities for satisfaction' include those, such as eating olives, plunging into icy water and watching football matches, which my personal preferences preclude from being a source of satisfaction even though they do provide opportunities which I am capable of taking. And this is an important point if we are to take seriously Regan's concern with the 'number and variety' of opportunities for satisfaction. After all, in Regan's lifeboat my inability to include olive eating, cold plunges and football matches on my score card might just tip the balance against my claim to a place. If the dog could claim all three Regan might have to revise his view.

Even if our ability to achieve satisfaction from all of the opportunities open to us were not limited by our personal tastes and interests, those privileged to have a great many opportunities would be unlikely to gain satisfaction from all of them. It is by no means obvious that the 'Jack of all trades' has a more satisfying life than the 'master of one'. To have many interests and talents in many fields can lead to frustration because there is never time or energy to do justice to them all. 'More' is not necessarily 'better', nor is variety necessarily better than depth.

## V

The American Utilitarian philosopher Raymond Frey believes that 'it is the sheer richness of human life, and in what this richness consists, which gives it its superior quality'[49] and he assures us that 'There is nothing speciesist about this; we find human life to have a much higher quality than animal life, not on the basis of species, but on the basis of richness; and the very high value we place on human life is a function of its quality'.[50] The 'us-ist' use of 'we' here is significant — Frey does not consider the possibility that some humans might disagree. His denial of speciesism, however, is no more than a willingness to include in the category of 'less valuable lives', not only those of animals but also those of human beings who 'deviate radically' from the norm and by con-

---

[49] Frey 1983: 109
[50] Frey 1983: 110

cluding that some animal lives may be more valuable than some human. But if, as the value-of-life philosophers claim, speciesism is analogous to racism, then Frey's insistence that his view is not speciesist is analogous to a claim that it is not racist to believe that the lives of all Asians are less valuable than 'ours' as long as we agree that at least some Westerners fall into the same category. Frey's list of 'things which give life its richness' includes many — such as looking at pictures, reading books, working and experiencing satisfaction in one's job, striving to make something of one's life, in terms of one's purposes and goals, seeking through years of training and hard work excellence in some athletic, artistic or academic endeavour — which are not only denied to animals but to many human beings as well. (Interestingly, Frey's list of exclusively human 'riches' also includes 'having children and watching and helping them to grow up' which is surely as much a richness in the lives of many mammals and birds as it is in some human. Not to appreciate this is to underestimate the wrong done to those who are deprived of their young.) And it is obvious that the class of human beings to whom these riches are denied is not limited to Frey's sufferers from 'severe mental and physical deformity or an irreversibly comatose condition',[51] but includes many healthy and intelligent people who are dispossessed, imprisoned or living under oppressive regimes, as well as many more whose cultures do not share Frey's values.

We might or we might not agree that such lives are less 'rich' than those which include many of the items on Frey's list, but even if we agree, I see no reason at all why this should lead us to accept Frey's case that the wrongness of killing is in proportion to the 'value' (i.e. 'richness') of the life taken. Few non-Moslem thinkers would deny that the lives of women under the Taliban regime were cruelly impoverished, deprived as they were of almost all of Frey's 'riches', but it would be extraordinary if we were to conclude that it would therefore be less wrong to kill them than to take the 'richer' lives of their oppressors.

Frey is conflating 'what makes life worth living' with 'what makes it wrong to kill', a tendency which is especially apparent in his example of the chicken as an animal which, he claims, 'the overwhelming majority of us' (that significant 'us' again) con-

---

[51] Frey 1983: 110

sider to have a life of 'exceedingly minimal' value.[52] Frey's reasons for this view are worth quoting in full, for they provide an excellent example of rampant 'us-ism':

> For chickens are mass-produced in their billions, rarely achieve any individuality in our eyes, are not noted for their behavioural, let alone intellectual affinities to ourselves, are rarely, if at all, considered to be self-conscious, are rarely contemplated for inclusion in the class of persons, and in general, lead us to believe that, for most purposes, one is pretty much as good as another.[53]

With minor adjustments to the rest of the paragraph it would only be necessary to replace 'chickens' with 'women', 'slaves' or 'non-whites' to have a fair representation of the views of the Taliban, sexists, racists and so on, which a less prejudiced observer might interpret as 'we treat them as if they were mindless, characterless and interchangeable, therefore they must be'.[54]

I imagine that Frey's opinion of chickens is based on a passing view of intensively farmed birds packed into broiler sheds or battery cages. A Martian's view of human beings based on a visit to a concentration camp would be equally ill-founded. The American philosopher Bernard Rollin describes the effect that mass deprivation of animals or humans can have on the perceptions of the perpetrators or observers:

> The animals become as indistinguishable as grains of sand, which in turn weakens both our sensitivity to signs of pain and our moral response. This is what happened in the concentration camps; shaved, starved prisoners, identically dressed, lacked individuality in the eyes of their captors and were thus more easily perceived as part of an endless flow of clones about which one need not feel moral concern.[55]

My own lengthy experience of chickens has been with family groups ranging freely in fields and stableyard, scratching for worms in the garden, dust-bathing in the yard, sunning themselves on the doorstep, roosting in the barn, laying eggs amongst

---

[52] Frey 1987: 109
[53] Frey 1987: 109
[54] For a discussion of the effects of treating 'as if', including Frey's treatment of his dog, see Chapter Four.
[55] Rollin 1989: 153

the hay bales or secretly in a hedgerow from which they eventually emerge with a piping brood of newly-hatched chicks to be fiercely protected, clucked over and educated in the arts of survival and gallinaceous etiquette. Far from 'one [being] pretty much as good as another', each member of the flock has her particular place in the social order. As for being 'not noted for their behavioural affinities to ourselves', how else are we to explain such everyday phrases as 'pecking order', 'hen-pecked' and 'ruling the roost' to describe human behaviour? That these have obviously become dead metaphors for Frey might well be taken as an indication that his own life is less rich than it might be. Frey's view of chickens illustrates the pervasive effect of impressions gained from animals kept in conditions which are either solitary or so crowded that social relations are impossible. Human beings in solitary confinement or crammed together into a cage would give an equally distorted impression. The use of space is of vital importance to social creatures, including humans. Human families on a public beach, like cows in a field, space themselves with unconscious care. Unspoken rules decree the optimum distance between guests chatting at a cocktail party, horses lounging in a paddock or dogs sharing a hearthrug. A stranger who stands or sits too close is disconcerting; so is an intimate friend who unexpectedly moves away. Social creatures — including chickens as well as humans — may want company but they also want to preserve their personal space and may become aggressive (or should it be defensive?) towards those who don't — or can't — respect it. That overcrowded chickens damage one another in their frantic attempts to defend a space for themselves is not evidence that they are unfeeling; rather it is evidence of the importance to them of social order and individuality. Further, even if it were true that chickens lack 'behavioural affinities with ourselves', it is not obvious that their moral status would be thereby reduced. That the behaviour of hostile chimpanzees shows 'behavioural affinities' to that of English football hooligans does not seem to justify their being granted enhanced moral status.

On Frey's argument we might well judge the lives of my chickens to be of higher quality than those of the concentration camp humans but surely our response should be that the lives of the deprived, whether human or chicken, should be improved, not that they are of such low value that if it is not *quite* alright to kill them then it is at least a very minor wrong compared to the killing of a well-fed and highly privileged western philosopher.

Frey's principle seems to be that 'from him that hath not, shall be taken away even that which he hath'. In arguing that the harm done in taking a life is in proportion to the value or quality of that life Frey allows that some animal lives may be of higher quality than some human lives, so that 'if we are confronted with the choice between saving the human or saving the animal, then we should be bound in terms of consistency to regard the animal's life as of greater value and to act accordingly'.[56]

Frey's observation that '[t]his point has serious implications in the matter of vivisection' would certainly seem to follow in cases where vivisection results in the killing of the subject, but I cannot see how it can be used to justify Frey's extraordinary leap from his view that one life may be more 'sacrificeable' than another to the assumption that the unfortunate livers of 'less valuable lives', whether humans or animals, are the right choice as subjects of painful — but not necessarily lethal — experiments, if such experiments are to be conducted at all. Frey uses the 'appeal to benefit' to argue in favour of non-frivolous experimentation, without offering any justification for the choice of the already less-favoured as victims for the infliction of pain and suffering. He does not suggest that either animals or those 'people [who] lead lives of a quality we would not wish upon our worst enemies'[57] are less susceptible to pain than 'normal' human beings, and it is hard to see how even utilitarianism can offer a justification for choosing the least fortunate in particular for the infliction of more suffering so that the fruits of their misery can benefit the most fortunate.

## VI

This brief examination of some aspects of the 'value of life' argument is not intended to be comprehensive, but I hope that it is sufficient to show the inadequacy of the suggested criteria for the assessment and comparison of the values of lives. In looking more closely at the various methods of 'valuing', whether Harris's 'personhood', Regan's 'number and variety of opportunities for satisfaction', DeGrazia's 'important or central interests', or

---
[56] Frey 1987: 111
[57] Frey 1987: 114

Singer's 'range of possible experiences', it has become obvious that they are neither acceptable nor workable and it is hard to avoid the impression that they merely articulate an assumption that the writers themselves and those who share their values — the 'us' so often referred to — are at the top of any hierarchy.

Squadrito's attack on DeGrazia could be directed equally at the 'value of life' argument in general:

> DeGrazia points out that the intuition persists that the killing of a human is more destructive of something objectively valuable than the killing of an animal. What kind of intuition is this? My guess is that it is based on a long history of speciesism, based primarily on our desperate desire to be important and powerful in a universe that cares as much about us as it does about a flea.

As the great eighteenth-century Scottish philosopher David Hume observed, 'the life of a man is of no greater importance to the universe than that of an oyster.'[58] Perhaps indeed a universal perspective would be value-free with no interest in life of any kind. Let us suppose, however, the existence of an 'impartial observer' who does value life, but has no bias in favour of any one species over any other. I can see no reason to suppose that such an observer would judge human life to be of greater value or human activity to be more important than that of any other species. If our impartial observer's concern was for the continuation of a diverse and flourishing ecosystem, he might well decide that the intrinsic value of human life was outweighed by the damage the human species is inflicting on the planet on which all life depends and which must be stopped by the removal — or at least the drastic culling — of Homo sapiens.

This point is recognised by Frey in his attack on Michael W. Fox's 'kinship and reverence for life' theory. Accusing Fox of inconsistency and implicit speciesism, Frey writes:

> I cannot forbear pointing out one obvious and very damaging implication of Fox's particular, reverence-for-life position. We are licensed to cull animal populations when serious over-population and, therefore, a disruption in the balance of nature is threatened. Why, then, are we not licensed to cull our own species, which in many parts of the world has long since outstripped its food resources? If a reverence for life is

---

[58] Hume 1904: 590

compatible with culling animals, why is it not compatible with culling humans? If I can kill animals in the name of an efficient well-managed ecosystem, why not humans? Is the reason ultimately that, though we are to revere all life, we are to revere the lives of members of our own species above all others? If so, then Fox's reverence-for-life ethic has a systematic bias in our favour built into it.[59]

Frey's purpose here, of course, is only to ridicule Fox's theory by pushing it to its logical conclusion and not to endorse the culling of humans. For Frey himself the 'reverence for life' position is absurd because his own 'us-ism' will not allow him to doubt the superior value of his own life and those of others like him. This really is a case of pots and kettles though, as Frey's own argument in favour of using 'less valuable' humans, as well as animals, in medical research to benefit the 'richer', is vulnerable to the same conclusion as Fox's 'license to cull'. Since Frey does not discriminate on grounds of species and since he defends the use of animals as food, it is odd that he does not suggest that 'less valuable' humans could also be killed and eaten by the richer. It is worth noting that none of the 'value of life' theorists mentions that to eat animal but not human flesh is speciesist.[60]

Let us now suppose that our impartial observer has decided that the human population must be culled before it destroys the ecosystem and eventually terminates all life, its own included. If some humans are to be spared, which should be chosen? From the environmental point of view, the obvious choice would be to spare those humans who are the least damaging to the environment and the ludicrous 'us-ism' of Frey's position is especially apparent when we realise that the least damaging are likely to be those that he considers to be 'least valuable' because their lives lack the 'riches' of his own. The significance of his talk of 'rich' lives assumes a new importance when it is seen to reflect the values of the rich western world with its constant search for new and varied experiences and its exploitation of the earth's resources to its own ends, regardless of the effects on the rest of the human as well as the non-human population. From a truly objective viewpoint, Frey's 'value of life' criteria might well be turned upside down and lives valued on a positive or negative scale according to the beneficial or harmful effects that they have

---

[59] Frey 1987: 108 (on Fox 1980)
[60] I discuss speciesism in Chapter Two.

on the environment and its many and varied inhabitants. The jet-setter and *bon viveur* who featured high in the 'value of life' hierarchy for his 'number and variety' of opportunities and experiences would then be high on the list for culling, while the simple hunter-gatherer or the self-sufficient peasant farmer, condemned by Frey for the poverty of his life, would be among the saved.

The philosophical view of man as 'the rational animal' would hardly be shared by an extra-terrestrial observer of life on earth, who would probably be struck by the extraordinarily *irrational* behaviour of the one species seemingly bent on the destruction of its own environment. To such an observer the most admirable species might well be found amongst the insects, none of which registers on the 'value of life' scale, which presumably regards the killing of a bee as of no importance at all. To the extra-terrestrial visitor, however, the bee would offer an impressive example of sustainable lifestyle, social organisation and integration in the ecosystem to the benefit of numerous other species, many of whose food crops depend upon pollination by bees. How irrational humankind would appear in its insistence on its own importance and its lack of regard even for those creatures on which its own survival depends.

## VII

A striking feature of the 'value of life' argument — that is, the view that the value of one life can be weighed against the value of another — is its determination to regard each life as somehow separate and its failure to recognise that lives, not only of individuals but of species too, are essentially interlinked. The emphasis is always on the pleasures, satisfactions and achievements of the individual for his own fulfilment and these are the criteria by which the value of his life is assessed. His contribution to the welfare of others — for good or ill — plays no part in the calculation, as is made clear by Regan, who argues: 'The most beneficent philanthropist is neither more nor less inherently valuable than, say, an unscrupulous used-car salesman. . . . A criminal is no less inherently valuable than a saint.' [61]

Regan introduces the idea of 'inherent value' as an 'egalitarian' alternative to the problems of utilitarianism and perfection-

---

[61] Regan 1983: 237

ism, and explains that 'inherent value is distinct from, not reducible to, and incommensurate with intrinsic values (e.g. pleasure)'.[62] Since, however, Regan has no hesitation in throwing the dog out of the lifeboat to protect the interests of the human beings, on the grounds that his 'opportunities for satisfaction' are fewer than theirs, his attempted egalitarianism is superficial to say the least. If life and death decisions are made on the basis of intrinsic values ('e.g. pleasures' — to quote Regan himself), then the insistence on equality of inherent value is a meaningless gesture, but the quotations above serve to illustrate the individualism that pervades Regan's view and is characteristic of the 'value of life' argument in general. Frey, for example, lists among his 'value' criteria, 'striving to make something of one's life, in terms of one's purposes and goals'.[63] For Singer, having plans for the future is so important that to kill a person will very often 'make nonsense of everything that the victim has been trying to do in the past days, months, or even years'.[64] (An extraordinary view, which seems to value the plan more than the life, which has become a means to an end. That having a life is obviously a precondition for having anything at all does not mean that life is a means to anything, but the 'value of life' argument seems inclined to regard life as a means for the acquisition of 'valuables' in the form of pleasures and satisfactions.)

Neither Frey nor Singer considers how the plans, purposes and goals of the individual are likely to affect others. Adolf Hitler certainly had plans for the future and did his best to 'make something of his life', but few of us would agree that his life was made especially valuable as a result. It is perhaps significant that any objection to the emphasis on individual importance is likely to be attacked as 'fascist'. Regan describes as 'environmental fascism',[65] Aldo Leopold's view that '[a] thing is right when it tends to preserve the integrity, stability and beauty of the biotic community. It is wrong when it tends otherwise'.[66] Regan objects to Leopold's description of man as 'only a member of the biotic team'[67] and insists that 'individual rights are not to be out-

---

[62] Regan 1983: 263-4
[63] Frey 1983: 110
[64] Singer 1997: 95
[65] Regan 1997: 362
[66] Leopold 1949: 217
[67] Leopold 1949: 209

weighed by such considerations',[68] without explaining what use 'individual rights' might be to anyone when the collective determination of human kind to exercise its rights has rendered the earth incapable of supporting life at all. If the dog must be thrown out of the lifeboat for the sake of the human beings, then presumably all animal life — together with the human 'marginal cases' — must be ejected from lifeboat earth if this is perceived as being in the interests of the 'normal adults'. Regan's 'animal rights' are just another fig leaf to conceal the us-ism that links him not only to Singer but to Frey as well.

In setting up his lifeboat case Regan was careful to specify that the four humans and the dog were all of approximately equal weight, and that the ejection of one would ensure the survival of the others. But the 'lifeboat earth' case is not like this. Its inhabitants are not all of equal weight and some of them — especially those judged 'most valuable' according to the 'value of life' criteria — use vastly more than their fair share of the available resources. With this in mind we might consider a variation on Regan's lifeboat case. Suppose that we have not a shipwreck but a flood caused by a combination of global warming and soil erosion as a result of the destruction of the rain forest. A river in Borneo, say, has burst its banks and is sweeping away all before it. Four 'normal' human beings, marooned on a rapidly submerging rooftop, manage to scramble onto a tree trunk which is floating downstream. The tree trunk is already occupied by two orang-outangs who cling to one another in alarm as they are joined by the humans. It soon becomes obvious that the load is causing the tree to float too low in the river to accommodate all its occupants, and that all will drown if the number is not reduced. The combined weight of the orang-outangs is about equal to that of each of the humans, all of whom are of equal weight. Regan will not hesitate: the orang-outangs must go. That this involves the loss of two lives, rather than one, is not relevant in his view, which strongly opposes any 'aggregation of interests'. In his own lifeboat example he claims that, since 'numbers do not count', it would make no difference if we had to decide between a million dogs and one human being — the human being must be saved. Nor would Regan allow any consideration of the fact that the orang-outangs are perhaps the last survivors

---

[68] Regan 1983: 362

of their species, whereas it is the very size of the human population that has resulted in the flood.

Stephen Clark writes:

> The simple answer to individualism is that there are no individuals. There are, to be sure, people, frogs and beech trees, breaths of wind and drops of acid rain, but none of these countable entities are self-sufficient, with essences and welfares atomically distinct from those of others.

Clark concludes that:

> My being and my welfare cannot be disentangled from the being and welfare of the created universe. . . . Claiming a spurious advantage for individuals at the price of damage to the whole is simply silly.[69]

## VIII

I want to challenge the validity of talk of 'independent value' of lives, not only from a global or environmental point of view but in our closest relationships too. Regan argues that, 'For either of us to treat the other in ways that fail to show respect for the other's independent value is to act immorally, to violate the individual's rights.'[70]

Am I then immoral in my inability to separate my fear that my husband might lose his life from my fear that *I* might lose *him*? Do I thereby violate his rights? I want to say that my attitude, far from indicating a flaw in our relationship, is an essential part of it. If my husband felt that, in the event of his life being threatened, my concern would be only for him and not for my losing him, our relationship would be entirely different.

Regan's view, crystallized in his lifeboat case, typifies the thinking of those who seek a formula by which they hope to assess the value of each individual life as quite separate from other lives, and the environment as a whole. To me the most extraordinary feature of Regan's lifeboat is that we are told nothing about its occupants other than their species (apart, of course, from being assured of the 'normality' of the human beings.) This is not, however, an oversight on Regan's part; it is crucial to his argument and he is confident that 'no reasonable person would deny that the death of any one of the four humans would be a

---
[69] Clark 1997: 81–2
[70] In Singer ed. 1985: 22

greater prima facie harm, than would be true in the case of the dog'.[71]

I may not be a reasonable person, but if I am expected to throw this individual to his death in order that that one might survive, I want to know more about those concerned than what species each belongs to. Are they all strangers or are there relationships between them? What is *my* involvement? How did the dog come to be included? Obviously they did not just find themselves adrift on the ocean in a small boat: I want to know how they got there. Was it everyone for himself or were some helped by others? Suppose that none of the humans could swim and that they had each in turn been rescued from the sinking ship by the dog? Suppose that two of the survivors are devoted partners, neither of whom would think life worth living without the other? I want to suggest that Regan's reasonable person would find it less easy to ignore these considerations than he imagines.

Regan's explanation for the apparent breach of his egalitarian principle is that:

> The selection of the dog does not conflict with . . . the dog's equal prima facie right not to be harmed . . . because recognition of the equal prima facie right not to be harmed requires that we do not count unequal harms equally. To throw any of the humans overboard to face certain death, would be to make that individual worse off (i.e. would cause that individual a greater harm) than the harm that would be done to the dog if the animal was thrown overboard.[72]

But the premise that a dead man is 'worse off' than a dead dog does not strike me as intelligible. Nor does it make obvious sense to speak of the dog as suffering less harm. Even on Regan's terms, if I hear that, of two individuals involved in an accident, one has been killed but that the other has been less harmed, I surely do not imagine that the 'less harmed' has also been killed, and I do not see that species has anything to do with this. Regan argues that '[t]o decide matters against the one or the million dogs is not speciesist. The decision to sacrifice the one or the million is not based on species membership. It is based on assessing the losses *each individual* faces *and* with assessing those losses *equitably*.[73]

---

[71]   Regan 1983: 324
[72]   Regan 1983: 324
[73]   Regan 1983: 325

But in Regan's lifeboat case nothing is done to assess the losses of individuals. He has told us nothing *about* the individuals concerned, other than their species. He does not say that we must eject whichever individual has the least to lose; he simply says that we must eject the dog — or the million dogs. To claim that this is 'not speciesist' is as absurd as the claim that it is 'not racist' or 'not sexist' to eject the non-whites or the women.

Regan's earlier example of unequal harms was simple enough:

> To say that two individuals, M and N, have an equal right not to be harmed, based on the equal respect each is owed, does not imply that each and every harm either may suffer is equally harmful. Other things being equal, M's death is a greater harm than N's migraine.[74]

Regan's conclusion that if M's death can be avoided at the cost of causing N to suffer a migraine, N's right not to be harmed can justifiably be overridden is unlikely to raise objections. But to move from a comparison between death and a migraine to a comparison between two deaths is illegitimate. N's migraine won't last more than a couple of days but the dog will be dead for just as long as the man.

A similarly misleading example is used to illustrate Regan's view on the relevance of 'the moral bonds between family members and friends'.[75] He allows that these qualify as 'special considerations' which can 'validly suspend' the application of the 'worse-off principle', but only in cases where the outsider will be made only slightly worse off than the friend. This seems all very reasonable and few would disagree with the force of the rider that, 'If the magnitude of the harms in question vary greatly (say it is a question of preventing the death of a stranger or a minor injury to a friend) then loyalty to one's friend (i.e. that type of special consideration) ought to be set aside and the normal application of the worst-off principle honoured.'[76]

But this example assumes not only that the friend and the outsider are both 'normal adult human beings' but also that we are comparing 'the ultimate harm'[77] that death would be to either with a trivial injury that would be serious to neither. What is not

---

[74] Regan 1983: 309
[75] Regan 1983: 316
[76] Regan 1983: 316
[77] Regan 1983: 100

addressed is a situation where we have to choose between death for one and death for the other and where the parties involved are *not* both 'normal adult human beings'. It does not seem to occur to Regan that loyalty to one's friends and family is not dependent on their being either human or 'normal'. In a case where the friend is a dog or the family member is a disabled human being, his theory, which holds that their deaths would be a lesser harm than the death of a 'normal adult', would hold that our saving their lives, rather than that of the 'normal' stranger, would not only be wrong but that the extent of the wrong would parallel the extent of the disability or 'sub-normality'. According to Regan's theory, the more vulnerable my disabled friend or my retarded child (that is, the more serious his disability), the greater my obligation to sacrifice him in the interests of the stranger. I want to argue that the greater the vulnerability, the greater the dependence upon me, the greater the wrong that I do in neglecting to honour the bond.

It might be the case that many people would share Regan's belief that in the lifeboat case it is the dog who should be cast overboard, but I doubt whether so many would support his view that if one of the human beings was 'retarded', he should be thrown off to make a place for the dog. Since Regan argues, however, that 'to persist in using animals in terminal research, when the magnitude of the harm for them is greater than it would be for a retarded human, is speciesist',[78] this would be his position. I would rather argue that our response to the retarded man's handicap should be to give greater consideration to his needs, not to decide that our killing him would be a lesser wrong than the killing of a more able person.

Regan is aware that his judgement in the lifeboat case might be seen as undermining the rights view's case for the protection of animals but argues that 'what a theory implies ought to be done in exceptional cases (and the lifeboat case is an exceptional case) cannot be fairly generalised to apply to unexceptional cases'.[79] My concern is that if a theory leads to such a definite answer, then the extreme case is not so isolated after all. It is not as though the answer to the ultimate dilemma were to be kept in a sealed envelope and only opened when required. If the theory requires that, in life and death issues which involve choices

---

[78] Regan 1983: 314
[79] Regan 1983: 352

being made between 'normal' humans, on the one hand, and animals and retarded humans, on the other, the latter categories be sacrificed to save the former, this prejudice cannot fail to affect attitudes in everyday life.

Squadrito concludes her attack on DeGrazia's version of the 'value of life' argument by saying:

> We are all worried about a philosophical framework which would throw us off a lifeboat. I would not throw a human being overboard in favour of a dog, not for DeGrazia's reason, but simply because I selfishly value humans more, I do not believe that our choices in these situations are justified by any ethical theory.

I would add that, not only are we wrong to expect to avoid such dilemmas by the construction of an ethical theory that provides answers for all eventualities but that we should regard with suspicion any theory that purports to do so. I believe that we should recognise that in the most difficult moral dilemmas there may be no right answers. In particular, a 'moral theory' which carries the implication that my attachment to John or Fido must always be tempered by the acceptance that, in a lifeboat situation, I would be morally bound to throw him overboard to make way for a stranger who happened to approximate more nearly to the paradigm of the 'normal human adult', is not worthy of consideration.

## IX

A particularly disturbing aspect of the views of those philosophers who attempt to place comparative values upon lives is the implication that the purpose of such measurement is to allow us to decide which lives can be 'sacrificed' to benefit other, more valuable lives. Competition, rather than co-existence, is the principle and selfish individualism triumphs over concerned involvement. The search for criteria for the granting of moral status carries the implication that any entity which lacks the specified characteristic is without standing and can be disposed of as 'we' wish, as if we were naturally inclined (and entitled) to destroy everything in our path unless we can be presented with a case to persuade us otherwise. For Singer and his followers, if pain is the criterion, then creatures which do not feel pain do not matter; if self-consciousness is the criterion, then creatures without it are 'replaceable', which means that if my kitten does not

match the new decor in the living room it can be killed and
replaced with another and no wrong will have been done as long
as the killing is painless. I find this view not only deeply offensive but breathtakingly arrogant; it also indicates the chasm
which separates the 'objective' view from that which regards all
creatures as important in their own right. It occurs to me that I
have no idea whether frogs, for example, feel pain — it is not a
question that I have ever thought to ask. I delight in the colony of
frogs in the pond in our garden and I do my best not to disturb
them. What possible difference would it make if I knew that they
didn't feel pain? Is it imagined that only the assumption that
they *do* could legitimately restrain me from draining their pond,
stamping on them or eating them? And if so, what if my human
neighbours were found not to feel pain . . . ? The anti-speciesist
claims of the value-of-life philosophers amount to no more than
a willingness to enlarge the class of 'beings less important than
us' to include not only animals but many humans as well. The
question 'is this being's life valuable?' has turned out to be just
another way of asking 'what can we do to it?', when a more
appropriate question might be 'what can we do *for* it?'. It is
important, however, that this should not be in a spirit of 'us and
them' in which we, as superior beings, demonstrate our magnanimity by generous gestures to our inferiors, but in acceptance of
our inter-dependence, our multifarious qualities and the fact
that none of us can survive in isolation.

Alasdair MacIntyre is concerned with the prevalent attitude of
philosophers to 'marginal cases':

> . . . when the ill, the injured and the otherwise disabled are
> presented in the pages of moral philosophy books, it is
> almost always exclusively as possible subjects of benevolence by moral agents who are themselves presented as
> though they were continuously rational, healthy and untroubled. So we are invited, when we do think of disability, to
> think of 'the disabled' as 'them', as other than 'us', as a separate class, not as ourselves as we have been, sometimes are
> and may well be in the future.[80]

For those concerned with values of lives, it is not as 'possible
subjects of benevolence' that 'they' are presented but as 'possible
subjects for throwing out of lifeboats', by comparison with

---

[80] MacIntyre 1999

which, the patronising attitude condemned by MacIntyre seems a very minor offence.

MacIntyre makes no mention of value of lives, or of weighing one against another, but stresses the essential interdependence of human beings and the importance of learning to receive, as well as to give, care and assistance as needed. He argues that a community only flourishes when it is the need of its members, including the most vulnerable that 'provides reasons for action',[81] and adds: 'Note on this account the good of the individual is not subordinated to the good of the community nor vice versa.' It is interesting to note that those most likely to be in need are those whose lives — at least at the time of their neediness — are of low value on the 'value of life' scale: the very young or old, the physically or mentally disabled.

Fortunately, the 'value of life' view is not universally accepted, and I am sure that I am not alone in believing (mindful of my charge of 'us-ism' against the 'value of life' writers, I hesitate to say that 'we believe') that in an emergency we should attend first to the most vulnerable rather than what some might judge to be the 'most valuable', and that this should be from a sense of fellowship, not superiority. That the 'value of life' view is irrelevant to many people is obvious from the regular reports in the British press of people risking, or even losing, their lives, when attempting to save the life of a companion animal. A recent case was that of a distinguished paediatrician whose working life had been devoted to saving the lives of children. He died in a fire at his home when, having escaped with his family, he realised that his elderly dog was still trapped inside the house and returned in an attempt to save her.

Supporters of the 'value of life' argument would presumably regard this as a waste of a valuable life (although they would judge the value of the doctor's life, not so much by his service to others, as by the satisfaction it afforded him) in a futile attempt to save a less valuable one — not only the life of a dog, but an elderly one whose capacities were limited not only by species but by infirmity too. I want to say that the good doctor was demonstrating one of the most admirable of human reactions — that of responding directly to the needs of the vulnerable without calculation. Even young children are capable of such responses; a

---

[81] MacIntyre 1999: 9

philosopher of my acquaintance told me of his four year old daughter's reaction to his swatting wasps at a family picnic. Not too concerned by the fate of the able-bodied wasps, she wept inconsolably when her cry 'Don't swat that one, Daddy — he's got a bad leg', went unheeded, sobbing over her sandwich, 'He had a bad leg, he had a bad leg.' I hope that the little girl grew up to care for the able-bodied, too, but that her first concern should be for the most vulnerable seems to me to be something to be encouraged, not replaced by theory and calculation. When a passer-by is so outraged by the sight of an elderly man being attacked in the street by a gang of thugs that he risks his own life by intervening, we do not regard his omitting to weigh up the value of the old man's life against his own as a failure on his part but rather as a precious virtue.

The 'goodness' of the Good Samaritan is that he responded directly to the needs of a vulnerable stranger without stopping to calculate values. As MacIntyre puts it, it was the need that provided the reason for action. The point of the story is to persuade us that such concern should not be limited to one's immediate circle of family and friends, but what it does not do is to face the Samaritan with a life and death choice between his son and a stranger. Nothing in the story suggests that in such a dilemma the Samaritan would be wrong to honour the bond with his son. Regan's conceding that such a bond counts as a 'special consideration' which allows a small margin of favour in non-serious cases seems to turn the natural order upside down. Surely the 'special consideration' would be needed to overrule the bond of close relationships, not to permit its validity as a reason for action. Few of us, I think (and the 'us' is certainly not intended to include the 'value of life' philosophers) would share Godwin's view that, in the event of Archbishop Fenelon and his chambermaid being trapped in a burning building, he would rescue the Archbishop on the grounds that his life was more valuable, and that, even if 'the chambermaid had been my wife, my mother or my benefactor, that would not alter the truth of the proposition. The life of Fenelon would still be more valuable than that of the chambermaid. . .'[82] Presumably Godwin would not have thought the point worth making but for the realisation that it was highly counter-intuitive. In the case of the paediatrician, the dog was not only especially vulnerable

---

[82] Godwin 1793: 41–2

because of her age but she was *his* dog with whom he had presumably shared part of his life and built up a relationship of trust which he could not betray. 'Trust' is not mentioned by those philosophers concerned with values of lives.

None of us can be certain how we might act in an imagined situation. I have never had to risk my life to save a dog: but if my six dogs were trapped in a burning building I imagine that my first concern would be to rescue the oldest. If asked to explain my choice I might think of a number of reasons: that because of her frailty she would have the least chance of getting out on her own; that she has always shown concern for me, staying with me and looking after me when I have been ill or temporarily disabled: that our shared history means that she represents a link with a substantial part of my life etc.etc. But to give reasons would be to attempt to justify an action which should need no justification. In answer to the objection that, at fourteen years old and in failing health, the old dog's life expectancy does not warrant her taking priority over the younger and fitter, I could only reply that the length of time we have spent together and the varied circumstances that we have shared have resulted in a particularly strong bond of trust between us. I would accept that a stranger might make a different choice, but I would feel that the betrayal of that trust would be unthinkable, just as it would be in the case of a human being with whom I have a similar relationship of trust. Singer argues that such partiality, although part of human nature, is something that we should strive to overcome, but MacIntyre writes:

> If and in so far as it is necessary, in order to take up an adequately critical attitude, to disengage ourselves from our relationships and commitments and to view them with a cold and sceptical eye, then at that point we will have distanced ourselves from our commitments in a way that may always endanger those commitments. It follows that, even if there is a time for criticism, there are also times when criticism has to be put aside . . .[83]

Anne MacLean, in her own version of the Bishop Fenelon story, goes further, saying that when the rescuer says that 'he *must* save his mother, because she *is* his mother. . . . This is not . . . his excuse for omitting to do what is morally required of him; it is his reason

---

[83] MacIntyre 1999: 153–4

for thinking that saving the charlady *is* what is morally required of him'.[84]

I have argued that those philosophers who seek a formula for the assessment of the value of a life are deceiving themselves into believing that they have achieved an objective and non-speciesist way of showing that 'normal human beings' (i.e. 'we') have lives which are of greater value than those of either 'marginal' human beings or animals. I have tried to show that Harris, Singer, Regan, Frey, and DeGrazia, far from offering an objective evaluation, are all guilty of an underlying anthropocentric speciesism. It has also become apparent that the desire to put a value on a life and to weigh it against other lives springs from a tendency to emphasise the individual without reference to others. I have argued that lives cannot, either practically or morally, be considered in isolation and that interdependence is a fact of life, both at a personal and a global level. An individual does not live well by trying to put his own interests before those of his family or community and humankind does not live well by trying to put human interests above all others.

## Conclusion

In this chapter I have discussed the work of a group of philosophers who, although differing widely in some respects, all agree that our moral concern should not be limited to members of our own species. Most embrace versions of the principle of 'equal consideration of interests'. This apparently radical view is tempered, however, by the belief that, although animals certainly have an 'interest' in avoiding pain, they cannot have an 'interest' in continuing to live. In other words, while suffering is suffering whoever suffers, it is apparently not the case that death is death, whoever dies. The truly radical feature of the value-of-life view is not, after all, that it enhances the moral status of animals but that it reduces the moral status of a large part of the human race.

I have argued that death is indeed death whoever dies and that none of the above methods of measuring values of lives has succeeded in proving otherwise. More than this, I believe that the perception of an animal's suffering as more significant than its death is symptomatic of a failure to recognise that there are — or should be — many more important things in the lives of animals

---

[84] MacLean 1993: 43–4

than the avoidance of pain. I have suggested that the desire to set values on lives and measure one against another springs more from a desire for a 'licence to kill' than from an interest in the livers of lives. I have also argued that the very idea of comparing values depends upon knowing what stands as a benchmark. None of the philosophers here has thought to question the assumption that the benchmark is the 'normal human being' or 'person'. The result of the 'assessment' is therefore a foregone conclusion.

# Chapter Two

# *Friends and Neighbours*

In the previous chapter I argued that the 'value of life' philosophers, although loud in their condemnation of 'speciesism', are in fact guilty of an even more pervasive prejudice, which I labelled 'us-ism'. In this chapter, I want to examine these prejudices more closely and to explore their relevance to personal relationships.

## I

'Notoriously', writes Peter Singer, 'some human beings have a closer relationship with their cat than with their neighbours'.[1] As a statement of fact this is undeniable — but why the condemnatory 'notoriously'?

Singer does not explain what he means by a 'close' relationship but given the habits of domestic cats and their liking for sitting on laps, sleeping on beds, sharing humans' meals, being stroked, petted and played with and enjoying the freedom of the house by day and night, it is hard to imagine that many people have closer relationships with their human neighbours. So what is Singer's point? Is it that the privileges accorded the household cat cannot reasonably be denied the human neighbours so that the cat owner should not object to coming home to find *them* curled up on her bed or sleeping on the hearth-rug, nor feel that her privacy is invaded by their unannounced entry into the bathroom while she bathes? Or is it, as I suspect, that Singer does not approve of close relationships between animals and humans?

---

[1] Singer 1997: 76

After all, it is only with reluctance that he accepts that the 'impartially grounded moral framework'[2] that he advocates needs to allow for personal relationships between humans, and throughout his writing there is a strong suggestion that complete impartiality is an ideal for which we should aim and to which personal relationships pose a serious threat: 'To act impartially, though it might be very difficult, is not impossible . . . we can therefore all come closer to the impartial standard proposed.'[3]

Since even relationships between human beings are thus regarded as an undesirable but, perhaps, unavoidable fact of life, and since any suggestion that our neighbours should be favoured above the rest of the population would certainly be inconsistent with Singer's general view, it seems reasonable to interpret his comment above not as an exhortation that we should be closer to our human neighbours, but that we should distance ourselves from our animals.

The context of Singer's comment makes clear that he is using 'neighbours' to mean 'people living in the vicinity of one's home' and not in the sense of the story of the Good Samaritan; and the difference is an important one. The Samaritan was a 'good neighbour' to the injured stranger because he responded directly to his need without considering such irrelevancies as rights, duties or relationship. But it is important to note that the Good Samaritan's neighbourliness did not require that he drop in for coffee, natter over the garden fence or admire the stranger's holiday snaps. That is, his being a good neighbour to the man did not necessarily entail having a 'close relationship' with him. Indeed it is crucial to the story that he was a stranger and therefore not considered as automatically entitled to the aid that would naturally have been offered to the people next door. Any community worthy of the name depends upon its members being ready to help one another when needed, but whether we have close relationships with the people who happen to live next door does not seem to me to be a matter of moral imperative. On the contrary, we may well consider that we have an important duty not to disturb our neighbours, to respect their privacy and to leave them to live their own lives as they wish — while hoping, of course, that they will show us the same consideration. I want to distinguish between 'neighbours' and 'those with whom we have close rela-

---

[2] Singer 1997: 244–5
[3] Singer 1997: 243

tionships' and to insist that animals can be included in both categories. If I define 'neighbours' as meaning both 'those who live in my vicinity' and 'those in urgent need of help whom I happen to come across', there are no reasonable grounds for excluding animals, whether wild or domestic. My duty to help applies to the injured cat or hedgehog just as to the injured human, as does the duty to leave in peace those whose lives do not require my intervention, whether the frogs in the garden pond or the human couple next door. In both cases there is a difficulty in drawing a line between non-interference and having sufficient knowledge of one's neighbours — of whatever species — to recognise that help is needed. My determination not to intrude upon my human neighbour's privacy may result in my being unaware that she is suffering from depression and needs someone to talk to. My anxiety not to disturb the nesting blackbird may mean that I do not see the fallen nestling that I could have replaced in the nest had I kept closer watch. These are difficult cases with no easy answer, but they do underline an important difference between cases which involve 'neighbours' and those which involve those with whom we have close relationships.

It is not just that we are more likely to be *aware* of the needs of those close to us but, more importantly, that the closeness of the relationship may make *our* help more acceptable, more desirable, and even more efficacious than the help of outsiders. If I am trapped in a burning building I don't much mind *who* comes to my aid; when I break my leg I need a *doctor* more urgently than I need a friend; but we all have more complex and subtle needs which can only be satisfied by those close to us so that the help of an outsider just will not do. The same is true of animals: the starving sheep on a snow-clad hillside don't care who drops the hay from a helicopter but the lost dog, running in panic and bewilderment through a crowded street wants to find its *owner*. The reciprocity of many human/animal relationships seems to be ignored by Singer. In condemning the closeness of human/cat relationships he does not comment on the parallel fact that some cats undoubtedly have a closer relationship with their humans than with their feline neighbours. In our household, where two humans are outnumbered by six dogs, it is very noticeable that the dogs will always seek the attention, company, comfort or help of the humans rather than of the other dogs. That animals living with their own kind may nonetheless show an obvious preference for human company is an important fact which is too often ignored by those who claim to champion their interests, and it is a point to which I will return. For now I want to explore the apparent incompatibility of Singer's remark about relationships with cats and his crusading stand against speciesism.

Singer defines the term 'speciesism' as 'a prejudice or attitude of bias towards the interests of members of one's own species' and adds that '[i]t should be obvious that the fundamental objections to racism and sexism ... apply equally to speciesism'.[4] But if we accept this analogy with racism and sexism we might compare Singer's earlier statement with: 'Notoriously, some people have a closer relationship with non-whites (or women) than with their neighbours' — which we might interpret as meaning either:

(a) that, in spite of his avowed opposition to speciesism, Singer is seriously speciesist, or

(b) that the condemnation of close relationships with non-humans/non-whites/women does not amount to 'a prejudice or attitude of bias towards the interests of members of one's own species' (race/sex).

In order to answer the charge of speciesism (and implied racism and sexism) Singer could answer (b) by claiming either:

(1) That he condemns *all* close relationships, or

(2) That close relationships are not in anyone's *interests*, so that condemning close relationships with cats, (non-whites/women) does not amount to denying them anything which is in their interests.

But answer (1) is not a possible interpretation of Singer's 'notorious' statement, which implies that close relationships with *neighbours* are at least desirable and perhaps obligatory.

Answer (2) is more complex, and in order to consider both its validity and the validity of my interpretation of Singer, we need to look at the 'notorious' statement in context. Perhaps surprisingly, it comes in the middle of a section on 'Equality for animals' purporting to attack speciesism. Having listed the various claims that human beings have an enhanced moral status by virtue of their alleged superior intellectual capacity, Singer raises the question of the status of 'severely intellectually disabled

---

[4] Singer 1976: 7

humans' whose intellectual capacities may well be inferior to those of many non-human animals. He examines and dismisses three widely-used arguments for the inclusion of such humans within the circle of moral concern from which animals are often considered to be excluded. Among these is the claim that such humans, although of lower capacities than some non-human animals, qualify for moral status because we have 'special relations with them that we do not have with other animals'.[5] Singer writes:

> This argument ties morality too closely to our affections. Of course, some people may have a closer relationship with the most profoundly disabled human than they do with any non-human animal, and it would be absurd to tell them that they should not feel this way. They simply do, and as such there is nothing good or bad about it.

The question that Singer raises here is 'whether our moral obligations to a being should be made to depend upon our feelings in this manner', but the contrast between his acceptance of the apparently morally neutral attachment to the disabled human and his condemnatory attitude to the attachment to a cat is hard to explain except as evidence of a deep-rooted speciesism. Also interesting to note is that Singer's tolerance of the close relationship with a disabled human is, according to his own argument, conditional upon its not being allowed to influence moral judgement. He writes:

> Ethics does not demand that we eliminate personal relationships and partial affections, but it does demand that when we act we assess the moral claims of those affected by our actions with some degree of independence from our feelings for them.[6]

Singer does not explain what 'partial affections' might amount to if they are not allowed to influence our actions, nor is it clear what is meant by 'some degree' of independence, but he continues:

> Notoriously, some human beings have a closer relationship with their cat than with their neighbours. Would those who tie morality to affections accept that these people are justified in saving their cats from a fire before they save their neighbours?

---

[5] Singer 1997: 76
[6] Singer 1997: 76-7

In a section in which Singer is arguing for the equal consideration of the interests of all sentient creatures, the vehemence with which the question is posed and its obviously rhetorical intention come as a shock. If, as Singer argues, suffering is suffering, regardless of who suffers, and a burned cat suffers as greatly as a burned human, why is it suddenly so obviously wrong to rescue the cat first? And if it would be wrong to rescue the cat before the neighbour would it also be wrong to put the 'profoundly disabled human' before either? If it is the influence of the close relationship that Singer objects to, perhaps he would find it morally acceptable to save the cat first as long as the decision were taken on the result of tossing a coin instead, but the diatribe continues:

> And even those who are prepared to answer this question affirmatively would, I trust, not want to go along with racists who could argue that if people have more natural relationships with, and greater affection towards, others of their own race, it is all right for them to give preference to the interests of other members of their own race.[7]

But this cannot — as Singer obviously intends — support an attack on speciesism as analogous to racism. The analogy has collapsed. In the cat case we have human beings putting the interests of their cats before the interests of their human neighbours — which is certainly not speciesist — whereas in the second case we have (say) a Frenchman putting the interests of other Frenchmen above the interests of foreigners. In the race case there is a move from individual relationships to a generalised bias in favour of a whole race, but in the cat case there is no such generalisation. It is not suggested that the cat lover, putting the interests of her own much-loved cat before the interests of her human neighbour, would therefore put the interests of all cats before the interests of all humans. She regards her cat as an *individual* rather than as a member of a particular species, which is exactly what Singer himself advocates just two paragraphs earlier, when rejecting the argument that 'severely intellectually disabled humans' are entitled to the privileged status of human beings on the grounds that, although they do not themselves 'possess the capacities that mark the normal human off from other animals ... they belong to a species, members of which normally do possess

---

[7]   Singer 1997: 76

them'.[8] Singer dismisses this argument on the grounds that 'we ought to treat people as individuals and not according to the average [IQ] score for their ethnic group' and that since 'membership of a species is not more relevant than membership of a group', 'we cannot insist that beings be treated as individuals in the one case and as members of a group in the other'.[9]

Not only is Singer's attack on speciesism confused but his definition of it as a 'prejudice or attitude of bias towards the interests of members of one's own species' is at odds with the usual understanding of the term 'racism' on which it is based. We surely do not limit our concept of racism to the behaviour of those who favour their race above *all others*. If I am obviously biased against the Chinese, I cannot expect to escape the charge of racism by pointing out that I favour preferential treatment for Eskimos. If we are to adopt the term 'speciesism', it should surely apply just as well to cases of giving preferential consideration to one species over another even when one's own species is not directly involved in the equation.

Writers on both sides of the 'animals issue' have remarked upon the inconsistency of human attitudes towards animals. The contrast between the Western affection for dogs and the abuse of the equally worthy pig has been highlighted by Serpell[10] and the willingness of the British to eat cows and sheep but their horror at the French liking for horse-meat has been widely ridiculed. Singer, determined to demonstrate his impartiality, declares:

> I am no more outraged by the slaughter of horses or dogs for meat than I am by the slaughter of pigs for this purpose. When the United States Defense Department finds that its use of beagles to test lethal gases has evoked a howl of protest and offers to use rats instead, I am not appeased.[11]

So it is clear that Singer is not concerned only with what he believes is a human tendency to discriminate against all non-humans. He is also very much concerned with the tendency to show a bias towards the interests of *some* species (such as the horse) and against the interests of *some* other species (such as the rat) and much of his scorn of 'animal lovers' (a description which

---

[8] Singer 1997: 75
[9] Singer 1997: 76
[10] Serpell 1986
[11] Singer 1976: ix

he always places in inverted commas and uses as a term of abuse) is directed at this perceived inconsistency.

Notwithstanding his own arguments against speciesism, discussed above, Singer fails to see animals as *individuals* rather than as mere members of a species. He fails to see how closely our attitudes to animals parallel our attitudes to our fellow human beings in that our prime concern is often not limited to a particular race, sex or even species, but to those closest to us.[12] It simply isn't true that most human beings give consideration to the interests of all human beings before showing any concern for animals. Nor is it true that we all care more for dogs than for rats. Rats may not be as popular as pets but a surprising number of people are fascinated by them, keep them in their homes, pet and play with them, teach them tricks and are charmed by their intelligence and affectionate behaviour.

Singer's book *The Expanding Circle* (1981) takes its title from a quotation from W.E.H.Lecky's *The History of European Morals*:

> At one time the benevolent affections embrace merely the family, soon the circle expanding includes first a class, then a nation, then a coalition of nations, then all humanity, and finally, its influence is felt in the dealings of man with the animal world.

What Singer and Lecky both fail to realise is that for many people, not only the much-despised English animal lovers, but throughout the world, animals are not restricted to the outer fastnesses beyond the rim of the circle but are at its hub as part of the family, forming the nucleus from which our 'benevolent affection' must develop before it can expand to cope with concern at an impersonal level. As Stephen Clark writes:

> The first charge upon our moral account is to care for those who are in our care, to be loyal to those with whom we have bonds of affection and familiarity. Only a doctrinaire humanism can ignore the obvious fact that among those domestic ties are ties of friendship and family loyalty to animals not of our species.... Historically and philosophically, children and dogs have rights before any notionally human stranger does.[13]

Singer appears to regard attachments to individuals as a violation of his principle of equal consideration for the interests of all

---

[12] What 'closest to us' amounts to is discussed in Chapter Three.
[13] Clark 1997: 106

but this need not be the case. The belief that all individuals — of whatever species — are equally entitled to have their interests considered does not conflict with the belief that *I* have a particular obligation to attend to the interests of those in *my* care. It is not, however, only *obligations* that are involved here. Like other social mammals, we have a *need* for relationships that involve caring and being cared for. The 'personhood' view in which our only relations with others are characterised by a detached respect for their wishes and welfare, gives a distorted picture of human nature and relationships, in which concern for another may be inseparable from one's own interests. We are not content merely to have our welfare and wishes respected as our due; we want to know that those we care for also care for us and that their concern for us springs from love rather than from a sense of duty. Regan's claim that we act immorally if we do not treat another as having essentially 'independent value' (see Chapter One) denigrates something that most of us think important — that another's joys can be our joys and his grief, our grief. But close caring relationships — although perhaps in everyone's 'interests' — cannot be handed out on a basis of equal distribution. A mother's belief that all children are equally entitled to have loving, caring parents cannot entail her having to try to be a loving, caring parent to all children. Dickens's Mrs Jellaby, who dedicated her life to letter-writing on behalf of underprivileged children in Africa while neglecting the emotional needs of her own children, is not an admirable character. Singer seems to believe that concern for animals is only valid when it is impartial, impersonal and all-embracing and that individual relationships between people and animals are necessarily trivial and demeaning to both. He rejects any suggestion that his position is threatened by his lack of love for, or interest in, animals by arguing:

> No one, except a racist concerned to smear his opponents as 'nigger-lovers', would suggest that in order to be concerned about equality for mistreated racial minorities you have to love those minorities or regard them as cute and cuddly. So why this assumption about people who work for improvements in the conditions of animals?[14]

A good point and one with which few would disagree — I argued above that being a 'good neighbour' need not involve a

---

[14] Singer 1976: ix

close relationship — but it is sad that Singer cannot resist yet another sneer at those who do not share his coldly impartial view but regard animals with interest and affection. Of course we should be concerned about equality for mistreated racial minorities, but would our concern be any the less genuine or valuable if it were aroused by our taking an interest in members of the minority group and perhaps coming to know and love them? And if I am right in suspecting that few of us share Singer's ability to act purely from reason without the driving force of emotion, surely love and interest are more likely than indifference to result in right action.

But is 'right action' all that matters here? Singer seems to think so, and that the important thing is that we send the relief supplies or campaign for human rights. He does not seem to consider whether our *attitude* matters to those who benefit. In recent years international aid agencies have shifted the emphasis from impartial 'right action' to personal involvement, encouraging direct links between donors and recipients, building partnerships and fostering friendship and affectionate concern. Oxfam's slogan 'Helping people to help themselves' and the various direct sponsorship schemes are typical of this change in attitude which many believe to be beneficial to both parties. Amnesty International does not limit its action to campaigning for human rights and justice but also encourages members to befriend prisoners by writing to them and many who are eventually released speak of the importance to them of the friendship shown in this way — of knowing that they were regarded not just as anonymous victims of injustice but as individuals of personal interest to others. That human beings care, not just about the actions, but about the *attitudes* of others is an important consideration.[15]

Singer's 'cute and cuddly' reference is typical of his determination to belittle the love that many people have for animals by representing it as superficial and sentimental. Human beings certainly have an inbuilt tendency to respond protectively to creatures displaying infantile features such as big eyes — the survival of human babies may depend upon this response. In Chapter One I noted Singer's condemnation of the protective attitude evoked by 'the helplessness or the innocence of the

---

[15] In Chapter Five I argue that partner animals also care about our attitudes towards them and that this is what makes possible the reciprocal relationships that we have with them.

infant Homo sapiens' and his suggestion that it misleads us by making us forget that babies — like animals — do not have the one feature that is required in order for them to be legitimate candidates for our full protection. In that chapter I concluded that Singer's argument failed. It is, in any case, a gross distortion to suggest that only the 'cute and cuddly', whether animal or human, arouse our concern. The 'cute and cuddly' factor can no more explain the life-long devotion between dog or horse and human being than between devoted long-term human partners. That some relationships are shallow is no reason to disparage all relationships.

Singer perhaps intends to smear animal lovers with the charge normally levelled at sexists — the accusation of stereotyping. The suggestion seems to be that the animal lover regards any attractive small animal as cute and cuddly and nothing more in just the same way that a sexist man may regard any attractive young woman as a bimbo. But surely Singer himself is guilty of something akin to sexism and racism in his sweeping claim that to him animals are neither interesting nor lovable: '[W]e were not especially "interested in" animals. Neither of us had ever been inordinately fond of dogs, cats or horses in the way that many people are. We didn't "love" animals.'[16] If I were to declare that, to me, Australians were neither interesting nor lovable, would my insistence on their right to equal consideration save me from an accusation of racism?

While accepting Singer's point that one can be 'concerned about equality for mistreated racial minorities without loving them' (although it might be argued that this type of concern *is* love of the kind shown by the Good Samaritan), I would argue that there is more to anti-racism than a concern for equality. No one who excludes from her circle a whole group, such as Germans or men, on the grounds that she finds them neither interesting nor lovable can escape the charge of sexism or racism. I suggest that in applying this attitude to animals, Singer is guilty of speciesism. Worse, in the quotation with which I opened this section, Singer is not only expressing a personal preference but condemning others who do have close relationships with cats.

I have argued that Singer's analogy between speciesism and racism results in his being vulnerable to a charge of something

---

[16] Singer 1976: viii

analogous to racism in his disapproval of close personal relationships between human beings and companion animals. Although I believe this charge to be justified, I do not believe that the analogy between speciesism and racism is, in most respects, valid because species are not analogous to races. All human beings are of a single species and what physical, psychological or cultural differences there may be between races are insignificant compared to the differences between all the many and varied species in the world. To deny the possibility — or worse, the morality — of having close personal relationships with members of any race other than one's own would be undeniably racist and I believe that it is speciesist to make the same judgement about all species other than one's own. The difference is that, whereas I have argued that it would be equally racist to exclude *any* race from the class of those with whom one might have such relationships, the same cannot be said of all species. The recognition that some species are capable of forming close and mutually beneficial relationships with human beings while many other species are not is not only consistent with giving equal consideration to the interests of all but is essential to it. In dismissing relationships as irrelevant, Singer is denying the importance of the most vital part of the life of almost any social mammal. He is also denying himself the opportunity of coming to know what the 'interests' of animals really are — for example that some, like the dog, can share our lives to our mutual benefit, while others, like the chimpanzee, cannot.[17]

Although I have suggested that getting to know individual members of a species can lead to an understanding of — and perhaps a concern for — the group as a whole, this is not always the case and to assume that it *should* be is to make the mistake of assuming that the race or species of the individual is a crucial factor in the relationship. Those who keep pet rats are likely to have a much better understanding of rats than those who avoid them at all costs but it is by no means obvious that their concern for *their* rats will be reflected in an interest in the welfare of the whole species. A doting cat owner may loathe the marauding tom cat next door just as she may love her own child while feeling murderous towards the school bully who makes his life a misery.

---

[17] The importance of this distinction is examined in the next chapter.

Perhaps Singer is anxious to maintain a safe distance between himself and animals because his impartiality depends upon it. For impartiality is like a windscreen which gives a clear view of the outside world but is shattered by the smallest stone when direct contact is made. It is essential in some situations — such as a court of law — but it cannot be applied to relationships between individuals. If we were to take seriously the demand that we care equally for all, denying ourselves the 'partial affections' and loving relationships of which Singer disapproves, it is hard to imagine that we would be moved to act at all — a view eloquently expressed by Dr. Johnson:

> To love all Men is our Duty, so far as Love is opposed to Hatred, and so far as it includes a general Habit of Benevolence, and Readiness of occasional Kindness; but to love all equally is impossible, at least impossible without the Extinction of those Passions which now produce all our Pains and all our Pleasures; without the Disuse, if not the Abolition, of some of our Faculties, and the Suppression of all our Hopes and Fears in Apathy and Indifference.
>
> The Necessities of our Condition require a thousand Offices of Tenderness, which mere Regard for the Species will never dictate. Every Man has innumerable Grievances which only the Solicitude of Friendship will discover and remedy, and which would remain for ever unheeded in the mighty Heap of human Calamity, were it only surveyed by the Eye of general Benevolence equally attentive to every Misery.[18]

Singer sometimes writes as if he regards personal relationships as analogous to cigarettes or alcohol: in an ideal world they should not be necessary, but since we lack the will power to rid ourselves of the habit, those who feel that these comforts help to make life worth living should not be too harshly condemned — as long as they do not allow their weakness to cloud their judgement. To make a moral judgement while under the influence of a 'partial affection', however, is as wrong as to drive a car while under the influence of alcohol. Against this, I want to argue that personal relationships and bonds of affection, kinship and love, far from being a hindrance to morality, are central to it.

---

[18] Johnson 1963: 223

## II

It is often more convenient to maintain a distance between ourselves and others than to get to know them as individuals. Life is much simpler if one can regard all men as beasts and all little old ladies as sweet, innocent and vulnerable. Personal relationships deny us the comfortable simplicity of stereotypes. For Singer they bring the threat of emotional involvement to challenge impartiality and the supremacy of reason. 'Reason, not emotion'[19] is his chillingly Orwellian battle cry. This suggestion that reason and emotion are mutually exclusive is hard to defend but given his lack of involvement with animals, Singer's strength of will in allowing his head to rule not only his heart but his stomach as well is truly remarkable; he feels no need to get to know animals as individuals because he already knows all he needs to know about them in order to decide that they fall within the 'limit of sentience ... [which] is the only defensible boundary of concern for the interests of others'.[20]

Is he afraid that closer acquaintance might persuade him that some animals are more equal than others? Whatever his motive, his determination to avoid direct contact with the creatures whose cause he champions strikes me as a curious inversion of the attitude of those meat eaters who prefer not to know about the animals which are likely to end up on their dinner plates. The disconcerting effect of being introduced to one's dinner is beautifully illustrated by Lewis Carroll in *Through the Looking Glass*.

> You look a little shy: let me introduce you to that leg of mutton,' said the Red Queen. 'Alice—mutton: Mutton—Alice.' The leg of mutton got up in the dish and made a little bow to Alice; and Alice returned the bow, not knowing whether to be frightened or amused.
> 
> 'May I give you a slice?', she said, taking up the knife and fork, and looking from one Queen to the other.
> 
> 'Certainly not,' the Red Queen said, very decidedly: 'It isn't etiquette to cut any one you've been introduced to. Remove the joint.' And the waiters carried it off and brought a large plum-pudding in its place.
> 
> 'I won't be introduced to the pudding, please,' Alice said rather hastily, 'or we shall get no dinner at all.'

---

[19] Singer 1976: x
[20] Singer 1976: 9

The experience of being 'introduced to the mutton' — of getting to know cows, sheep, pigs or poultry as individuals with lives of their own — has turned many meat eaters into vegetarians, and I have suggested that most people are more susceptible to this type of conversion than to Singer's purely rational argument. A *purely* emotional approach, on the other hand, can result in what Singer would regard as ridiculous inconsistencies, such as the behaviour of people who are happy to make friends with *some* 'food animals' as long as they are not the individuals to be eaten. A remarkable example of this type of double-think can be found on a deer farm in Scotland where visitors are encouraged to stroke and feed the deer in the paddocks before calling in at the farm shop to buy frozen venison. Any reservations about the 'etiquette' of this are apparently allayed by a notice on the counter to the effect that the venison on sale comes not from deer on *this* farm, but the one up the road — which presumably has a reciprocal arrangement! Similarly I have known a number of people who were happy to rear livestock for the table but could not bring themselves to eat their own and got round the problem by swapping with other producers.

But would it be right to call such behaviour inconsistent? Or is it just a different basis for discrimination — not 'thou shalt not eat sentient creatures' but 'thou shalt not eat any animals to which you have been introduced!'? This would certainly be universalizable, but I imagine that Singer would dismiss it on the ground that acquaintance is not a morally significant factor.

A more difficult case is that of people who treat their animals with care, concern and even affection and yet slaughter and eat them. This might not be a problem for Singer who is not concerned with relationships but only with the prevention of pain and suffering. He is not, in principle, opposed to the slaughter of animals for food as long as they are both reared and killed without suffering, though he suspects that 'practically and psychologically it is impossible to be consistent in one's concern for non-human animals while continuing to dine on them'.[21] Since Singer's own view sanctions the (painless) killing of animals, it seems odd that he doesn't think this inconsistent with concern for them. R.M. Hare, who describes himself as a 'demi-vegetarian', has no such reservations and argues that 'it is better for an animal

---

[21] Singer 1976: 172

to have a happy life, even if it is a short one, than no life at all'.[22] The title of Hare's paper is an interesting reflection of his attitude: could I claim to be a 'demi-cannibal' if I only ate people on Fridays?

My discomfort with the idea of killing and eating an animal which has otherwise been treated as a pet — perhaps a bottle-reared and hand-fed lamb — is partly at the betrayal of the trust that will surely have been built up between human and animal. I am reminded of Lewis Carroll's 'The Walrus and the Carpenter' (*Through the Looking Glass*) whose villainy consists not so much in their *eating* the oysters as in their doing so after gaining their trust and promising them a treat. Even the Walrus feels a twinge of guilt at this treachery when the oysters recognise his intention and cry:

> 'After such kindness that would be
> A dismal thing to do,'

and we remember the now poignant enthusiasm with which they had earlier

> '... hurried up,
> All eager for the treat.'

In real life, many would feel that, whereas to shoot a wild animal for food might be acceptable, to kill a tame and trusting one is not, and even those who do slaughter and eat their home-reared animals are selective: the most earthy of British smallholders will not treat his dog, cat or horse in this way. The complexity of such attitudes is ignored by those philosophers who constantly refer to 'our' attitudes when the first-person singular would be more accurate. In reality, relationships with animals are as varied as those with other human beings, which may be loving or violent, stressful or stable, based on equality or domination.

Among those who do not include animals in their lives, there are a number of popular myths about those who do. Perhaps the most widespread is the notion that animal lovers do not care for people or are so maladjusted that their fondness for animals is an attempt to compensate for a failure to form human relationships. This is not borne out by James Serpell's survey of pet keeping throughout the world which brings him to the conclusion that:

---

[22] Hare 1999: 239

> ... far from being perverted, extravagant, or the victims of misplaced parental instincts, the majority of pet-owners are normal, rational people who make use of animals to augment their existing social relationships and so enhance their own psychological and physical welfare.[23]

I have strong reservations about the assertion that we 'make use of' animals in this way, any more than we 'make use of' our human friends, but the *normality* of pet keeping, and the place of animals as part of a circle of relationships rather than as a substitute certainly supports my experience.

Richard Ryder (who coined the term 'speciesism') also attacks the notion that there is something unnatural about affectionate relationships between humans and animals, arguing that zoologists have reported such relationships between wild primates of different species, so that since 'relationships *between* species occur quite naturally, [they] should not be regarded as the one-sided prerogative of frustrated, decadent or inadequate humans'. [24] It is odd that Ryder should feel it necessary to *justify* human/animal relationships like this: we do not condemn human language, art or transport as 'unnatural' on the ground that they are not found among other species, nor do we justify cannibalism by noting that some species practice it but, that aside, Ryder clearly approves of close relationships between humans and animals and it is interesting that Singer, although sharing many of Ryder's views, should reject this view of animals as potential friends and partners and regard them only as objects of impartial moral concern.

Another myth which Serpell disposes of is the idea that pet keeping is a decadent invention of wealthy Westerners. In surveying widespread pet keeping in tribal societies, Serpell remarks on the puzzlement of Western observers who cannot believe that tribal peoples keep pets just because they like them and not for their usefulness. He suggests that pet keeping may have pre-dated livestock farming and mentions the finding of a 12,000 year old tomb in which a human was buried with a hand resting on a dog, as evidence that 'prehistoric man may have loved his dogs and his other domestic animals as pets long before he made

---

[23] Serpell 1986: 119
[24] Ryder 1975: 25

use of them for any other purpose'.[25] Tim Ingold suggests that systematic mistreatment of animals started with early farming. His thesis is that pre-agricultural hunters treated their prey with great respect: 'For they are not regarded as strange alien beings from another world, but as participants in the same world to which the people also belong.'[26] By contrast to this, 'the relationship of pastoral care, quite unlike that of the hunter towards animals, is founded on a principle not of trust but of domination'.[27] With increasing intensification of agricultural methods, farm animals have less opportunity than ever for participation in the world in which we live. Animals and poultry kept in vast overcrowded flocks become indistinguishable even to the people who attend to them. Since it is impossible to identify individuals there is no opportunity to *treat* them as individuals, no opportunity for them to *be* individual, and the vicious circle is complete.

Serpell comments:

> It isn't so much that we avoid killing the animals with which we are friendly. It is more the other way around. Unconsciously or deliberately we avoid befriending the animals we intend to harm, or we fabricate elaborate and often mythical justification for their suffering that absolves us of blame.[28]

I am tempted to suggest that the various 'value-of-life' views examined in Chapter One amount to an 'elaborate and often mythical justification' of the assumption that 'we' are superior beings. Taken together, the theories of Ingold and Serpell offer a plausible alternative explanation of the rise of the anthropocentrism which many philosophers attribute to Judaeo-Christian belief in man's 'dominion over the rest of creation'. It is a failure to accept animals as 'participants in the world to which the people also belong' which has led many philosophers to reject as 'anthropomorphic' any talk of the feelings and emotions of animals. The feeling that animals are outsiders is also responsible for a quite common view that anything bestowed upon an animal — whether food, affection or a place by the fireside — amounts to a squandering of resources which should rightfully be reserved for humans.

---

[25] Serpell 1986
[26] Ingold 1994: 12
[27] Ingold 1994: 16
[28] Serpell 1986: 170

Whether man's fall from grace in his dealings with animals was a cause or an effect of his conversion to an agricultural lifestyle, it is obvious that farming today involves the use of animals as marketable produce and robs them of their individuality. It might be argued that there are still some farming situations in which a farmer needs to get to know his animals to some extent. Anyone milking cows, for example, will have problems if he doesn't remember which of them is nervous, greedy, quarrelsome, or inclined to kick. But if he doesn't consider their needs 'for themselves', but only instrumentally, this 'relationship' amounts to nothing more than he has with his tractor. He may regard his cows as expendable, replaceable machines, to be scrapped when no longer useful. Indeed he may well be less attached to his cows than the motorcycle enthusiast is to his machine. For the farmer's need to make money inclines him to denigrate the keeping of non-profit-making animals as sentimental nonsense whereas the bike enthusiast, like the pet owner, is happy to lavish his time, attention, and much of his income on his charge without any thought of recouping his investment. We do not, however, think of the biker as 'having a relationship' with his machine because we normally think of a relationship as interactive, which requires that both partners are not only sentient but that they also respond to one another.

The relationships which we have with animals kept for pleasure rather than for profit are many and varied, ranging from those in which the non-human interest in the human is only as a supplier of food to those in which the parties not only recognise and greet one another as individuals but seek each other's company for its own sake. Some are also capable of cooperating in joint enterprises and sometimes sharing the same goals so that a true partnership is formed. I will refer to these animals as 'partner' animals. Dogs and horses are man's most obvious partners and, since I will be arguing for the value of experience over theory, I will concentrate on these two species in particular, drawing on more than fifty years experience of sharing my life with them. This is not to deny that other species may qualify as partners; the elephant almost certainly does, the dolphin is a possible candidate and there may be others, but since the possibility of forming a partnership depends not only on psychological compatibility but on the ability to share an environment, opportunities for such relationships with marine creatures or those of vast size are obviously limited.

Because we live with human beings and are socially and emotionally involved with them, we come to know them, and we come to know these animals in the same way. A detached, objective study might result in our knowing a great deal *about* a particular species or even a particular individual, but this is a very different matter from knowing *him*. If we want to know whether John is interested in sport, whether Fido likes playing ball or whether Tiddles would object to a new kitten in the house and we are not in a position to ask them directly, we would be well advised to ask someone who knows them well. So it seems extraordinary that a philosopher like Singer, committed to giving equal consideration to the interests of all, should feel that getting to know those whose interests are under consideration is not only unnecessary but undesirable as well. In this chapter I have suggested that Singer's objections to relationships with animals, although ostensibly arising from a concern to maintain an objectivity of judgement, are more complex than this. I will be exploring his views further in later chapters, but as the desirability of an objective approach is widely accepted it can be addressed here.

Where relationships are concerned, the distinction between objective and subjective views becomes blurred and not only because we have a particular attitude towards those with whom we are involved. It is not only our attitudes which are changed; in any close relationship both parties are themselves also changed. The demands of a marriage or bringing up a baby are very different from those of studying philosophy; I am not sure whether it even makes sense to ask which are greater. The demands of bringing up young horses are different again; it is not a 'soft option' for those who cannot cope with human beings. Nor are adult horses comparable to infant or defective human beings, as some philosophers seem to suppose. Young horses, like young people, have to learn their place in their social group, to explore their world, to learn from their elders and get on with their peers and they may also have to learn to adjust to the demands of humans and to accept their authority. The humans, if they are to be worthy of their horses, must also learn to adjust and adapt and to accept that the authority is not always theirs, for, like the guide-dog, the ridden horse will sometimes have to take charge and be responsible for his rider. It is a humbling and educational experience to give oneself into the safe keeping of a partner and to know that the trust will not be broken. Sadly, it is also an experience which seems to be beyond the imagination of many of the philosophers writing on the animals issue. Nonetheless, partnerships between humans and guide-dogs or ridden horses are a publicly observable reality which cannot be dismissed as 'anthropomorphism' or 'wishful thinking'. As evidence of the capacities of dogs and horses they are at least as valid as the observations of the ethologist and much more valid than the laboratory tests of the scientist.

Life for many domestic animals, whether farmed sheep, cattle and poultry or pet rabbits and cage-birds, is much less demanding than for their wild forebears. Deprived not only of the opportunity to find their own food and shelter but also of the possibility of forming lasting — or even any — social relationships with their conspecifics, their psychological potential is unrealised and likely to atrophy. In sharp contrast to this, it is obvious that the demands that we make on our partner animals are perhaps greater, and certainly very different, from those made by their conspecifics, and that they are, as a result, changed in ways which are not only psychologically but morally relevant. It is not just that through relationships we learn things about our partners — and ourselves — that we would not otherwise know; it is that through relationships they — and we — become what we would not otherwise be.

It is not anthropomorphic to recognize that animals and humans can often work together to achieve a genuinely shared goal. When I watch shepherd and sheepdog bringing in the sheep together I am left in no doubt that they share the same purpose, even if they disagree about tactics. Even in play, there is a discernible difference between a man playing with a dog, a dog playing with a man, and dog and man playing together. This ability to engage in a joint project is a defining characteristic of our partner animals and it may depend as much on different abilities and attitudes as on similarities. When my horse and I are caught in a storm in a distant part of the forest and want to take the shortest route home, we each contribute our particular skills (her strength, speed and sense of direction; my map-reading and knowledge of which routes may be closed today) to our joint project. Frey would dismiss my notion of such partnerships as an illusion since only the human can be credited with having any idea of what he is doing: the behaviour of the dog or horse is a matter of 'instinct or innate behaviour-responses'. Frey's determination to deny the similarity of feeling, attitude and response of humans and animals results, as mentioned in Chapter Four, in his being unable to understand the behaviour of his own dog.

Some animal liberationists, rightly outraged by the injustice of vivisection, factory farming and other exploitative practices, are inclined to condemn *all* human/animal relationships as essentially based on exploitation and domination and to regard the keeping of companion or pet animals as self-indulgence on the part of the owner at the expense of the animal. Sadly, this may be a justified criticism in many cases where 'pet' animals are regarded rather as if they were animated toys for the amusement of humans than as creatures with lives of their own to live. My claim that we come to know animals by living with them depends very much on the rider that this involves social and emotional *involvement*. The solitary caged rabbit, canary or white mouse is denied the opportunity to live its life rather than merely exist and its keeper, denied the opportunity of coming to understand what is important to and about his charge, is likely to assume that eating, sleeping and gazing blankly through the bars is all that such creatures are capable of. In fact there are many species which, although not likely to form the partnerships with humans that I have described, can live very well in their own social groups alongside humans beings and other species. My own principle is to keep only such creatures as can be allowed almost complete freedom to live as they please with others of their kind while co-existing peacefully with all other residents, human and non-human. Over the years the group has included families of goats and Jersey cattle, a flock of white doves and generations of ducks and poultry — all of which have lived happily not only with the human family but with the ten-generation dynasty of Bearded Collies and the extended family of Arab horses who have been with me for almost a lifetime.

By living with these creatures I have learned that all of them are 'like us' in some very important ways. Perhaps most significant is that they — like us — are all social creatures so that, regardless of the extent to which they may form relationships with humans, their relationships with each other are at least as important to them as food, drink and shelter. This is not to say, of course, that physical comfort is not important to them but here again I am constantly aware of how many of their pleasures and discomforts we share. All of us enjoy warm, dry, sunny weather and dislike wet, cold, windy conditions. All of us are bored and frustrated when bad weather makes us seek shelter. Sitting in the sun on a summer afternoon I cannot think my contentment any greater than that of the hens, dogs and horses sunbathing around me. Washing up at the kitchen sink and seeing through the window, a group of hens and cockerels scratching busily for insects in the hedgebanks, I cannot see that my occupation is more important than theirs. What is clear is that all of us — hens, humans, horses, dogs and all the other social creatures — have needs and priorities which are broadly similar despite the differences in detail. The important things in all of our lives are our families, especially our partners and children; freedom of movement in surroundings which offer both a safe retreat and an opportunity to explore; an occupation — which may be as basic as literally scratching a living or as cerebral as writing philosophy. Freedom of choice, as mentioned briefly in Chapter One, is also of importance to us all and it is important to me that I do not impose on the animals *my* ideas as to what they should want. For example, when — even in mid-winter — two Dorking hens choose to sleep in a beech tree rather than under cover with the rest of the flock, having tried various 'better' roosts, it is not for me to prevent them.

While agreeing, then, that many 'pet' animals are hardly less deprived than those kept commercially, this need not and should not be so. In particular this criticism cannot be applied to the type of relationship that can develop between human beings and partner animals, a relationship based not on domination or exploitation but, like the best human/human relationships, on mutual understanding and trust. That some human/human relationships are exploitative does not imply that all relationships are suspect. That some parents abuse their children does not, I hope, blind us to the value of parental love — rather it makes us more aware of its importance.

Some will feel, nonetheless, that the guide-dog and the ridden horse are slaves — even if happy ones — and that in referring to them as examples of the capabilities of partner animals I am condoning the very anthropocentric bias that I challenge. Certainly these two animals perform an invaluable service to human beings but my interest is not in the service that they give but in the relationship which makes it possible. As explained above, they are important examples because they provide publicly observable evidence of a type of relationship which, although by no means unusual, is in most cases a private affair dismissed by critics as an illusion of doting horse and dog owners. In the following chapters, I will support my case with many examples drawn from my own experience of living with dogs and horses as a mixed social group in which there is no question of the animals being kept as service providers and where the most important joint enterprise is that of maintaining social harmony.[29]

Singer's arguments, however, do not suggest that it is concern about the possible exploitation of dogs, cats or horses that motivates his disapproval of the place that these animals have in the affections of many humans. It is not self-indulgence of the owner that worries him, so much as the perceived indulgence of the animal, with the implication that this is at the expense of other equally deserving but less favoured animals. Yet there seems to be no evidence to suggest that if the owners of dogs and horses were deprived of *these* relationships they would instead devote themselves to the cause of rats or hyenas, and I believe that Singer's comment that 'people tend to care about dogs because they have dogs as pets'[30] turns the case upside down. As I argue in the next chapter, people live with dogs because they get on well with dogs: the 'caring' is probably a 'chicken and egg' phenomenon.

## Conclusion

Singer's tirade against cat-lovers, with which this chapter opened, is typical of a number of such comments which betray what appears to be a deep vein of anthropocentric speciesism running through his work. Singer would deny this by arguing that what might appear to be a prejudice against animals is in fact the application of his principle of equality which demands, not equal *treatment* for all but equal consideration of the *interests* of all. As I noted in Chapter One, Singer believes that although persons have an interest in continuing to live, cats do not, but I argued that his arguments in support of this claim were *based* on

---

[29] That the animals are active partners in this is explained in Chapter Five.
[30] Singer 1976: 31

his prior assumption of the superior value of the lives of persons and could not therefore be used to *justify* it.

Singer's 'neighbour and cat in burning building' is a resurrection of Godwin's 'archbishop and chambermaid'. To rescue the cat first would be to fail to accept that the neighbour's life was more valuable or to allow a personal relationship to outweigh the recognition of a truth. I have argued that personal relationships of trust, affection, loyalty and expectation are themselves of great moral significance. This wider examination of Singer's attitude to relationships in general and those with animals in particular confirms the impression gained in Chapter One from an examination of the concept of a 'person' as an introspective, detached and unemotional individual, whose only relationship with others is one of impartial respect for their interests. Concern is only perceived as genuine if it is properly grounded — and emotional attachment is not considered a proper ground for anything. Concerns for cats and babies, for example, are therefore not *real* concerns at all but sentimental, superficial and contemptible.

In the next chapter I will examine Singer's claim that, although cats and babies fail to qualify for personhood, there is one group of animals — the great apes — which does.

## Chapter Three

# *Nearest and Dearest*

---

*There are, it may be, so many kinds of voices in the world, and none of them is without signification. Therefore, if I know not the meaning of the voice, I shall be unto him that speaketh a barbarian, and he that speaketh shall be a barbarian unto me.   (I Cor. 15 vv. 10–11)*

In the previous chapters, I argued that many philosophers writing on the animals issue, including some of those who argue for animal rights or equal consideration of animal interests, show a deep-rooted anthropocentric bias. I challenged the view that the life of a 'normal human being' or 'person' provides the paradigm of a valuable life against which all other lives are to be measured and placed on a scale according to how closely they resemble 'us'.

I now want to examine more closely what is meant by 'like us' and to question its validity as a criterion for enhanced moral status. As we have seen, a major concern in the 'personhood' view is to decide which creatures can legitimately be killed and which cannot. Singer comments '[s]o in discussing the wrongness of killing non-human animals it is important to ask if any of them are persons'[1] and points out that

> [w]hat we are really asking is whether any non-human animals are rational and self-conscious beings, aware of themselves as distinct entities with a past and a future.
> 
> Are animals self-conscious? There is now solid evidence that some are. Perhaps the most dramatic evidence comes from apes who can communicate with us using a human language. The ancient dream of teaching our language to

---

[1]   Singer 1997: 110

another species was realised . . . when the Gardners raised Washoe as a human baby and taught her sign language.[2]

So impressed was Singer by the possibilities that the language-project apes seemed to offer that he launched the 'Great Ape Project', demanding that the great apes be granted equal moral status with human beings. Curiously, the arguments put forward in this work make no mention of personhood, but concentrate on the apes being 'the species that are our closest living relatives and that most resemble us in their capacities and their ways of living.'[3] In an extraordinary *volte-face* the previously impeccably impartialist Utilitarian now demands privileged status for our 'closest relatives'. Further, not only is he prepared to indulge in nepotism to gain legal recognition of the apes' superiority over other animals, he is excited at the prospect of having *relationships* with them.

Remembering my discussion in Chapter Two of Singer's apparent disapproval of relationships with cats and implied criticism of close relationships with any animals, this is highly significant. He writes '[t]he appearance of apes who can communicate in a human language marks a turning-point in human/animal relationships'. Previously his talk has been limited to 'our way of seeing ourselves in relation to animals'[4] rather than examining our *relationships with them*. It seems that Singer, having previously regarded animals only as objects of moral concern, sees in the language-project apes a hitherto unimagined possibility of interactive relationships. That the interactive relationships which have existed between humans and languageless non-humans since prehistoric times are of no significance to Singer seems to confirm an anthropocentric view that privileges language. But the above quotation continues: 'Washoe, Loulis, Koko, Michael, Chantek and all their fellow great apes cannot directly demand their general enfranchisement — although they can demand to be let out of their cages, as Washoe once did.'[5]

Singer is skating over a very significant detail here; why *are* these apes in cages? If their ability to communicate *really* 'marks a turning-point in human/animal relationships', why are they behind bars? Indeed, what does the ability to communicate amount to if their requests are not answered? The answers to

---

[2] Singer 1997: 111
[3] Singer & Cavalieri ed 1993: Preface
[4] Singer 1976: cover note
[5] Singer & Cavalieri ed 1993: 309

these questions will, I believe, show that neither self-consciousness nor being 'our closest relatives', nor 'resemb[ling] us in their capacities and ways of living' are sufficient to enable the apes to be members of our 'community'. Further, I will suggest that these characteristics are not even necessary for such inclusion and that dogs, who apparently share none of them, might be more promising candidates.

Apes behind bars, calling in vain to be let out were not part of the 'ancient dream' of popular stories and legends which tell of characters as diverse as King Solomon and Dr. Dolittle 'talking to the animals'. Interestingly, these stories tell of humans learning to understand the language of animals rather than expecting them to learn ours, but whichever way the communication was to go, it was imagined to involve not just an exchange of words, but a much deeper understanding between man and beast. No one imagined that 'if a lion could talk', he would simply use his ability to exchange a few pleasantries before biting off one's head ('Now this isn't going to hurt', perhaps). Two hundred and fifty years ago when De La Mettrie put forward the idea of teaching sign language to apes, he was confident that a language-using ape would be transformed to be not 'a wild animal, nor a defective man, but he would be a perfect man, a little gentleman'.[6]

But even being able to exchange words with another *human* does not guarantee an understanding. Don't we sometimes say of a person whose values and interests differ from our own that he 'doesn't speak our language'? When a teenager complains that he 'can't talk to' his parents, he doesn't mean that there is no exchange of words but that there is not the mutual understanding which is involved in communication.

In the previous chapter it became apparent that language is not a necessary condition for satisfactory personal relationships. I now want to suggest that it is not a sufficient condition either and that the language-project apes' apparent inability to maintain relationships with humans calls into question their ability to be part of Singer's 'community of equals'. In examining the evidence I will argue that some animals are already an integral part of our community and that there are very good reasons for this.

One of the most important lessons that I learned in the course of growing up with an increasingly varied assortment of animals

---

[6] Quoted in Rumbaugh et al. 1994

was that although many species have been domesticated and many more are often kept in captivity, the number that can live freely and happily with human beings and enjoy relationships of mutual trust with them is quite small. As a child I dreamed of having a pet cheetah, bear or tiger with which I imagined I could enjoy the same kind of relationship that I had with the family cats and dogs. My mistake soon became apparent when, having trained some of my own animals to act in films and on television, I was asked to handle big cats and apes in studios and on film sets. I rapidly learned that whereas my dogs loved the whole business of learning their roles and making friends with the people involved and could always be relied upon to behave appropriately, the more exotic species could only be manoeuvred, coerced, or bribed into an appearance of cooperation which I abhorred. The distinction between wild and domestic animals is not an arbitrary one. Most would agree that domestic animals are those which have been selectively bred by man for behavioural or physical traits that suit human needs. Most wild animals can be tamed, especially if they are hand-reared by humans so that they accept contact with humans as the norm, but their basic instinctive responses remain unchanged.

This is not to suggest that instinctive responses are any less important in the behaviour of domestic animals and indeed of humans too. Even the most sophisticated behaviour grows out of our basic needs and emotions.[7] The difference seems to be that some domestic animals, most notably the dog and the horse, have the ability to extend the behavioural repertoire that they — or their wild ancestors — use with their own kind. They are thus able to cope with the probably greater demands of living in close relationships with modern man in a way that does not seem to be possible for their wild cousins such as the wolf and the zebra.

I believe that a serious misunderstanding arises from the popular notion of man as an essentially civilised creature whose task in domesticating animals is to impose a veneer of his civilisation on savage nature. This is the attitude that lies behind the recent spate of popular books aimed at the owners of pet dogs and which — with titles like *The Wolf at Your Fireside*, claim that, since Fido is 'really' just a tame wolf, his owner must assume the dom-

---

[7] This point reappears in Chapter Four in a discussion of philosophers who seem to regard animals as driven entirely by blind instinct in contrast to humans who are seen as being guided entirely by reason.

inant role of the savage 'alpha wolf' if he is to get the better of the brute. These writers show little understanding of either dogs or wolves and make a serious mistake in accepting the popular myth that most wild animals, including wolves, are constantly locked in a violent power struggle to establish dominance. In reality, ethologists report the social life of the wolf pack as being typically peaceful and characterised more by cooperation, affection and group loyalty than by the ferocity of the popular imagination. Michael Fox,[8] who has reared wolves in his home, found that the greatest problem in living with them was not ferocity but their restlessness, inability to relax in a household situation and their extreme nervousness, especially of unfamiliar humans.

I suspect that the popular 'dog psychologists' base their theories on an experience of dogs which is generally limited to dealing with individual pet dogs living in a human-dominated situation and largely deprived of relationships with other canines. My own experience of living almost my whole life with a ten-generation family of dogs (six to twelve adults at any one time, plus occasional litters of puppies) has shown their social life to be — like that of the wolf pack — essentially peaceable, affectionate and cooperative. As is explained in more detail in Chapter Five, our living with them in a mutually agreeable way is therefore a matter of building on their natural (i.e. pre-existing) readiness to modify their behaviour in order to be accepted and to avoid friction, rather than imposing on them an order which is alien to their nature. But although the success of the man/dog relationship may depend upon the highly developed social skills of canines it is important to recognise that the relationship between dog and human is very different from that between dog and dog, not to mention wolf and wolf. The important difference here is precisely that I do *not* need to adopt the manner of a wolf — alpha or otherwise — in order to live happily with my dogs, because dogs, like horses, cats and a few other species are not limited in their interaction with *us* by the behavioural repertoire that they use with other animals. In this way they differ very significantly from the tamed wild creature which seems only to be able to interact with humans on the basis of its stock behaviour. This results in amusing but rather sad misunderstandings such as that of Konrad Lorenz's pet jackdaw

---

[8]   Fox 1971

which was determined to feed him with worms and which, when Lorenz refused to open his mouth, resorted to stuffing them into his ears.

My dogs do not treat me as a dog, nor do my horses treat me as a horse, any more than I treat *them* as people. We are all able to adapt to each other, both as species and as individuals, and it is this ability to form real social relationships with human beings that distinguishes what I call 'partner' animals from those of wild species. And it is this ability to adapt their behaviour in their interaction with human beings that is missing in the great apes. The language-using apes are behind bars because they do not 'speak our language' in the sense of having an understanding with us. De La Mettrie was wrong. Language use has not made a 'little gentleman' of the chimpanzee. He remains a truly wild animal and his language teachers have the scars and missing fingers to prove it. Singer was wrong, too. The 'turning-point' in human/animal relationships that he envisioned has not been reached, because the mere ability to use words, unsupported by social understanding, is irrelevant to such relationships.

A human-reared chimpanzee will accept his human 'mother' as will many young wild animals when hand-reared, but as the chimpanzee grows up he becomes increasingly dangerous because he seems to have no way of adapting the 'might is right' rule of chimpanzee society, and a rudimentary use of language seems irrelevant here. (Significantly, Jane Goodall's account of chimpanzee society reveals that it is here, rather than in the wolf-pack, that life is a perpetual fierce power struggle.) Sadly, the chimpanzee who has for his first few years been treated as a pampered child in a human family will inevitably spend his adult life as a lonely prisoner behind bars. A number of the sign-language chimpanzees have even been sold to laboratories for medical research when they became unmanageable.[9] Paradoxically, the chimpanzee language projects which so impressed Singer and led him to demand for the great apes the right to life, to freedom and to protection from torture, have inevitably violated those very rights. None of the language work could have been carried out had not the chimpanzees been deprived of their freedom and those who were passed on to laboratories suffered torture and death as well. If the teaching of language to chimpan-

---

[9]   Linden 1986

zees cannot be done without these appalling consequences then it should not be done at all. The philosopher Mary Midgley, a leading figure in the animals debate, writes:

> It is no privilege, but a misfortune, for a gorilla or a chimpanzee to be removed from its forest and its relations and brought up alone among humans to be given what those humans regard as an education.[10]

Compare this sorry tale with that of the domestic dog who becomes increasingly reliable as he grows up. His lack of language is no bar to his acceptance as a loved and trusted member of the family and given the right training he may take on the responsibility of police work or become a guide for a blind person. One only has to consider the example of the guide dog to appreciate the gulf between the domestic dog and such wild creatures as the chimpanzee and the wolf. A wolf can be bullied into performing some of the responses expected of a dog. He will sit, lie down, come to call, but his attitude remains that of a wild pack member — there is no sense of partnership between him and his trainer. Vicki Hearne, a trainer of dogs and horses, who has also trained wolves, writes:

> The wolf has wolfish social skills, but he has no human social skills, which is why we say that a wolf is a wild animal. And since human beings have for all practical purposes no wolfish social skills, the wolf regards the human being as a wild animal, and the wolf is correct.[11]

That the lack of common ground affects the way that *each* regards the other is important, and Hearne's case is that the same is true of chimpanzees. She continues:

> The wolf is not alone in his regard for the commitments talking with humans implies. Even Lucy, the chimpanzee whose (true) story is told in *Growing up Human*, turns out on examination not to have learned from her family, the Temerlins, who brought her up as their 'child', as much about not biting and toilet training as the family dog.[12]

The chimpanzee can be bribed to learn an impressive array of tricks, but is no more a 'partner' than the wolf is.

---

[10] Midgley 1983: 99
[11] Hearne 1987: 23
[12] Hearne 1987: 23

The guide dog requires neither bribes nor bullying. He forms a partnership with his trainer and then with his blind owner and devotes himself to his job without material reward. Bruce Johnston, a blind psychologist who has been looked after by a succession of guide dogs, writes that good training demands

> a questioning of some of the assumptions we hold about the necessity of human dominance for effective control of the dog. The deep attachment the dog has for its owner, and its nearly insatiable desire to please, means the need to resort to physical punishment to gain pack leadership for the purpose of behavioural control is unnecessary.[13]

Indeed the guide dog is often required to take charge of a situation and to overrule his owner's instructions if they cannot be safely carried out. It might be worth noting here that the owner's instructions are of course verbal and that the dog's inability to reply does not prevent him from responding. No amount of training would turn a wolf into a guide: the difference between wolf and dog is certainly more than skin-deep. The difference of DNA between the two is just 3% which sounds small until we realise that the DNA difference between man and chimpanzee is a mere 1.6%

Much has been made of the claim that the chimpanzee is 'our nearest relative' and a study of chimpanzee behaviour certainly offers an interesting comparison with human culture and may give useful insight into the origins of some human behaviour, but we do not not limit our expectation of human behaviour to what we know of chimpanzees and we should not limit our expectations of dogs to what we know of wolves.

So what of Singer's claim that the great apes are entitled to privileged status by virtue of being 'our closest relatives and [that they] most resemble us in their capacities and their ways of living'? Since Singer does not explain in what sense the great ape species are 'our closest relatives', I will explore some possible interpretations. Perhaps the most likely is that he is referring to the fact that chimpanzees and humans share a larger percentage of their genes (Dawkins speaks of more than 99%) than either does with any other species and that their last common ancestor was comparatively recent (Dawkins says 'as recently as five mil-

---

[13] Johnston 1995

lion years ago').[14] But Singer himself has argued forcefully that our biologically evolved tendency to favour our kin is not to be accepted as moral behaviour. In *Practical Ethics* he recognizes that a parent who gave his last bowl of rice to a stranger when his own child was starving would be considered unnatural, but adds 'whether it would be wrong is another question altogether'. So by Singer's own ethics, our closest relatives have no special claim on us.

Setting aside this inconsistency, I want to challenge Singer's assumption that being 'our closest relatives' gives the great apes an entitlement to greater consideration than other animals. In our relations with other human beings it is by no means obvious that genetic closeness either is or should be more influential than personal relationship. Similarly, in our dealings with non-humans, our first duty is surely to those with whom we have close relationships rather than those with whom we share the most genes. Singer's assumption, in the above remark about children, is that our natural inclination is to favour those to whom we are genetically most closely related, but this is demonstrably untrue. Genetically, the closest possible relationship is between siblings whereas the parent/child genetic match is only fifty per cent, but the concern of a parent for a child will usually take priority over concern for a sibling, and this is the case not only in humans but in most, if not all, other species too. If close emotional ties were dependent upon genetic closeness, how could we explain the equal love and concern of parents for both natural and adopted children? In the case of the parent/child relationship the importance of the close involvement required in the day-to-day care of the dependent child cannot be overestimated. Although, in most cases, it is obviously true that 'this is my child' is the main reason for involvement in the first place, there is also a very real sense in which any child can *become* 'my child' by virtue of my bringing it up. This has been poignantly illustrated in cases where mothers have been sent home from maternity hospitals with the 'wrong' baby and the mistake has only come to light after a considerable time. Part of the shock for the mothers involved is the realisation that the child that they have cared for has *become* 'their child' and that the biological child is a stranger. That shared history is more important here than shared DNA is

---

[14] Both quotations from Dawkins 1986: 263

something that seems to be ignored in the recent interest in the possibility of cloning human beings. The parents who want to replace their dead child with a clone are confused if they believe that they will be somehow regaining the lost individual. This is even more apparent if we imagine that in the future it might be possible to produce a fast-growing clone of an adult, so that shortly after the death of a loved partner, one could take delivery of a genetically and visually identical 'replacement'. The horror of being faced with a replica which was *not* the same person because lacking the shared history which constituted the relationship is the stuff, not of dreams, but of nightmares.

Whether intentionally (as in adoption or marriage) or accidentally (as in the hospital mix-up) we often find that our closest relationships are with individuals to whom we are not biologically related at all (except in as much as we are all related to some extent — but then so are all mammals related). Genetic relationship only seems to be relevant in medical cases where close relatives are most likely to be able to supply matching tissue, such as bone marrow. Suppose I am contacted by a tissue-matching agency on behalf of a sister whose existence was previously unknown to me and who is now suffering from leukaemia, from which she can be saved by a bone marrow graft. I may feel obliged to provide it, but not more obliged than I would feel to another stranger to whom I was not related. My sense of obligation arises from the knowledge that I am in a special position to help, not from our being related.

Similarly, that it is important that I visit my elderly mother arises partly from my understanding that what she wants is not just a 'visit' but *a visit from me*. What is important here is not the fact that we are genetically *related* but that we have an emotional *relationship*. I didn't choose to have a mother but people *do* choose to have children so they have a special and inescapable responsibility towards them, not only to support them materially, but to give them the care and interest that they need. Exactly the same applies to adopted children or to the children produced from donated eggs or sperm. The important bond is the emotional, not the genetic. Similarly, in taking on an animal, one has a special obligation to care for it and that this was a 'free choice' does not make it less binding.

The responsibility involved in accepting the role of parent or carer is two-fold. Initially there is an obligation to provide for the needs of the dependant, to see that he is fed, housed and cared for, but as a relationship develops it involves an acceptance of the importance that one has personally for the dependant and an obligation not just to provide for his needs but to give of oneself. The pet gerbil may not care *who* looks after him as long as he is fed but most dogs, like children, regard their people as irreplaceable. A child whose parents fail to turn up to watch his performance in a school play is unlikely to be consoled if they pay someone else to stand in for them: my dogs are disappointed if I am not home in time for an anticipated walk but nothing will persuade them to go for a walk with a friend instead. This type of personal attachment is a defining characteristic of those animals capable of having social relationships with us and it entails a particular obligation to recognise its importance to the individual. Genetic closeness does not seem to count for very much here.

Perhaps Singer is not so much concerned with the genetic closeness of the species as with the 'family resemblance' between humans and apes. It has been suggested that human sympathy is aroused by the humanoid appearance of these 'relatives', but this is not a universal feeling and many people find the physical similarity repulsive because the behaviour of apes — particularly chimpanzees — is seen as a parody of all that is least loveable in human beings. This attitude is used to great effect by Jonathan Swift in *Gulliver's Travels*, contrasting the loathsome ape-like Yahoos with the noble, rational horses or Houyhnhnms (who seem to embody Singer's ideal of rational, emotion-free beings). Physical similarity can arouse either sympathy or revulsion, depending on how the other characteristics of the species are viewed, but it does seem to be more significant than genetic closeness. Imagine that a species were to be found that resembled us in appearance much more closely than does the chimpanzee, but which, when DNA tested, proved to be no more related to us than herrings are. Evolutionary convergence has produced many such examples which 'have arrived at a very similar endpoint, from a very different starting point'.[15] I imagine that our attitude to this new species would depend far more on its ability or inability to form social relationships with us than on either its DNA or its physical appearance.

---

[15] Dawkins 1986: 95

As for 'capacities and ways of living', there are certainly remarkable similarities of behaviour between chimpanzees and humans but unfortunately some of the 'ways' we share are those regarded as most undesirable in humans — not just bullying but warfare, genocide and despotic rule. Jane Goodall's long-term observation of chimpanzees in the wild has given us a detailed picture of their social life in which power is achieved by domination and terrifying displays of violence. Top ranking males (it is a male-dominated society) are overthrown and often savagely injured as soon as they show the least sign of weakness. Such behaviour may be acceptable among politicians but not among civilised people.

Goodall has dedicated her life to the study of chimpanzees and is accepted by them as an inoffensive observer but being accepted includes being attacked if she gets in the way of an angry chimp. When she returned to Gombe after the birth of her child she kept him in a cage to protect him from attack. She knew the chimpanzees too well to have any illusions about them. She had seen them kill and eat each other's babies.

She writes,

> I cannot conceive chimpanzees developing emotions, one for the other, comparable in any way to the tenderness, the protectiveness, the tolerance and the spiritual exhilaration which are the hallmarks of human love . . . For chimpanzees usually show a lack of consideration for each other's feelings which, in some ways, may represent the deepest part of the gulf between them and us.[16]

This observation may explain the crucial difference between chimpanzees and our partner animals, for the 'lack of consideration of each other's feelings' contrasts sharply with the attitudes of my dogs and horses within their own family groups. Members of both these groups show not only a keen awareness of one another's feelings but also a willingness to adapt to them without confrontation and this basic inclination is vital to the success of their relationships with humans. If this ability is absent from chimpanzee society it is not surprising that captive chimpanzees fail to develop satisfactory relationships with humans. There are certainly 'capacities and ways of living' which resemble our

---

[16] van Lawick 1971: 178

own, but they are not the capacities and ways of living that we want in our friends.

An infant chimpanzee throwing a tantrum when he fails to get his own way is so exactly like a toddler in Tesco's denied a tube of Smarties that we may be enchanted by the resemblance but both are using displays of rage and violence to intimidate and manipulate others. The toddler must learn more acceptable ways to influence; the chimpanzee is practising a vital skill for chimpanzee life.

Singer does not explain *which* 'capacities and ways of living' he has in mind when he refers to the great apes as the 'species which most resemble us' in this. It might be argued that the daily life of the chimpanzee bears far less resemblance to the daily life of the average human being than does that of the domestic dog for example.

But in any case why should this be relevant for Singer? 'Capacities and ways of living' may be of considerable significance in our choice of partners, especially if we are to share our homes and lives with them, but they are not acceptable criteria for granting or withholding moral status. Your wanting to dance until dawn every night and sleep until two every afternoon may be incompatible with my habit of being out with the horses by six a.m. and fast asleep by ten p.m., but this has no bearing on our respective rights to life, liberty and protection from torture. The 'similarity of ways of living' argument suggests a favouring of our own kind, be it class, sex, race or species, in a way vehemently opposed by Singer himself in his attacks on racism, sexism and speciesism. Those who know dolphins well tell of their intelligence, their communication skills and their generosity towards the uninvited human beings who regard them as unpaid psychotherapists. That their 'capacities and ways of living' are so unlike ours does not seem any excuse at all for withholding from them the protection demanded for our 'closest relatives'.

So much for 'ways of living' but what about the similarity of capacities? Again Singer does not say which capacities he means. We have seen that chimpanzees certainly do resemble us in their capacity for savagery and treachery towards their own kind, but perhaps Singer is thinking of the capacity for more sophisticated skills such as tool use, which, like language, was once thought to be a uniquely human ability. No one who has witnessed, as I have, examples of primitive tool use by a philosopher, using a concrete block to hammer out a dent in the wing of his motor car before inserting a flattened baked bean tin into the resulting hole could fail to be impressed by the finesse with which a chimpanzee uses a stick to fish for termites. I wouldn't trust either of them with a chain saw but is this similarity morally relevant?

Much has been made of the similarities between human children and young chimpanzees. The teachers of sign language to apes report with excitement that early language learning is remarkably similar and the lengthy dependence on the mother makes them both appealing, vulnerable and playful. A two year old chimp, like a two year old child, may be mischievous, affectionate, demanding, inquisitive and totally irresponsible. A two year old dog may be responsible for guiding his blind owner through city streets, coping with bus and train journeys, ignoring distractions, constantly taking decisions as to which is the best and safest course of action. His owner's life depends upon his reliability. The difference between dog on the one hand and child or chimp on the other is striking — it will be many years before the child can be allowed even to cross the road on his own and no one would want to trust his decision-making skills in a life or death situation.

By four years old the child can dress himself, has an impressive vocabulary and a lively imagination and is becoming more amenable to reason. The chimpanzee will still throw tantrums and is already showing a growing tendency to intimidate those around him. A four year old horse may be carrying a rider safely across country or on busy roads. A police horse may be involved in riot control, stoically facing terrifying situations while a pony in the 'riding for the disabled' scheme will be carrying frail and uncoordinated children with amazing care. In each case the life of the rider depends upon the reliability of the horse.

These examples demonstrate the danger of making comparisons between creatures of such disparate character and capacities and make a nonsense of Singer's anthropocentric determination to preserve the traditional view of the normal adult human being as the pinnacle of creation against which the value of all other lives can be measured. To compare animals with 'severely intellectually disabled humans', as Singer frequently does, is to be guilty of a deep anthropocentrism. In *Animal Liberation* he assures us that, 'As long as we remember that we should give the same respect to the lives of animals as we give to those of humans at a *similar mental level* (my italics), we shall not go far wrong'.[17] But this is to assume that we are comparing like with like and this is exactly where Singer is so seriously wrong.

In *If a Lion Could Talk*, the scientific journalist Stephen Budiansky writes that

> an honest view of animal minds ought to lead us to a more profound respect for animals as unique beings in nature, worthy in their own right. The shallow and self-centred view that sees what is worthy in nature as that which resembles us seems vapid and petty by comparison.[18]

We have been given no reason to accept Singer's claim that similarities in capacities and ways of living justify enhanced moral status. They may contribute to the possibility of forming a close relationship with another individual, human or animal, but the very different capacities of human adults and children, for example, although they *can* make living together difficult, are certainly not an obstacle to the formation of close relationships. And as I want to suggest — against Singer's utilitarian and impartialist principles — that we *do* have special moral obligations to those with whom we have close relationships, I shall now examine the qualities that make such relationships possible. I am not referring here to biological relationships in which we have no choice but to those partners we choose for ourselves, from among our own kind or others.

Primatologists Quiatt and Reynolds argue that cross-species social relationships lack 'a substantive basis in shared experience for mutual rapport and intimate communication of mood, motivation and intended action' and give as a main reason for this the fact that

> [t]he conversations which dogs initiate with their masters and mistresses most frequently have to do with acquiring food and going outdoors; many of the conversations which apes initiate with human trainers in experimental settings appear to be similarly orientated.[19]

---

[17] Singer 1976: 24
[18] Budiansky 1998: 194
[19] Quiatt & Reynolds 1993

To the first quotation I would like to ask how the writers think that guide dogs and ridden horses manage to work with their human partners if not through mutual rapport and intimate communication of mood, motivation and intended action? As for the dismissive reference to 'food and going outdoors', they seem to have overlooked the importance of food and going out to most humans. One only has to look at the number of books, newspapers and magazine features, television and radio programmes devoted to various aspects of 'food and going outdoors' to appreciate how large a part these concerns play in the lives of most humans. Indeed a quick survey of newspaper personal columns reveals that so many of the advertisers WLTM someone who shares an interest in eating out, travelling, sport etc. that I can't help thinking that many of them would be happiest with a dog.

Shared interests are important but when it comes to *skills* a partnership may best be served not by *shared* but by *complementary* skills. If you have a passion for cooking then wouldn't you be happier with an appreciative eater than with someone who was always pinching the grater or fighting for space on the stovetop? Dogs may not be great cooks but that doesn't mean that they aren't *interested*. Anyone cooking in our house can be sure of an enthusiastic but wonderfully uncritical audience which never notices when the souffle collapses but *is* hugely appreciative of anything that gets spilled, burned, or dropped on the floor, which is more than you can say of the humans in the family.

I do not for a moment want to suggest that the interests of the great apes are of less importance than the interests of our dogs and horses. But I do want to say that our dogs and horses have a special place in our affections because of their special ability to form social relationships with us and that this ability is lacking in the great apes. For this reason a life with humans, though acceptable and perhaps even advantageous to dogs and horses, is not a satisfactory option for the great apes — it is not in their 'interests'. So what *can* we do for them? In an ideal world we would simply leave them alone to live their lives in their native forests. Sadly our own species has over-populated the world to such an extent that those native forests are disappearing at an alarming rate. In addition the great apes are being killed and eaten by their human neighbours. Extinction in the wild seems inevitable. The only hope of survival for these species is probably in managed reserves in the developed world. There is just one other possibility — that an attempt be made to domesticate them through a selective breeding programme. Purists will be appalled but as man sweeps the rest of creation into extinction it may well be a case of 'domesticate or die'. In fact I doubt whether it would be possible to domesticate the great apes. Selective breeding has certainly contributed to the domestication of the dog and, to a lesser extent, to that of the horse, but if the wild ancestors of these species had not been amenable to domestication in the first place the process would never have got off the ground.

There are various stories told about the origins of the man/dog relationship. Perhaps early dogs were attracted to man's camp by the bones and scraps thrown away: perhaps it was man who scavenged from the kills of hunting dogs. What is likely is that they formed a partnership because of shared interests and needs and an ability to work together for a common goal. These common interests were important but it was the *differences* in abilities that sealed the bond, bringing together the scenting and tracking ability of the dog and the strength and weapon power of man to form a partnership which benefited both.

Few of us use our dogs for hunting today but we and they still enjoy exercising the skills and following the interests that we depended upon in our hunting together. Together we explore the countryside, enjoy a game of ball on the beach or travel to new territory (and the dog, not much of an inventor himself, is greatly appreciative of man's favourite toy, the motor car, as a useful alternative to slogging his way over the plains). The evening meal may come from the supermarket now but the old partnership, built on shared interests and complementary skills, is as strong as ever.

There are no stories of the chimpanzee creeping unbidden to man's fireside or helping man to fill his cooking pot. And indeed, what would the two have to offer one another? It may be that the very similarities between ape and man that Singer thinks so important are what make it impossible for them to form partnerships or to enjoy real social relationships. Isak Dinesen writes of human relationships

> [i]n order to form and make up a Unity, in particular a creative Unity, the individual components must needs be of a different nature, they should even be in a sense contrasts. . . .

> A hook and an eye are a Unity, a fastening; but with two hooks you can do nothing.[20]

I have argued that the same is true of human/animal partnerships.

The significance that Singer places on the language use of some apes appears to be ill-founded. His belief that it makes possible animal/human relationships of a kind beyond anything previously possible has proved false. As for his additional claims, that the great apes are 'our closest relatives and . . . most resemble us in their capacities and their ways of living', not only are these ill-defined but to regard them as grounds for privileged status would be to violate Singer's own previously stated principles of equality and impartiality.

Although, in the preface to *The Great Ape Project*, Singer allows that 'some people, among them some of the contributors to this book, would like to see a much larger extension of the moral community, so that it includes a wider range of non-human animals', the fact this 'larger extension' is not a part of the project seems to betray a deeply anthropocentric attitude, accepting that 'our membership of the human species gives us a precious moral status'[21] and limiting inclusion within the charmed circle to our 'closest relatives'. In spite of his revolutionary stance, Singer continues to accept man as the gold standard against which all other creatures must be measured.

It is debatable whether the great apes' use of language does in fact provide the evidence that Singer wants, but this is not my only concern here. My worry is with both the use of humanoid characteristics as the only criteria of personhood and with the notion that persons are entitled to greater consideration than non-persons. In *Animal Liberation*, Singer supports Bentham's view that

> the ability to use language is not relevant to the question of how a being ought to be treated — unless that ability can be linked to the capacity to suffer, so that the absence of a language casts doubt on the existence of this capacity.[22]

---

[20]  Blixen 1987: 281
[21]  Singer & Cavalieri 1993: Preface
[22]  Singer 1976: 15

Singer examines, and rejects, various arguments which claim that there is such a connection, and also recognises the difficulty of comparing capacities for suffering between members of different species, allowing that different levels of intellect increase rather than solve the problem. Since he offers no firm argument for ascribing a greater capacity for suffering to the great apes than to other creatures, it is hard to see the grounds for singling *them* out, as the 'Declaration on Great Apes' does, for 'protection of individual liberty and the prohibition of torture'.[23] Even if we were to accept (which I do not) Singer's claim that 'persons' have a right to life which is not appropriate for 'non-persons', we are given no explanation as to why protection from imprisonment and torture should not be extended to all creatures. There seems to be a quite unsupportable suggestion that some animals are, after all, more equal than others.

For Singer, the apes' use of language demonstrates an awareness of past and future which is crucial to his claim for enhanced moral status for them. His account of the evidence, however, tells us more about his own bias than about the abilities of the apes:

> Apes also use signs to refer to past or future events, thus showing a sense of time. Koko, for example, when asked, six days after the event, what had happened on her birthday, signed 'sleep eat'.[24]

One would have thought that even a philosopher in the grip of a theory might have realised that 'sleep eat', if it refers to anything at all, could refer equally well to any and every day in the monotonous life of a captive gorilla; but Singer continues with mounting excitement: '*Even more impressive* [my italics] is the evidence of temporal sense shown by the regular festivities held by the Fouts for the chimpanzees at Ellensberg', and goes on to recount the report that one of the chimpanzees took the first fall of winter snow as a sign that Christmas goodies might not be far behind, which is interesting, but not more so than that our dogs take the first hot afternoons of summer as a sign that trips to the seaside might be expected to follow.

That life may be enhanced by the expectation of pleasures to come seems indisputable; that expectation of pleasures — or pains — to come should be the exclusive preserve of language-users is

---
[23] Singer & Cavalieri 1993: 4
[24] Singer 1997: 112

absurd, and that the claim should be used to argue that the lives of language-users are essentially of greater worth is insupportable. Given the importance that Singer attaches to self-consciousness, it is curious that he should remark, 'It is notoriously difficult to establish when another being is self-conscious.'[25] This is reminiscent of Harris's reference to self-consciousness as an 'inner quality', but if that is what it is, rather than something manifest in behaviour, it is hard to see how it is to affect our attitude to the individual concerned. It is not as though self-consciousness were on a par with an unseen but vitally important physical feature, such as a serious allergy which might result in a doctor, unaware that his patient is allergic to penicillin, unintentionally causing his death by inappropriate treatment.

For Singer, however, evidence that a being is self-conscious may indeed be used in making life or death decisions. His claim that 'the grounds for not killing persons do not apply to new born infants' is followed by a discussion of the difficulty of deciding at what stage a child might be classed as a person and therefore entitled not to be killed.

> It would, of course, be difficult to say at what age children begin to see themselves as distinct entities existing over time. Even when we talk with two and three year old children it is usually very difficult to elicit any coherent conception of death, or the possibility that someone — let alone the child herself — might cease to exist.[26]

Singer's difficulty in establishing whether another being is self-conscious is an inevitable consequence of his defining self-consciousness according to essentially introspective criteria. 'A self-conscious being is aware of itself as a distinct entity, with a past and a future'.[27] This view of the individual as a self-contained unit is one that I criticised in Chapter One.

Singer's definition of self-consciousness, however, is not the only one. Charles Darwin, for example, recognised that it may take different forms.

> It may be freely admitted that no animal is self-conscious if, by this term, it is implied, that he reflects on such points, as whence he comes or whither he will go, or what is life and

---

[25] Singer 1997: 119
[26] Singer 1997: 171
[27] Singer 1997: 90

death, and so forth. But how can we be sure that an old dog with an excellent memory and some power of imagination, as shewn by his dreams, never reflects on his past pleasures or pains in the chase? And this would be a form of self-consciousness.[28]

But although Darwin allows that there may be more than one kind of self-consciousness his definition is still an introspective one. While I have no wish to dispute his insistence that a particular kind of reflective self-consciousness is a uniquely human attribute — it certainly seems to require linguistic ability far beyond anything approached by the great apes — I do want to suggest that consciousness of self can also be defined as awareness of oneself as one among other selves. Once we recognise individuals as essentially interrelated and interdependent the question of self-consciousness, so important to the individualist, becomes less important than the question of awareness of other selves. Stephen Clark writes:

> There is reason to think, within the framework of educated assessment and empathy, that animals who live in social groups, with relatively long lives and a need to resist temptation in an environment where purely stereotyped behaviour will be maladaptive, will have some degree of self-awareness. Awareness itself does not have any clear evolutionary rationale, but self-awareness does. It does not 'pay' such aware creatures as do not need to live long and varied lives if they are to leave genetic replicas to have any self-awareness. It does 'pay' aware creatures that need to regulate their actions in accordance with relatively long-term goals and under the eyes of their fellows. Accordingly some non-human animals are self-aware.[29]

And Clark concludes, 'part of the very self-awareness of which I have spoken is the recognition of a self (even, if you like, a sleeping self) in others'.

Clark doubts that self-awareness can be limited to language-users, and his talk of *degrees* of self-awareness is important. It may also be that degrees of language-use are significant here, since our companion animals, although not language users themselves, certainly regard our language use as an important

---

[28] Darwin 1872
[29] Clark 1997: 41

part of our behaviour and as of especial interest when it refers to them. It would be absurd to suggest that the names we give to our dogs, for example, are only for our own ease of reference: that they are of great importance to the animals themselves is especially obvious in a household such as ours, which includes several dogs. Each dog knows, and responds to, not only her own name but those of her companions. Her response to her own name varies appropriately according to whether it prefixes a question, a greeting, a command and so on: she responds to the names of the others by looking at each of them as they are mentioned, asked to do something, or called. Similar responses were noted among wild vervet monkeys studied by Cheney and Seyfarth, but it is possible that our giving names to our dogs results in their developing a keener sense of self and of others than they would otherwise have.

Particularly significant may be the way in which they respond to hearing their own names mentioned in the course of conversation — when, that is, they are being *referred to*, rather than *addressed*. Any dog mentioned by name in our household will acknowledge the reference, usually with a turn of the head and a slight wag of the tail — a very different response to that elicited by a direct address. (I am thinking here of references which are not of particular interest to the dog, such as 'Branwen is Nan's great-grandmother'. A remark such as 'I think I'll give Brighde a bath' or 'I'll take Small with me to town' can be guaranteed to send the first running for cover and the second racing out to the car to claim her favourite place in the front passenger seat.) But an animal's ability to respond in this way surely entails her recognising not only that *something* is being referred to but that she is that something. If, as Clark suggests, the demands of living socially among con-specifics require 'a degree of self-awareness', it seems likely that the intellectually greater demands of living socially among human beings and being engaged in their language use might result in the development of a greater degree of self-awareness. The celebrated philosopher of mind Daniel Dennett writes:

> Dogs, and only dogs among domesticated species, respond strongly to the enormous volume of what we might call 'humanizing' behaviour aimed at them by their owners. We talk to our dogs, commiserate with our dogs, and in general treat them as much like a human companion as we can — and

we delight in their familiar and positive response to this friendliness.[30]

Part of this 'familiar and positive response' is the dog's response to his own name and his ability to distinguish between its use to refer to him, to address him and so on. What are we to make of the particular response he makes when he is referred to or addressed in a critical manner and turns his face away, squirming uncomfortably? In a human being we would call it embarrassment, or indeed, self-consciousness. Interestingly, this is the only way in which we do use the term in everyday speech; if I tell you that John is self-conscious you will probably not immediately think of him in terms of distinct entities or musings on life and death but as someone who feels uncomfortable when he is the centre of critical attention or fears that he might be. That Fido cannot say to himself, 'They are looking at me, Fido, who was born and will one day die but is at this moment hiding under the kitchen table in number three Acacia Gardens,' does not invalidate my claim that in *this* sense of the word, his self-consciousness is comparable to John's.

I have mentioned several different forms of self-consciousness and there are probably more. Only the reflective form mentioned by Darwin is obviously language-dependent and therefore beyond the capacity of non-language-users, whether human or non-human. It seems that self-consciousness cannot reasonably be used to make the sort of distinctions that Singer wants and I propose that the obsession with it springs from a mistaken belief that it is the most important factor in our dealings with one another. But in a relationship with a friend, whether human, dog or horse, I am not so much concerned with his introspective view of himself — or even whether he has one — as with his attitude to *me*. My being persuaded that he is a Lockean 'person' is of little significance compared with my knowing that he trusts me and I can trust him; that we have an understanding of, and sympathy for, each other's emotions and that he is in my company from choice, free to leave if he wants to. In a relationship, the ability to be a friend is arguably more important than the ability to introspect.

Stephen Budiansky comments (*If a Lion Could Talk*):

---

[30] Dennett 1996: 165

There is a certain flavour of anthropocentric bias in the very hunt for self-awareness in other animals, a hint that conscious self-awareness is the best thing evolution has yet to produce and we want to know how animals stack up against this standard of ultimate perfection. Yet it is not an insult to animals that they might do what they do without self-awareness as we understand it: nor is it a particular compliment to animals to see how closely they share our peculiar cognitive abilities.[31]

Mary Midgley is also critical of the tendency to use intellectual criteria such as language to decide whether creatures are worthy of consideration and writes:

> What makes creatures our fellow beings entitled to basic consideration is surely not intellectual capacity but emotional fellowship. And if we ask what powers can justify a higher claim, bringing some creatures nearer to the degree of consideration which is due to humans, those that seem to be most relevant are sensibility, social and emotional complexity of the kind which is expressed by the formation of deep, subtle and lasting relationships. The gift of imitating certain intellectual skills which are important to humans is no doubt an indicator but it cannot be central.[32]

Singer wants a two-tier system which, although giving basic consideration to all sentient creatures, offers admission to the human 'sphere of moral equality' only to the great apes on the grounds that they are the species 'most like us' — a claim which seems to depend upon their alleged capacity for language use and consequent categorisation as 'persons'. Midgley, by contrast, argues that the ability to form relationships offers a more justifiable criterion for enhanced moral status. Interestingly she does not distinguish between intra-specific relationships and those between animals and humans and this is important: in concentrating on the particular significance of human/animal relationships, I do not wish to suggest that animal/animal relationships are in any way less important. With reference to my earlier discussion of Singer's ambivalent attitude towards the possible significance of language to the capacity for suffering, I would suggest that the ability to form relationships certainly

---

[31] Budiansky 1998: 162
[32] Midgley 1985a: 60

makes a creature more vulnerable to acute suffering not only as a result of the loss of or threat to its partners but also because of the greater psychological development required for social interaction. But I want to go further than Midgley's criterion for 'basic consideration'. As far as our own special responsibilities to those with whom we have close relationships are concerned, I have argued that we do have a particular concern for dogs, horses and other animals of that group that I want to call 'partners', and I have also referred to Singer's dismissal of such concerns as 'sentimental appeals for sympathy towards "cute" animals'.[33] In choosing the examples of guide dog and police horse to contrast with human child and chimpanzee I was taking two cases of animals whose long-standing connection with man and genetic selection by him, has resulted in a capacity to develop abilities and skills which go far beyond those of their wild forebears.

In *Kinds of Minds*, Daniel Dennett discusses the case of the dog in particular and considers the possibility that our special concern for dogs is based not on favouritism but on 'our recognition of a greater capacity for suffering in dogs than in other animals'. He argues that this may well be the case and offers an evolutionary explanation in the dog's long and intimate connection with man, and concludes:

> Among other traits we have unconsciously selected for, I suggest, is susceptibility to human socialising, which has, in dogs, many of the organising effects that human socialising also has on human infants. By treating them as if they were human, we actually succeed in making them more human than they would otherwise be. They begin to develop the very organisational features that are otherwise the sole province of socialised human beings. In short, if human consciousness — the sort of consciousness that is a necessary condition for serious suffering — is, as I have maintained, a radical restructuring of the virtual architecture of the human brain, then it should follow that the only animals that would be capable of anything remotely like that form of consciousness would be animals that could also have imposed on them, by culture, that virtual machine. Dogs are clearly closest to meeting this condition.[34]

---

[33] Singer 1976: ix
[34] Dennett 1996: 165–6

If Dennett is right, he offers a *morally significant* reason for favouring those animals which 'are most like us', not by virtue of their genetic inheritance, physical appearance or ability to use tools, weapons or language but as the animals most capable of what Dennett describes as 'serious suffering'. While I do not accept what is one reading of Dennett, that other animals, including the great apes, are *not* capable of 'serious suffering', his reference to the changes effected in dogs 'by treating them as if they were human' is especially relevant to the language-project apes, who, having been reared as human infants have been treated even more 'as human' than the family puppy. As I have described, the results are remarkably different; the puppy grows up to be a trusted family member and possibly a useful member of society while the ape seems incapable of responding in this way. This is the difference which Singer ignores in the 'Declaration on Great Apes' which sets out the objectives of the Great Ape Project, and in which he refers to the apes as '*members* of the community of equals' (my italics) and not merely as the passive beneficiaries of protection. The Declaration explains that '"the community of equals" is the moral community within which we accept certain basic moral principles or rights as governing our relations with each other and enforceable at law', from which it is evident that *every* member is under an obligation to respect the rights of every other member and will be legally accountable for any failure to do so. The paragraph on the 'Protection of Individual Liberty' is similarly ambitious; it starts: 'Members of the community of equals are not to be arbitrarily deprived of their liberty; if they should be imprisoned without due legal process, they have the right to immediate release.'

In answer to which I turn to Eugene Linden's description of the lives of the language-project apes, most of whom had been reared as human infants:

> [A]s they grew up, the people in contact with them discovered that they were neither domestic animals nor people. Their great strength necessitated restrictions on their freedom; at a point at which the animals were maturing and therefore eager to explore their world, they would find their freedom decreasing. The freedom to roam through a private house would be replaced by confinement in various forms of cages. Trips outside cages would become more and more

infrequent, and on those rare occasions, the ape would have to suffer the indignity of a leash.[35]

And things could only get worse after that, as described by Vicki Hearne, who tells of accompanying two of Washoe's former teachers on a visit to their erstwhile pupil, after her transfer to a cage in a wild-animal park:

> I watch, early one morning, while Ken and Roger take her out of her cage for a walk. This entails the use of leashes, a tiger hook and a cattle prod. I am instructed to watch from a distance and to be very still.[36]

One cannot but agree that the treatment of these animals is very wrong, but it is not a wrong that can be righted by simply unlocking the cages, as Singer would know if he had looked more carefully at the wealth of available information on the language projects. Having criticised philosophers on the other side of the animals issue for attempting 'to do philosophy from the armchair on a topic that demands investigation in the real world',[37] he seems to be doing the same thing himself. Picking out the bits of evidence that support one's theory and discarding the bits which can't be made to fit is a temptation to which even philosophers occasionally succumb. De La Mettrie had no way of testing his theory that a language-using ape would be 'a little gentleman'; Singer's naive faith in the civilising effect of language acquisition cannot be so easily excused. The 'immediate release' he demands would inevitably be followed by immediate reincarceration as Washoe and company breached the Declaration's own rules of conduct which are to be 'enforceable at law'.

Singer believes that language acquisition is the key to the 'moral community', membership of which entails not only rights but obligations too, whereas non-language-users can never progress beyond the 'sphere of moral concern'.[38] But Singer's claim that the great apes have 'mental capacities and an emotional life sufficient to justify inclusion within the community of equals'[39] is unfounded. Certainly they have 'mental capacities and an emotional life' which make it wrong to deny them the

---

[35] Linden 1986: 53
[36] Hearne 1987: 39
[37] Singer 1997: 114
[38] Singer 1976: 23
[39] Singer & Cavalieri 1993: 5

opportunity to live their complex lives with their own kind and without human interference, but these are not the sort of mental and emotional capacities that enable them to be members of a human or multi-species community.

In this chapter I have tried to show that the psychological and social capacities of the great apes make it impossible for us to have with them the mutually satisfying close personal relationships that we have with 'partner animals', based on mutual understanding, affection and trust. I have argued that language — at least in the form that they have displayed — is irrelevant to this. I also want to suggest that the 'mental and emotional capacities' most likely to indicate something that we might recognise as morality are not those of the great apes but those of our partner animals. This is not to rule out the possibility of a capacity for altruistic behaviour within the apes' own community, as shown by Goodall's accounts of chimpanzee orphans being adopted by their kin. But this is not sufficient for them to function in a human or multi-species community.

Despite claims for his language use, self-consciousness and 'personhood', the chimpanzee lacks one vital attribute for inclusion in a human community — we cannot trust him. Since I believe trust to be crucial to any worthwhile relationship within or between species, it is perhaps worth considering why it is so important and what forms it may take. All creatures like to feel secure and human beings are no exception. Those — like the dormouse, for example — for whom a solitary existence is the norm, may find security in a safe nest hidden from predators but for social creatures security entails being part of a group and isolation causes insecurity and anxiety. At a simple level the group offers the advantage of many eyes to spot danger so that individuals can enjoy some relaxation. Group members may also join forces to drive off predators or rival groups and may cooperate in rearing young and — in the case of predators — in hunting. None of this would be possible if individuals could not trust one another.

Similarly, human society can only function against a background of trust, not only between those who know each other, but also between the individual and businesses, service providers, police, government and fellow citizens. Close personal relationships may be defined by the level of trust between the parties. My friendship with Mary will be shaped by my knowing that although I can trust her judgement on some matters and rely on her help when needed I cannot trust her to keep a secret or not to get drunk at parties. Mary's partnership with John may survive her knowing that she cannot trust him not to flirt with other women, but if she cannot trust him not to beat her up I would feel that this is no longer a partnership worthy of the name. In the same way, whereas a human/animal partnership may be able to accommodate one knowing that the other cannot be trusted not to chase tractors, if each cannot, at the very least, trust the other not to attack or knowingly injure him or her, the description of this as a partnership must be questionable. In many cases, of course, the trust goes far beyond this; the guide-dog and the ridden horse which are literally entrusted with our lives are not merely required to refrain from injuring us but to deliver us safely to our destination, which involves not only resisting the temptation to chase tractors but making judgements and choosing a safe route.

It seems likely that only social creatures which normally have relationships of trust with their own kind are capable of forming partnerships with humans. Certainly dogs and horses in social groups rely heavily on trust. For example, a single mare with a foal will not lie down to rest but remains constantly on her feet keeping watch. But in a group of mares and foals the mothers take turns at sentry duty and it is not unusual to see a number of mares and their off-spring all stretched out asleep on the grass under the watchful — and obviously trusted — eye of the one on guard. (I've often wondered whether the mares agree on a rota or whether it is a case of the crafty ones lying down first on the understanding that the last one left standing accepts the obligation which her situation entails.)

The relaxed atmosphere in which six dogs share our home would not be possible without the trust which they have not only in us but in each other too. Even their play depends on trust since youngsters enjoy chasing and wrestling with one another (though not in the house!) with mock ferocity and much clashing of jaws without ever causing so much as a scratch. That they all share in the rearing of puppies depends on the mother's ability to trust the others with her babies and I, of course, know not only that I can trust them to treat me with care but also that any creature — human or non-human — that I introduce into the household will be tolerated, regardless of whether I am present. The newcomer will not, however, be *trusted* unless or until it has earned that trust for itself.

That dogs can be trusted in this way is crucial to the central role that they have in our multi-species household and to the role that dogs in general have in many human societies. It suggests an ability to internalise the principles of the group in which they live, even when the group is predominantly human, to an extent not found, perhaps, in any other species. The cat, by contrast, although a delightful friend and companion, who can certainly be trusted not to use her claws on her friends, cannot — in my experience at least — be trusted with the canary or the tame robin.

Singer was excited by the expectation that the language-project apes would 'convey to us, in more detail than any non-human animals have ever done before, a non-human viewpoint on the world'.[40] Experience has shown, however, that the only 'viewpoint on the world' that these apes have is from behind bars. And what they can — and do — 'convey to us' is that they want to be let out. Fido and Tiddles, without the benefit of language, can also convey to us that they want to be let out: the difference is that we can safely do as they ask and open the door.

## Conclusion

Singer argues that language use and the 'personhood' that depends upon it are sufficient to elevate a being from the status of passive object of moral concern to that of a full member of the 'community of equals'. Although he recognises that this involves responsibilities as well as rights, he ignores the evidence that the great apes lack the psychological and social qualities that would make it possible for them to 'accept certain basic moral principles or rights as governing our relations with each other and enforceable at law'.[41]

This calls into question the definition of 'personhood' accepted by both Singer and Harris. On the one hand we have a 'person' who is apparently able to converse with us but only through the bars of a cage, while on the other we have a companion who is a loved and trusted member of the family, a playmate and protector of the children and perhaps a working partner as

---

[40] Singer & Cavalieri 1993: 309
[41] Singer & Cavalieri 1993: 4

well, who is denied the moral status of the first on the grounds that he cannot introspect.

There are some unfortunate human beings who, although able to use language and aware of themselves in the Lockean sense, have no sense of social responsibility and who, like Goodall's chimpanzees, 'show a lack of consideration for each other's feelings, which . . . may represent the deepest part of the gulf between them and us'. We call such humans 'psychopaths', and accept that, because they cannot be held responsible for their actions, they cannot safely be part of our community. Whether they are 'persons' in Singer's and Harris's sense, I do not know, but I do know that they are not normal human beings. For chimpanzees, however, such behaviour *is* normal, not an aberration. Chimpanzees are not 'like us' in this respect and this fact seems to outweigh the significance of the ways in which they are or are claimed to be 'like us' in terms of genetics, self-consciousness, 'ways of living' and so on.

It is not only the notion of personhood that is challenged by this comparison. Talk of 'equal consideration of interests' and 'speciesism' is also implicated. To classify the great apes as 'persons' is to expect of them a reciprocal acceptance of responsibility which is beyond their capabilities. To classify them as persons is therefore not in their interests. Since there is no race of humans of which this can be said, the notion of speciesism as analogous to racism is also in doubt. Singer's demand that the great apes be protected from being killed, imprisoned or tortured is to be applauded but his claim that they are more worthy than other creatures of such protection is insupportable.

The 'personhood' theory gives a distorted view not only of animals but of humans too. It is significant that the introspective, unemotional and 'rational' individual who seems to exemplify the ideal 'person' could well be regarded as 'inhuman' by others. An example might be that of Dr. Pannwitz, described by Primo Levi in his account of life as a prisoner in Auschwitz. Dr. Pannwitz, a fastidious, meticulous, and coldly detached man, has the job of deciding whether Levi, a chemist, has skills that can be made use of by the regime and Levi writes of the doctor's manner towards him that

> the brain which governed those blue eyes and those manicured hands said: 'This something in front of me belongs to a

species which it is obviously opportune to suppress. In this particular case, one has first to make sure that it does not contain some utilisable element.'

For Levi, the impression of inhumanity was indelible.

> From that day I have thought about Dr. Pannwitz many times and in many ways. I have asked myself how he really functioned as a man; how he filled his time, outside of the Polymerisation and the Indo-Germanic conscience; above all when I was once more a free man, I wanted to meet him again, not from a spirit of revenge, but merely from a personal curiosity about the human soul.
>
> Because that look was not one between two men; and if I had known how completely to explain the nature of that look, which came as if across the glass window of an aquarium between two beings who live in different worlds, I would also have explained the essence of the great insanity of the Third Germany.[42]

Compare Dr. Pannwitz with another individual who came into contact with Jewish prisoners in Nazi Gemany. Bobby was not a person, nor even a human, but a stray dog who befriended the prisoners working in a forest lumber camp, yet it was Bobby's recognition of them as essentially *human* that helped them to *remain* human in spite of the dehumanizing attitude of the people 'who also passed by and occasionally looked at us — they all stripped us of our humanity . . . we were no longer a part of the world'.[43] As the author, Emmanuel Levinas, writes of Bobby, however, 'For him — without question — we were men.'[44]

---

[42] Levi 2000
[43] Levinas 1990
[44] The passages from Levi and Levinas were collated in Finkelkraut 2000

## Chapter Four

# *Beyond the Pale*

---

*Next to the ridicule of denying an evident truth, is that of taking much pains to defend it; and no truth appears to me more evident than that beasts are endow'd with thoughts and reason as well as men. The arguments are in this case so obvious, that they never escape the most stupid and ignorant.*

(David Hume. *A Treatise on Human Nature*)

### I

So far I have challenged the views of those philosophers who, while presenting their theories as radical, retain the traditional hierarchical system which places humans at the top. I have argued that their obsession with a particular type of introspective self-consciousness and the language with which it is identified gives a distorted view of what is important to humans and fails to recognise that many animals have much more in common with 'us' than an ability to feel pain. Singer does want a revolution but the equality of living creatures is compromised; there are special privileges for the great apes on the grounds that they are 'like us' in the most important ways of all.

I will now turn to those who want to retain the status quo where animals are concerned on the grounds that language use affects every aspect of perception and experience, so that languageless animals experience the world so differently from humans that it is anthropomorphic to think of them as significantly 'like us' in even the most basic ways. These philosophers, like those discussed earlier, have an over-intellectual view of what is involved in emotion whether human or animal, but they go further in arguing that even pain is radically different in non-human species. Their attempts to illustrate the differences between animals and humans, however, serve only to emphasise the similarities.

There seems to be a gulf between people whose interactions with animals make it impossible for them to doubt that animals have thoughts, intentions, beliefs and emotions and those theory-driven philosophers whose belief that language is the *sine qua non* for any mental capacities at all leads them to deny that animals have any of these. Although the view of the seventeenth-century philosopher Descartes that animals lack even sentience is rarely voiced (Carruthers's theory comes close, though, as discussed later), there are a number of philosophers who argue that animal behaviour is adequately explained in terms of simple stimulus/response mechanisms.

This is the view of Raymond Frey, who argues that the attribution of desires, beliefs, emotions etc. to animals is the foolish weakness of 'lonely people'[1] who, 'for understandable reasons'[2] indulge in such 'anthropomorphism' in order to persuade themselves that their pets really care about their owners and feel affection for them. Not so Frey, of course. Arriving home to be greeted by a barking, bouncing, tail-wagging dog, he insists that he has no way of knowing whether the animal's behaviour is occasioned by his owner's arrival or by an eclipse of the sun. After all, he argues, 'if other dogs are like my dog, the behavioural repertoire of dogs is itself limited; and wagging its tail, barking and jumping back and forth comprise a large part of this repertoire'.[3] The explanation of Frey's determined failure to comprehend the dog's behaviour is that he is himself the victim of a philosophical theory, which is that belief is essentially propositional and therefore impossible without language. Frey insists that

> if someone were to say, for example, 'The cat believes that the laces are tied', then that person is holding, as I see it, that the cat believes the sentence 'The laces are tied' to be true; and I can see no reason for crediting the cat or any other creature

---

[1] Frey 1980: 84
[2] Frey 1980: 85
[3] Frey 1980: 115

which lacks language, including human infants, with regarding the sentence 'The laces are tied' as true.[4]

Frey explains his use of 'sentence' rather than the generally accepted 'proposition' 'as having the effect of avoiding the implication that the believer must [entertain] the concept of a sentence' but since it does 'commit him to knowing the use of a sentence'[5] this does not help the cat.

The introduction of 'human infants' into the argument raises a new problem for Frey. If a human infant's belief that he is about to be fed depends upon his believing the sentence 'I am about to be fed' to be true, then clearly he can have no such belief. But if, prior to the acquisition of language, he can have no beliefs, how is he ever to acquire language at all? Prelinguistic beliefs — together with desires and emotions — are the essential hooks on which language is hung, but Frey, determined to show the validity of his theory, defies such common-sense views by arguing that non-linguistic creatures 'do not have desires, beliefs, emotions, reasons etc'.[6]

The distinguished American philosopher of language and mind, John Searle, writes illuminatingly on this. His dog is a fortunate animal by comparison with Frey's. His owner has no difficulty in understanding him and warns that to deny canine beliefs and desires is to render canine behaviour unintelligible[7] which is exactly what Frey does, with disastrous results, especially for the dog. Frey insists that we do not need to attribute desires and beliefs to animals in order to understand their behaviour. Ethologists, he argues, don't need to consider 'subjective states' and we should follow the example of Tinbergen who 'develops the concepts of instinct and innate behaviour responses' which he finds quite adequate 'to explain, for example, the rather stylized reproductive behaviour of sticklebacks or the intricate feeding behaviour of goldfish'.[8]

My experience of sticklebacks and goldfish is limited and I am prepared to accept that Tinbergen's objective approach may be adequate to explain their behaviour but my experience of dogs will not allow me to accept that the same is true of them. Frey's

---

[4] Frey 1980: 87
[5] Frey 1980: 88
[6] Frey 1980: 163
[7] Searle 1998
[8] Frey 1980: 83

own inability to understand the behaviour of his dog would seem to support the commonsense view that what might work for sticklebacks will not work for dogs because dogs and sticklebacks are very different kettles of fish. Frey's theory, however, cannot recognise that there may be very significant differences between dogs and sticklebacks because it insists that the role of language is an all-or-nothing matter. A creature that lacks language *cannot* have beliefs, desires, emotions etc. Frey's theory admits of no degrees here; the impossibility is absolute and a languageless dog is as much limited to 'instinct and innate behaviour responses' as a languageless stickleback. In effect, Frey's view of animals differs from that of Descartes only in that Frey does allow that 'animals feel pain, or, as I would prefer to say, since I think they lack this concept, have unpleasant sensations'.[9] At least then, Frey does not believe animals to be insensate, but his claim contains two absurdities. Firstly, it is untrue that the ability to feel pain depends upon having a concept of pain and secondly, to replace 'pain' with 'unpleasant sensations' is to imply a relevant difference between the two locutions where none exists. If their lack of the concept of pain prevents animals from feeling pain, it must surely follow that their lack of a concept of unpleasant sensations prevents them from feeling unpleasant sensations.

Given his view of the capacities of animals, from sticklebacks to dogs, as so uniformly limited, it is not surprising that Frey does not even consider the question of human/animal relationships, other than to dismiss them as an illusion of lonely people. One cannot have a relationship or partnership with a creature that one believes to be bereft of desires, beliefs, emotions etc. One cannot communicate with a creature whose behaviour one believes to be mechanical. Frey's dog is obviously in an unenviable position. His owner even denies that the dog has preferences, arguing that

> in response to the question whether my dog desires or prefers eating to chasing sticks, I can only say that he does both when the situations are to hand and no other impulse interferes. Several times, I have tried putting food before him and

---

[9]  Frey 1980: 163

throwing a stick at the same time; each time he has sought neither the food nor the stick but stood looking at me.[10]

The choice of this example to illustrate an allegedly significant difference between animals and human beings is extraordinary. I am tempted to ask what Frey's own response would be if, having an appetizing meal set before him at the end of a hard day, he were at the same moment invited to play a game of squash. I imagine that he would gaze in disbelief at the speaker, unable to make sense of the situation. Frey would dismiss my comment as anthropomorphic, but I want to say that it is his anthropocentricity which prevents him from recognising the fact that dogs and humans often react in strikingly similar ways to similar situations because there are significant similarities between them. As for the countless human beings whose daily lives depend upon the ability of dogs and human beings to communicate with each other and to form partnerships based on mutual understanding — the owners and trainers of guide dogs, sheepdogs, police dogs and hearing dogs for the deaf, to mention just a few who can hardly be dismissed as lonely victims of illusion — Frey simply ignores their existence: his theory cannot tolerate it.

Frey argues that it is not the philosopher's job to seek out new facts but allows that 'he can and doubtless should concern himself with and even soak himself in the factual material pertaining to the specific arguments under his gaze'.[11] I want to say that the partnerships I have listed *are* part of that factual material and cannot legitimately be ignored. If a blind man who relies upon his guide dog's ability to lead him safely though a busy city centre were a victim of an illusion he would very soon be the victim of a road traffic accident. The dog's inability to agree to the truth of the sentence 'it is not safe to cross the road yet' is demonstrably irrelevant to his ability to make the necessary judgement. Frey's argument that the dog's behaviour can be adequately explained in the same terms as 'the rather stylised reproductive behaviour of sticklebacks' seems to depend upon a culpable ignorance of some very important 'factual material'.

The title of his book, *Interests and Rights: The Case against Animals*, indicates the reason for Frey's refusal to consider any evidence which might challenge his theory: his purpose is to deny

---

[10] Frey 1980: 137
[11] Frey 1980: 2

that animals have either interests or moral rights. Since he denies that humans have moral rights either, Frey's withholding them from animals is not necessarily to allow that animals can be treated with less concern than should be accorded to humans. To deny that animals have *interests*, however, has much more serious implications, since it destroys the foundation on which Singer bases his argument that morality demands that animals be accorded equal consideration of their interests. Frey states that 'if animals do not have beliefs or desires or rational desires or emotions or a moral psychology, and if they do not grasp propositions or make judgements or act for reasons, they do not have interests at all'.[12] Having defined all of these criteria so as to make them language-dependent, Frey concludes that animals cannot have interests. Only human beings have interests because only human beings have language:

> [W]e deem human beings to have a stake in certain things; and what we deem them to have a stake in we deem them to have an interest in. Since we do not deem pigs and chickens to be human beings (or, for that matter, if one wants to distinguish, to be persons), we do not on this view concede them interests.[13]

If we had accepted Frey's arguments so far we might expect that the statement above would be followed by another which recognised that, because of the vital role of language in the 'interests' issue, being human, although a necessary condition for having interests, could not be a sufficient condition and that humans who lacked language would be classified with animals as being without interests. It therefore comes as something of a surprise to learn that this is not Frey's view at all, and that he is happy to grant interests not only to human beings who are permanently comatose but to foetuses and 'future beings' not yet conceived. This is inconsistent with his claim, when discussing values of lives, that his view is not speciesist because he believes some animal lives to be 'more valuable' than some human. But he now claims that

> [t]he ascription of interests in these cases ... is grounded upon our identifying the creatures in question as human beings; therefore ... unless doubts can be raised about whether a par-

[12] Frey 1980: 139
[13] Frey 1980: 156

ticular creature *is* a human being . . . we shall concede it a stake and so an interest in those things typically desired by human beings (in respect of their general well-being).[14]

But even if we could make sense of conceding desire-based interests to the permanently comatose, foetuses and the as yet unconceived, why should we imagine that these would be interests in 'those things typically desired by human beings'? I would suggest that a list of the most typical of such desires would include a desire for freedom of movement, for company, for interesting surroundings and occupation and for a place in a social relationship or group. I cannot see that a list of 'those things typically desired by human beings' will be other than a list of those things desired by typical human beings and I do not consider the permanently comatose, foetuses or the as yet unconceived to be typical human beings.

An indication of the strength with which Frey is gripped by his theory can be gauged from his answer to the question as to how we *know* what human beings 'typically desire'. His explanation that 'we know what sorts of things *these* are by having been among and coming to know something of human beings'[15] might suggest that if he were to spend time in the company of dogs so as to 'come to know something' of dogs, he would be equally aware of the typical desires of dogs which might well include those things on my list above. But to Frey this would be a pointless exercise since his theory tells him that dogs cannot have desires and no amount of experience of their behaviour will persuade him otherwise. His being among human beings only helps him to identity *their* typical desires because his theory tells him that they do have desires.

What are we to make of a theory which, having denied interests to animals on the grounds that interest is 'bound up with desire'[16] and that desire is dependent on language, none the less extends interests to *all* human beings, regardless not only of their linguistic status but even of such basic criteria as consciousness or existence? Having followed Frey's argument through all the steps designed to show that only language users can have interests, we learn that this requirement is to be waived for any creature which can be 'identified as a human being'. One cannot help

---
[14] Frey 1980: 156
[15] Frey 1980: 156
[16] Frey 1980: 157

wondering, therefore, what purpose the argument served since it is not, after all, the case that the class of 'beings with interests' consists of all and only language users, but rather that it consists of all and only human beings. Frey offers no argument to support this favouring of the human species: he begs the question by 'deeming' all human beings to have interests while animals have none and expecting us to accept this without demur. But what reason — apart from *self*-interest, perhaps — have we to accept *this* as a moral basis for our relations with animals any more than the basis offered by Singer et al., of which Frey writes '[t]he major difficulty with the claim that being able to feel pain is a sufficient condition for the possession of interests is that it is an unargued claim'.[17] The trouble with claims of this kind, says Frey, 'is that a value judgement about the intrinsic evilness of pain has come to take the place of argument'.[18] He goes on

> One wants to say, 'Show me that pain is an intrinsic evil; to find the issue unargued, or to be told that it is not the sort of thing which can be argued and shown, and then to see that the value judgement that pain is an intrinsic evil plays a vital role in the case for a moral basis to vegetarianism, is at the very least bound to make the philosopher and anyone else in search of arguments sceptical about the case erected upon such a basis.[19]

> In Roman Catholic and Anglican orthodoxy, for example, though cardinal sins are regarded as intrinsically evil, the mere having of unpleasant sensations is not.... It is sin, not pain, which exercises the orthodox Christian, sin and not pain which he is anxious to guard against.... [S]in is not to be committed merely in order to avoid inflicting pain, either upon oneself or others.[20]

But the introduction of 'intrinsic' here seems to be irrelevant. While it might reasonably be argued that pain itself is not always an evil since it does have an important function in, for example, discouraging the use of a damaged joint and so allowing injuries to heal, it is hard to imagine a convincing argument to show that in other cases pain is *not* evil. If Frey cannot accept that torturing a 'heretic' to death is evil, then I cannot imagine that any *argu-*

---

[17] Frey 1980: 158
[18] Frey 1980: 159
[19] Frey 1980: 161
[20] Frey 1980: 161–2

*ment* would convince him. For such an argument to carry weight the premises would have to be stronger than the conclusion. But what could be stronger than that this is evil? Wittgenstein commented that arguments have to stop somewhere. This seems to be just such a place.

## II

The controversial English philosopher, Peter Carruthers, aims to challenge '[t]he assumption ... that animal experiences (particularly pain) are sufficiently similar to our own to be appropriate objects of moral concern',[21] and argues that:

> Mental states admit of a distinction between conscious and non-conscious varieties that is best accounted for as the difference between states that are and states that are not, regularly made available to conscious (reflexive) thinking. Then since there is no reason to believe that any animals are capable of thinking about their own thinkings in this way, none of their mental states will be conscious. If this account were acceptable, it would follow almost immediately that animals can make no moral claims on us. For non-conscious states are not appropriate objects of moral concern.[22]

Carruthers does admit that 'further research' would be needed before this principle could be accepted 'as a secure basis for moral practice' but I want to suggest that the passage quoted above contains so many assumptions which are either highly suspect or obviously false that it will not do even as a basis for further research, let alone moral practice.

The assumption in the opening sentence that only experiences 'similar to our own' are of moral concern, betrays the anthropocentric prejudice which is a main target of my thesis and which I have challenged in preceding chapters, so I will now move straight on to examine Carruthers's definition of consciousness.

Carruthers's distinction between conscious and non-conscious mental states corresponds to that more often made between aware and self-aware or conscious and self-conscious. But even if we accept his use of 'conscious', not, as in ordinary language, to contrast with unconscious but as equivalent to 'self-aware', his definition of this as an ability to 'think about one's own think-

---
[21] Carruthers 1992: 170
[22] Carruthers 1992: 193

ing' sets a higher threshold for self-awareness than that used by many writers and his assertion that any creature not capable of this high level of self-awareness is incapable of having any conscious states at all is to deny the existence of any mental state equivalent to what we normally refer to as consciousness or awareness. Carruthers gives examples of non-conscious mental states in human beings, concentrating particularly on the phenomenon of blindsight, in which sufferers are able to respond to visual stimuli of which they are not consciously aware, and on the ability of experienced car drivers to drive safely, responding to familiar road conditions, without being aware of what they are doing. I will examine the car-driving case first, in order to show that, for at least two reasons, it will not do as an analogy to illustrate Carruthers's theory of animal consciousness.

My first objection is that a driver is only able to drive 'non-consciously' after a long and very *conscious* learning process. For the inexperienced driver, the occasional realisation that he has just negotiated a stretch of road without thinking about it is an encouraging sign of gradually increasing proficiency. It would not be possible to learn to drive a car without the ability to focus one's attention on the mechanics of the task. Since animals can and do learn complex tasks, it seems unlikely that their permanent mental states are comparable to the non-consciousness of Carruthers's driver. Like children, animals can only be taught by being first persuaded to attend to the task in hand; and this can best be achieved by removing distractions as far as possible. Only by concentrating on what he is doing during the learning period will a dog, horse or child eventually acquire the ability to carry out his tasks 'automatically', even in a public, noisy or unfamiliar situation, when his attention may well be divided. In this case the animal — or the child — is, like the car driver, only able to perform his task 'non-consciously' because he learned it consciously, therefore Carruthers's analogy fails to support his case that animals are permanently 'non-conscious' or even to explain what he means by saying that they are.

My second objection to Carruthers's example is that he describes the non-conscious driver as 'thinking deeply about some aspect of her work or fantasizing about her next summer holiday'[23] — that is, she is not *not thinking* — on the contrary she

---

[23] Carruthers 1992: 170

is 'thinking deeply' — it is just that she is not thinking about what she is doing. How is the example supposed to parallel the animal case — unless Carruthers intends to suggest that the dog is unaware of catching the Frisbee because he is thinking deeply about getting even with the cat next door tomorrow?

The examples that Carruthers offers in support of his claim that animals are non-conscious are unconvincing, but what is his reason for making such a claim? It might be imagined that Carruthers's aim in attempting to persuade us that animals are permanently locked into a non-conscious mental state, similar to that which occasionally occurs as a temporary phenomenon in human beings, is to argue that this makes them unable to feel pain, but this is not his object, since he does not deny that animals feel pain, only that their pain need concern us:

> [I]n the case of brutes: since their experiences, including their pains, are non-conscious ones, their pains are of no immediate moral concern. Indeed since all the mental states of brutes are non-conscious, their injuries are lacking even in indirect moral concern. Since the disappointments caused to the dog through possession of a broken leg are themselves non-conscious in turn, they, too, are not appropriate objects of our sympathy. Hence, neither the pain of the broken leg itself, nor its effects on the life of the dog, have any rational claim upon our sympathy.[24]

But Carruthers's description of the 'non-conscious' mental states of animals is inadequate to justify this conclusion. No grounds are offered in support of the claim that the ability to 'think about one's own thinkings' is a prerequisite for acceptance as an 'appropriate object for moral concern'. I suggest that the only explanation for Carruthers's bizarre theory is his prior commitment to contractualism as 'the most acceptable framework for moral theory'[25] in spite of its exclusion of animals on the grounds of their 'failing to qualify as rational agents'.

Carruthers's reasoning seems to be as follows:

(1) Contractualism offers an acceptable basis for a moral system.

(2) Contractualism cannot accord moral standing to animals.

(3) Therefore animals have no moral standing.

---

[24] Carruthers 1989: 268
[25] Carruthers 1992: 194

But why should we accept this when we could just as well replace it with:

(1) Animals must be accorded moral standing.

(2) Contractualism cannot accord moral standing to animals.

(3) Therefore contractualism does not offer an acceptable basis for a moral system.

This would still satisfy Carruthers's own requirement for a moral theory:

> [O]ur moral beliefs can only be acceptable if they form part of a coherent body of such beliefs, linked together by general principles having at least a powerful intuitive appeal. It follows that a considerable part of our task, when it comes to determining the appropriate moral treatment of animals, will consist in seeing how principles concerning such treatment might fit acceptably into an overall moral theory.[26]

There is nothing here to indicate that only contractualism can fulfil the requirements and my suggested formula has arguably as much 'powerful intuitive appeal' as Carruthers's bizarre conclusion that 'non-conscious animals are not appropriate objects of moral concern'.

Carruthers's case against animals has some unfortunate implications for humans too and his examples of non-conscious mental states in humans are worth closer examination. He explains blindsight as a non-conscious visual experience which sufferers use non-consciously 'to help in the control of their actions'. Since Carruthers reports that blindsight sufferers 'prove remarkably good at describing features of objects presented to them in their [blind] area',[27] although they were not aware of seeing anything, it would presumably be possible for such a person to receive a signalled message in the blind area without being aware of seeing it. If the message were such as to be deeply distressing to the recipient, would not her resultant non-conscious mental state be an appropriate object of moral concern?

Carruthers does not discuss the moral status of human beings during temporary states of non-consciousness, but, to be consistent, he would have to deny that we should be concerned about

---

[26] Carruthers 1992: 5–6
[27] Carruthers 1992: 172

them. Yet mental distress is not rendered less real by the sufferer's inability to 'think about his thinking'. And what of physical pain? Should the pains of Carruthers's absent-minded driver not concern us? The answer to this question confirms the inadequacy of Carruthers' theory, since, rather than supporting his attempt to show the difference between human and animal experience, it underlines the similarity.

Carruthers accepts that animals suffer, feel pain and even disappointment, while arguing that these are non-conscious states, like the state of the non-conscious driver. But are non-consciousness and feeling pain compatible? If the driver is stung by a wasp he will be abruptly awoken from his reverie. If normally painful stimuli did not have this effect we would conclude that the subject was either affected by a local anaesthetic or was *un*conscious rather than merely distracted. Although apparently effective methods of controlling pain by hypnotism, acupuncture and so on, do seem to offer the possibility of redirecting attention away from pain, this is not something that most of us can do for ourselves. I might try to concentrate hard on something else to distract myself from the pain caused by the dentist's drill, but although this may be effective in reducing the *unpleasantness* of my experience, I am brought sharply back to full awareness of it as soon as the pain becomes severe. That this ability to distract myself is beyond the capacity of any animal[28] would seem to suggest that animals, like children, are likely to suffer more acutely than adult humans.

Not only does Carruthers's argument fail to show that the pains of animals are non-conscious but his own analogies can be used to support my counter-claim that non-conscious states and the feeling of pain are incompatible, and that, since animals clearly *do* feel pain (as Carruthers allows) their pains must be conscious. Since Carruthers limits conscious mental states to those capable of reflexive thinking, it follows that not only the temporarily unaware, such as the absent-minded driver or the dreamer, but the permanently senile, the mentally defective and all young children will also be classed as non-conscious and therefore fail to qualify for moral concern. Given Carruthers's

---

[28] That an animal cannot *deliberately* distract itself does not mean that its attention cannot be divided; indeed, the ability to remain alert to possible danger while searching for food is often essential for survival.

own insistence that 'a powerful intuitive appeal' is one of the criteria for an acceptable moral belief, surely even those who might agree with him on the intuitive appeal of the belief that animals do not matter would have some misgivings about a belief which excludes the most vulnerable humans from the circle of moral relevance.

Carruthers falls back on contractualism to argue that those human beings who are not rational agents can be brought within the domain of moral concern either by the argument from social stability or 'slippery slope' argument. Thus, explains Carruthers:

> Contractualism withholds moral rights from animals while at the same time granting them to all human beings. Yet contractualism can explain our common-sense belief that animals should not be caused to suffer for trivial reasons, since causing suffering is expressive of a cruel character.

And Carruthers adds approvingly, 'this position is sufficiently plausible to be acceptable under reflective equilibrium'.[29]

So much the worse for reflective equilibrium and its supposed coherence, we might add, for this view is surely incoherent. If causing suffering is not in itself a bad thing, how can it be bad to behave in such a way? Carruthers never denies that animals both feel pain and suffer, yet he avoids describing the infliction of pain and suffering on them as 'cruel' and prefers the less direct locution 'expressive of a cruel character'. But is there a difference here? Can an action be 'expressive of a cruel character' without *being* a cruel action? I think not, because it is the object of the action rather than the action itself which is crucial to our judgement of a particular act as cruel. Compare this with the notion of violence. A violent character can be expressed, not only by punching a policeman or pounding the table with one's fist but also by shouting, stamping or gesticulating. The violence is in the action, irrespective of its object. But in the case of cruelty, the relevance of object and action is reversed. To hurl objects at a wall is probably a violent action but whether it is also a cruel one depends upon the objects. If they are pots and plates the action is not cruel; if they are babies and puppies it certainly is. (If the pots and plates form part of your prized collection of porcelain it might be cruel of me to hurl them at the wall, but in that case it is you, not they, who are the object of my cruelty.) A cruel character

---

[29] Carruthers 1992: 169

is one inclined to perform cruel actions and an action is cruel if it causes, or is intended to cause, suffering 'for trivial reasons'. The words 'cruel' and 'cruelty' are value-laden: to be a cruel person or to commit a cruel action are both necessarily wrong. If causing suffering to animals is, as Carruthers says, 'expressive of a cruel character' it is cruel and therefore wrong in itself and we have no need of further implications to 'explain our common-sense belief' that this is so. What Carruthers has done is to transfer the basic moral charge from where it belongs — the causing of suffering to the innocent — to something secondary, namely the character of the agent.

Carruthers's claim that 'contractualism can explain' this belief appears to depend upon the 'slippery slope' argument used by the German philosopher of the Enlightenment, Immanuel Kant, and others who argue that cruelty to animals, although not of importance itself, is liable to lead to cruelty to humans, but since Carruthers is attempting to persuade us that animals are too unlike us to warrant moral concern themselves, why should he fear a slide? If the two cases, of causing suffering to animals and causing suffering to humans, are not comparable, it is not only that there is no reason to suppose that the first might lead to the second but also no reason to suppose the first to be expressive of a cruel character. My tendency to neglect my car and forget to fill its radiator has no bearing on my care of my horses because the two cases are not comparable. The car is not an 'appropriate object of moral concern' because it has no feelings and cannot suffer;[30] the horses have feelings and will certainly suffer if deprived of water, so common sense would surely grant them moral status. Carruthers cannot coherently argue that animals are too unlike us to warrant moral consideration while at the same time holding the view that to cause them suffering is likely to lead to cruelty to humans. And, indeed, this concern is in conflict with the belief expressed in Carruthers's statement:

> I regard the present popular concern with animal rights in our culture as a reflection of moral decadence. Just as Nero fiddled while Rome burned, many in the West agonise over

---

[30] I do not wish to imply that these are the only criteria for objects of moral concern, but they are the relevant ones here.

the fate of seal pups and cormorants while human beings elsewhere starve or are enslaved.[31]

Here he seems to suggest that concern for animals and concern for human beings must conflict, a view which is not only totally unsupported and highly implausible but one that lies uneasily beside the suggestion that cruelty to animals is likely to lead to cruelty to humans. Given his view of concern for animals as decadent, it is curious that Carruthers also mentions, without criticism, that contractualism might entail 'indirect duties towards animals, owed out of respect for the legitimate concerns of animal lovers',[32] since it is difficult to see how his arguments allow the 'concerns of animal lovers' to be anything other than illegitimate and entirely reprehensible. He concludes:

> The most important practical conclusion of this book is that there is no basis for extending moral protection to animals beyond that which is already provided. In particular there are no good moral grounds for forbidding hunting, factory farming or laboratory testing on animals.[33]

In the passage from *Brute Experience* quoted earlier, Carruthers argued that the 'non-consciousness of all animal experience, including their pains' results in their failing to qualify for moral concern either direct or indirect. I have examined this claim and have argued that the notion of non-conscious pain is unintelligible and that the fact that animals clearly *do* feel pain — which Carruthers does not deny — shows that they *are* conscious in the normal sense of the word and should therefore be accorded moral consideration. I suggest that, because of Carruthers's prior commitment to the contractualist theory, his arguments here are prompted, not by a genuine desire to assess the moral status of animals, but from an attempt to justify the contractualist exclusion of animals from the area of moral concern. I have argued that this exclusion is a sufficiently serious flaw to disqualify this form of contractualism from consideration as an acceptable moral system.

---

[31] Carruthers 1992: Preface xi
[32] Carruthers 1992: 121
[33] Carruthers 1992: 196

## III

Like Kant before him, Carruthers is committed to an ethical theory which excludes animals. But whereas Carruthers tries to justify the exclusion by claiming that animal experiences are so unlike those of humans that they are 'not appropriate objects of moral concern', Kant was unable to ignore similarities between animals and humans and was troubled by the implications of his theory. It is interesting that, although Kant is famous for his suspicion of emotion as a motive for moral action, it was the reality of animal/human relationships that particularly concerned him.

> If a dog has served his master long and faithfully, his service, on the analogy of human service, deserves reward, and when the dog has grown too old to serve, his master ought to keep him until he dies. Such actions help to support us in our duties towards human beings, whence they are bounden duties.... If a man shoots his dog because the animal is no longer capable of service, he does not fail in his duty to the dog, for the dog cannot judge, but his act is inhuman and damages in himself that humanity which it is his duty to show towards mankind.[34]

Having excluded animals from his Kingdom of Ends, Kant could not condemn callousness towards them except by suggesting that it might lead to callous treatment of human beings, but I suspect that this is the attempt of an humane man to make a loophole in his rigid system of ethics to allow the condemnation of something which he felt to be wrong though it did not breach his rules. Like Singer, he allowed his adherence to the principle of 'reason not emotion' to lead him to some very bizarre conclusions.

Perhaps it was an underlying unease with this principle that caused the ambiguity and inconsistency in the paragraph quoted above. It is certainly very odd to argue that the dog *deserves* reward and that 'his master *ought* to keep him' (my italics) while maintaining that the master 'does not fail in his duty to the dog' if he shoots it when it is no longer of use to him. Surely we would expect the claim that the dog's service deserves reward should entail a duty on the part of his master to provide that reward. It is also unclear whether the reference to his not failing in his duty is intended to convey that he *has* no duty or whether he does have a

---

[34] Kant 1924: 241

duty to the dog but that shooting it would not constitute a failure in that duty. Even less satisfactory is Kant's explanation for the master's not failing in his duty, which is that the dog 'cannot judge'. If a doctor ignores the needs of his patient or prescribes inappropriate or harmful drugs we would not consider that the patient's inability to judge the matter was any bar to our saying that the doctor had failed in his duty to him. On the contrary, we normally feel that the duty is particularly binding when the other is *not* able to judge, which is why a failure in a duty towards a child or senile person is held to be particularly reprehensible.

Even Kant's attempt to condemn mistreatment of animals on the 'slippery slope' argument is suspect because it depends upon an analogy with human cases. Such an analogy can only be valid if there are significant similarities between animals and humans but if there *are* such similarities, surely they entail direct duties to animals themselves and the analogy becomes redundant. If there are no significant similarities how can our treatment of animals 'support us in our duties towards human beings'? Equally, how can our humanity be damaged by our treatment of creatures which lack the features that would demand that we treat them well *for themselves?* No one imagines that my neglect or abuse of my car might damage my humanity or lead to neglect and abuse of humans. Because my car has no significant similarities to human beings there is no analogy. Kant's view that the dog's service should be valued 'on the analogy of human service' depends upon significant similarities between dog and human which are lacking in the case of the motor vehicle. The problem might seem to be solved by Bentham. The question is not 'Can they *reason?* Nor can they *talk?* But *can they suffer?*'

But this will not settle Kant's difficulty because his concern is not so much the avoidance of suffering as the bestowal of a reward for services rendered. He would not be appeased by the argument that the ungrateful master could shoot his dog without causing it any suffering. Because his ethical framework places animals beyond the pale of moral concern, Kant cannot acknowledge any direct duties towards them. At the same time, he cannot ignore the similarity between the master's relationship with his dog and that with a human servant. It is the relationship with the individual which matters and in this respect I find myself much more in sympathy with Kant than with Singer, who is concerned only with generalisations. Indeed, Kant is not only moved by the man/dog relationship, but also by relationships between animals, and the passage I quoted above continues '[t]he more we come into contact with animals, and observe their behaviour, the more we love them, for we see how great is their care of their young. It is then difficult for us to be cruel in thought even to a wolf'.

I have said that Kant's discomfort with the case of the dog arises from his exclusion of animals from the Kingdom of Ends, the inhabitants of which are 'ends in themselves' and are not to be treated only as 'means to ends'. I have suggested that Kant's desire to find a justification for giving the deserving dog the same reward as the deserving human servant is an indication of a deep flaw in this distinction. If the human servant is an end in himself, he must not be valued only for the service he can give and when he is too old to serve he must continue to be valued for himself. Since the dog, according to Kant's system of ethics, can only be of value as a means to an end, his value is inseparable from his ability to serve his master and cannot outlast it. Kant regards the master as having a duty towards the human but not towards the dog (although I have noted an ambiguity in his wording here), but I am inclined to think that talk of 'duty' only arises in the absence of appreciation or affection for the individual. When an elderly relative worries about 'being a burden' to her family, she reveals a fear that she was only ever valued for what she could do and not as an 'end in herself'. The thought that her family have a *duty* to care for her will be little comfort. We would all prefer to think that our friends and relatives are bound to us by ties of love and interest rather than by a sense of duty. It seems appropriate to think of duty in such contexts as a safety net which may avert disaster when affection and concern fail. Appeals to duty should not arise in a concerned relationship and if they do they indicate that something has gone badly wrong. I see no reason why this should not apply to relationships with animals just as much as to human relationships.

Again, a difficulty arising from a theory which seeks to emphasise a difference between human and non-human has served to underline the similarities. The particular similarities between the cases of the old lady and the old dog are worth closer examination as they highlight the central role that relationships play in the lives of both humans and dogs. In drawing an analogy between the long and faithful service of the dog and a human servant, Kant overlooks an important difference. The human servant probably has family and friends of his own with whom he will be glad to spend his retirement on the pension that the good master supplies. For the dog, his master is not just an employer, but probably takes the part of friend and family too, so that a pension of food and shelter will not ensure a happy retirement if he no longer has the company, friendship and approval for which he has worked. The dog's case is therefore more analogous to that of the elderly relative mentioned above, for whom the greatest distress of old age and infirmity is not the pain and reduced mobility but the loss of the role in her family on which her identity depended. When our old bitch, Branwen, suffered a stroke, it was her determination to continue to oversee the doings of the household that motivated her to overcome the physical handicap and, I am sure, made her life worth living. When a final seizure reduced her to the role of patient rather than carer, only euthanasia could end her obvious distress which was caused, I believe, not by pain but by the loss of the role she had played for so long.

Many human nursing home residents, having been removed from their homes to be 'properly looked after', deteriorate rapidly in their 'improved' situation and it is by no means obvious that western sensitivity which demands that the failing animal be 'put to sleep' and the elderly human tidied away to vegetate, is to be preferred to that of other cultures where the elderly remain part of the family, even when that means their struggling to help with the work.

## IV

Like Carruthers, the philosopher Michael Leahy believes that in the debate on the ethical treatment of animals the question of their self-consciousness is of crucial importance. In *Against Liberation* he considers several of the claims for self-consciousness in animals, such as responding to personal names or images in a mirror, and dismisses them all, saying, 'Self-awareness, even in an absolutely minimal form, is not merely to recognise oneself, but to be aware of recognising oneself *as oneself* with much of what that implies'.[35] Leahy argues that this is only possible for language-users and adds, with an unfortunately ill-assorted metaphor; 'Language is the key which unlocks horizons light-years beyond those of animals' [36] and goes on to list the benefits of language, such as our ability to 'make the thoughts of others our own', 'share their hopes' and 'contemplate our personal past and future'. Most of this is uncontroversial, although I have argued at length against the implication that non-language users are unable to communicate their feelings and desires or to have any notion of past and future. But the most significant part of Leahy's claim is that although language brings great benefits it also brings a much greater capacity for suffering. 'The presence of self-consciousness guarantees that we are prone to a range and intensity of suffering light-years from that of brute beasts'.[37] And he dismisses 'Bentham's over-exposed retort that what calls forth our moral concern, no matter their capabilities, is that animals suffer'. Leahy's argument is not that animals are unconscious or insensitive to pain, indeed he argues forcefully against any suggestion that this could be so.

> The grounds for attributing sensation to animals and human beings are equally imperative. To be sceptical over the susceptibility of mammals to pain ... is to find oneself in the counter-intuitive position of implying that the screaming astronauts in their defective capsule were just conceivably all play-acting. ... Similar strategies can be used to reject indecision over brute consciousness; as opposed to *self-*

---

[35] Leahy 1991: 145
[36] Leahy 1996: 200
[37] Leahy 1991: 256

consciousness which involves far more than the ape's merely responding to a mirror-image by signing 'Me Washoe'.[38]

So far Leahy has stated his views clearly but unfortunately his linguistic competence weakens as his argument progresses, making accurate analysis difficult. He has stated his case that animals are conscious and susceptible to pain but that, lacking language and therefore self-consciousness, their capacity to suffer is much less than ours. 'If it can be shown that the susceptibility of animals to suffering is diminished by the implications of their inability to use language, then this too is of moral importance, since it is agreed that suffering is.'[39] But how are we to draw a distinction between 'suffering' and 'susceptibility to suffering'? Surely the suffering results from a susceptibility to the *pain* in the same way that my feeling cold results from my susceptibility to cold. I suffer as a result of my susceptibility to cold, not as a result of my susceptibility to suffering. Leahy, however, proceeds to list four ways in which, he claims, human suffering is greater than that of animals. Since I want to challenge each of these claims, I will examine them in detail, quoting the relevant passages from *Brute Equivocation*.

> 1. An injured dog will lick the affected part, may whimper or shriek, or betray sympton (sic) that are the stock-in-trade of veterinarians. It tends to recover quickly. A beast's pain is surprisingly short-lived, in part because of the effects of thanatosis; a temporary paralysis, akin to hypnosis, brought about by the shock of confrontation. . . . But humans are far more discomforted by pain, however intense.[40]

This passage seems to contain several points which are crucial to Leahy's argument and which I want to challenge. Unfortunately it also contains so many linguistic errors that the meaning is often obscured, which makes my task difficult.

The reference to 'symptons' might appear to be a straightforward typing error for 'symptoms' but the reader's ability to make allowances for minor errors depends upon the correct word fitting the context and 'symptoms' will not do here, since symptoms are not the 'stock-in-trade' of the veterinarian. The only occupation for which symptoms might be the stock-in-trade

---

[38] Leahy 1996: 198
[39] Leahy 1991: 256
[40] Leahy 1996: 200

is that of the professional malingerer. 'Thanatosis' is a medical term for gangrene,[41] but at least Leahy explains his idiosyncratic use of the term, as 'temporary paralysis brought about by shock', so we do know what he means by it. But knowing what he means by the term does not help to clarify his argument here, as there is no explanation as to how 'temporary paralysis' could result in a rapid recovery from pain. Leahy refers elsewhere to 'Dr. Livingstone's paralysis of feeling when seized by the lion'[42] and also to the 'injuries in war and disasters [which] provide numerous anecdotes of the anaesthetic effect of shock'. But these are cases where the shocked victim is not *immediately* aware of his injuries: once the shock wears off he may well be in great pain, for the effect of the shock is to delay the *onset* of pain, not to reduce its duration. Leahy's dog is described as licking its wound, whimpering or shrieking and therefore in obvious pain and certainly not numbed by shock. 'Thanatosis' is not only the wrong word here, the explanation it is intended to offer is wrong too. It is also odd that Leahy, anxious to show that humans suffer *more* than animals, should choose to illustrate his case with these examples of *absence* of pain in humans, but he repeatedly uses the 'shock' theory to raise the 'serious questions to be asked about the extent and nature of the alleged suffering' of animals. However the 'thanatosis' phenomenon does not seem to be essential to the argument presented in Leahy's first paragraph (no. 1 quoted above) to show that animal suffering is much less than that of humans. The argument there seems to run as follows:

(a) A dog in pain shows symptoms of pain such as licking the wound, shrieking etc.

(b) A dog which does not show such symptoms is not in pain.

(c) Dogs do not lick and shriek for long

(d) Therefore their pain is 'surprisingly short-lived'.

(e) Conclusion. Pain causes much more suffering to humans than to animals.

---

[41] I am grateful to Dr. William Ritchie, researcher, and Dinah Roberts, Librarian, both of Dyfed-Powys Health Authority for their advice on this.
[42] Leahy 1991: 217

The suggestion that the injured dog is only in pain as long as he continues to 'lick the affected part, . . . whimper or shriek etc.' seems to come from Leahy's interpretation of Wittgenstein's question as to whether there can be pain without pain behaviour. Leahy has argued that to believe this possible would be to be guilty of 'philosophical dualism; the assumption that pain is an ineradicably mental event, available only to private introspection, and for which no publicly specifiable criteria (whether neurological, organic or behavioural) is necessary'.[43]

Leahy goes on to acknowledge Wittgenstein's influence here in 'rejecting dualism. Private mental events, including the mind itself, are, in the absence of publicly observable criteria, corrosive myths bred of linguistic confusion'.

I cannot tell whether Leahy's reference to both 'publicly specifiable criteria' and 'publicly observable criteria' in the same passage is itself a 'linguistic confusion'. He does not differentiate between the two which suggests that he regards them as synonymous but this is plainly false. That a square circle is not publicly (or even privately) observable does not prevent me from publicly specifying that that is what I want to draw.

In spite of his reference here to 'neurological, organic or behavioural criteria' of pain and later to 'tell-tale symptoms', Leahy seems otherwise to regard the absence of the most dramatic pain behaviour as evidence of absence of pain. He fails to recognise that 'publicly observable criteria' may be much more subtle than the licking and shrieking which he seems to regard as the dog's standard response to pain. No wonder that he finds the speed of recovery of injured dogs surprising since he equates the abatement of the immediate and very obvious reaction to *injury* with the cessation of *pain*. He confuses the initial reaction with the 'learning to live with pain' process that follows it. Although taking his lead from Wittgenstein, whose comment that 'only of a living human being and what resembles (behaves like) a living human being can one say: it has sensations; it sees; is blind; hears; is deaf is conscious or unconscious'[44] has been so often quoted, Leahy does not seem to consider whether the dog he describes *is* behaving like a human being in pain. Why should he believe that the dog's pain *ceases* with the cessation of its licking and shrieking when we do not assume that human pain has

---
[43] Leahy 1996: 199
[44] Wittgenstein 1953: I. 281

abruptly ceased because the sufferer has stopped yelling and writhing? Human pain behaviour takes many forms, from screaming and thrashing about to lying hunched up and silent or just being uncharacteristically gloomy or irritable. The same is true of canine pain behaviour: if my dog and I both burn ourselves on the stove, we will probably both yelp and jump back and while I suck my burned finger she will lick her burned nose. Even a minor burn may be quite painful for some time, but neither of us will continue to yelp, jump or lick. But Leahy seems to imagine that shrieking and licking (or attempting to soothe the injury) are the paradigm of pain behaviour in all species and that their absence can only be explained either by absence of pain or by a deliberate suppression of this natural behaviour. He states his case in the fourth of his paragraphs on the differences between human and animal pain, but since the argument follows naturally from the above I will deal with it next.

> 4. Human beings can suffer in silence. Are animals capable of it? Babies appear not to be. Mothers, almost intuitively, diagnose specific cries and whimpers as symptoms of needs of which the baby is unaware. But as infants mature they note the advantages of adopting a 'stiff upper lip' and so regulate their vocalising on this or that occasion and for this or that *reason*. Even the most optimistic liberationists are wary of attributing this competence even to chimpanzees.

Leahy then quotes Wittgenstein's doubts on the possibility of a dog simulating pain before continuing

> So if we claim that the creature *can* inhibit pain, we imply that it knows the reasons why it is doing so. This seems excessively anthropomorphic in the absence of language. But if we *deny* it then . . . it becomes difficult to sustain the tempting claim that creatures which have appalling injuries, but which are nonetheless quiescent and not betraying other tell-tale symptoms *must be* in pain. But if they cannot suffer in silence they cannot be in pain.[45]

Leahy follows this with a catalogue of the 'highly misleading' stories of animal suffering in 'alleged atrocities in some modern US research laboratories', of 'neglected cattle awaiting slaughter' and crated veal calves, the significance of which he believes to be undermined by his argument, and dismisses 'the perennial

---

[45] Leahy 1996: 201

protests in the UK over the export of live cattle as sentimental hot air'.

As I suggested in my analysis of his first paragraph, Leahy is wrong not only in his description of animal pain and pain behaviour but also in his representation of the human case in that he implies that only our intentional suppression of pain behaviour prevents us from screaming and writhing for the duration of the pain. While I agree with Leahy's initial assertion, that human beings can suffer in silence, I find it difficult to reconcile this with his earlier statement that 'private mental events, including the mind itself, are, in the absence of publicly observable criteria, corrosive myths bred of linguistic confusion' which suggests that absence of publicly observable criteria indicates absence of pain. His suggestion that babies are unable to suffer in silence seems to be right, although it is hard to imagine an infant – even a 'mature' one – being able to 'note the advantages of a stiff upper lip' and even adult humans only deliberately suppress their 'cries and whimpers' in particular situations, such as in the dentist's chair. In *this* case, they may well 'regulate their vocalising for this or that *reason*', but Leahy follows this with an unjustified conclusion that 'if we claim that an animal *can* inhibit pain (sic) we imply that it knows the reasons why it is doing so'. I will assume that Leahy's reference to the ability to 'inhibit pain' is a mistake and that he intended to refer to the inhibition of pain *behaviour*, although the possibility that the suppression of pain behaviour might lead to the inhibition of the pain itself is an interesting one.

Leahy's reasoning seems to be as follows:

(a) Pain is always expressed by crying and whimpering unless a conscious effort is made to suppress it.

(b) Babies cannot suppress their cries and whimpers because they are not self-conscious.

(c) Self-conscious humans can suppress their cries and whimpers when there is a reason for them to do so.

(d) Therefore, only a creature which 'knows the reason why it is doing so' is able to suppress its cries and whimpers.

(e) Because animals lack language they are not self-conscious and cannot know their reasons for acting.

(f) Therefore animals cannot suppress their cries and whimpers.

(g) Therefore a silent animal cannot be in pain.

There are two major flaws in this argument. Firstly I believe that Leahy's basic premiss (my 'a') is simply wrong, and secondly, 'd' does not follow from 'c', since acting for a reason does not necessarily entail knowing the reason (where 'knowing' is defined as being able to *give* the reason), nor does the fact that I sometimes act for a reason preclude my sometimes acting for no particular reason. When my dog goes to the door, barks and looks expectantly at me, I know that she wants me to open the door so that she can go out, but is she acting for a *reason*? Well, obviously not if we define 'having a reason' as being able to put it into words, but this does not mean that her case parallels that of Leahy's infant emitting 'cries and whimpers as symptoms of needs of which the baby is unaware'. In the case of Leahy's baby, the infant is unaware of its need and is dependent upon its mother to identify the cause of its distress. In the case of my dog she is aware of her need — this does not entail *self*-awareness — and she knows how it can be satisfied — by going out. She also knows that this requires the door to be opened (she never attempts to walk through the closed door) and she also knows that she cannot open it for herself (she has tried in the past but the handle on this door cannot be opened by nose or paw: she knows that she can manipulate the handles of other doors in the house and if she wants one of *those* opened, she doesn't bother to 'ask' me.) That she depends upon me to understand what she wants is a very different matter from the baby's dependence on its mother's 'almost intuitive' (presumably as opposed to 'learned') diagnostic ability. I have learned to understand what my dog wants: she has learned how to enlist my cooperation and if I fail to respond to her initial signals she will try others (gaining my attention by a paw on my knee or by nosing my hand and then returning to the door with a 'woof' while wagging her tail and looking at me again). If the baby's mother fails to respond appropriately to his cries he does not change his tactics because he neither knows what he wants nor that his mother can be persuaded to provide it: all he can do is to continue to cry, but not for a reason.

But even without this objection Leahy's argument fails to support his conclusion because his basic premiss (my 'a') is false both in the case of animals and in the case of adult humans. Since, even in the absence of inhibition, pain is not always expressed by crying and whimpering, it cannot be the case that the absence of vocalization indicates its deliberate suppression. When the dentist's drill causes me pain, do I need a *reason* not to cry out? (A fear of offending the dentist perhaps.) Might not the reverse be the case; that I *do* cry out because I have a reason to do so? (To let the dentist know that he is hurting me.) To insist that I suppress my cries in order not to offend the dentist implies that I *would* cry out if I were alone, but would I?

Leahy's implication that animals cannot 'suffer in silence' betrays a serious ignorance of animal behaviour. In the next chapter I examine the way in which the emotions of different species are typically displayed in very different behaviour, as illustrated by the Cheshire Cat's observation that dogs and cats express their pleasure and annoyance in ways which are diametrically opposed. From Leahy's point of view, both cats and dogs at least get *one* thing right, in that they do sometimes vocalise when in pain but, as I have already noted, Leahy is mistaken in assuming that when the yelps and cries cease the pain has gone. It is significant that our two favourite companions, dog and cat, are predators as we are and, like us, use their voices to communicate their pleasure and pain, contentment and distress. The hungry cat will mew hopefully by the fridge door and purr with pleasure when her plea is answered. The dog waiting in eager expectation of a walk will whine impatiently by the door and yelp in pain when it is inadvertently opened on his toes. Vocalization in pain or fear seems to be much more common in predators than in prey species, which would only increase their problems if they cried out when pursued or injured. So although red deer stags, for example, are extremely vocal when defending their breeding territory against their rivals, the hunted individual runs in silence. By contrast, the baying of the pursuing hounds serves not only to keep the pack together but also for communication between hounds and huntsman. If the hounds lose the trail they will cast about in silence until one picks up the scent, giving tongue and alerting his fellows as he sets off again. Unfortunately for the stag, a cry from *him* would result not in an avenging herd of his fellows racing to the rescue, but only in a greater advantage to his pursuers.

A lack of vocalization then, can hardly be taken as evidence for lack of distress and Leahy's[46] claim that animals are incapable of 'suffering in silence' is clearly absurd. Leahy makes the mistake of failing to realise that, for the reasons given above, many animals, particularly prey species, *must* 'suffer in silence' to avoid drawing attention to their increased vulnerability. Leahy seems to assume that vocalization is an essential part of pain behaviour and that its absence must indicate either a lack of pain or an attempt to deceive. He then reasons that, since an animal cannot pretend to be in pain, neither can it pretend not to be in pain. Therefore, he concludes, a quiet animal isn't in pain.

It is not because they have a *reason* to remain quiet that prey species rarely cry out but because evolution has resulted in the development of a behavioural repertoire which excludes anything — such as screaming when injured — that would make the creature more vulnerable by attracting the attention of predators. Leahy's account entails that the injured deer, if in pain, has a *reason* for remaining silent but what sense is there in seeking a reason for the absence of behaviour which is, in any case, not part of a creature's repertoire? That the deer does not 'know the reason' for its silence is irrelevant. Talk of reasons is not appropriate here.

Leahy is rightly critical of the anthropomorphism of interpreting animal behaviour in terms only legitimately applicable to human beings, but his ignorance of animal behaviour leads him to make the more serious mistake of thinking that only animals which show what he thinks of as typically *human* pain behaviour can be in pain. As Rollin says

> It is not the people who impute pain to animals who are anthropomorphic; they have good evolutionary, physiological, and behavioural reasons to do so. It is, rather, those who *deny* pain to animals on the grounds that their behaviour is unlike ours who are anthropomorphic; for who else besides someone guilty of the grossest anthropomorphism would expect expressions of animal feelings to be precisely like ours, would expect a cow in pain, for example, to run about beating its breast and bellowing 'Oy vay'? (even Gentiles don't do this) . . . [and later the same page] . . . People who deal with horses a great deal and who follow the dictates of experience and common sense are aware that in some cases

---

[46] Leahy 1996: 200–1

mere tightening of the palebral (eyelid) muscles eloquently bespeaks great agony, but obviously not to the person who is expecting the full range of human pain behaviour from the horse.[47]

Nor, one might add, to Leahy, who tells us that he avoids horses on the grounds that he 'finds their smell repulsive'. Rollin's comment supports my argument that the ability to 'read' behaviour, of whatever species, is dependent upon experience which is both wide and deep — experience which cannot be gained by avoiding the animal in question.

The next part of Leahy's argument deals with the possibility — or for Leahy the *im*possibility — of mental suffering in animals.

> 2. Humans can of course suffer where there is no pain at all or very little. Unexpected lumps that do not hurt can nevertheless have catastrophic consequences and reduce people to the depths of despair. This is all beyond the wit of animals.[48]

Few would argue with Leahy's claim that only humans can suffer the mental anguish of worrying about the implications of the painless lump which might be a tumour, but from this uncontroversial example Leahy makes the unjustified leap to the assumption that animals are never capable of suffering anxiety or fear about the future, and dismisses any suggestion that they suffer mental distress through fearful anticipation when, for example, waiting at a slaughterhouse. Leahy's claim is that, without language, animals cannot anticipate future events and he acknowledges the influence of the British philosopher Stuart Hampshire in this. Hampshire argues

> It would be senseless to attribute to an animal a memory that distinguished the order of events in the past, and it would be senseless to attribute to it an expectation of an order of events in the future. It does not have the concept of order, or any concepts at all.[49]

But Hampshire is here applying the same Procrustean method that led Peter Carruthers into such difficulties — the formulation of a theory, followed by a denial of the validity of any evidence that might disprove it. Hampshire seems to have first decided

---

[47] Rollin 1989: 146
[48] Leahy 1996: 200
[49] Hampshire 1959: 199

that neither a memory of the order of events in the past nor an expectation of the order of events in the future is possible without a 'concept of order', and thus finds himself obliged to deny any such memory or expectation on the part of animals, which, as non-language users, are incapable of having concepts in Hampshire's linguistically defined sense.

Only a prior commitment to the necessity of a 'concept of order' and a particular understanding of what that comes to could explain Hampshire's determination to ignore the evidence that animals *do* both remember and anticipate the order of events: their ability to predict the behaviour of others depends upon their being able to do so. Owners of pet dogs are all too aware of the ability of dogs to remember the order of events in the past and to use this to predict the order of future events: mounting excitement in anticipation of a walk results from the dog's observation of the pattern of 'events' in the owner's behaviour. In this case the dog's reaction is one of delight and eager anticipation, but it is just as likely that his memory of unpleasant events leads to him predicting − and fearing − unpleasant events in the future. Wittgenstein suggests that a dog can only be concerned with its immediate situation. 'One can imagine an animal angry, frightened, unhappy, happy, startled. But hopeful? And why not?'.[50] It is clear from the sentences following this quotation that the question is to be answered in terms of the animal's supposed inability to look forward to events removed in space or time:

> A dog believes his master is at the door. But can he also believe his master will come the day after tomorrow? And *what* can he not do here? . . . Can only those hope who can talk? . . .

'The day after tomorrow' may be a notion only available to language users, but it would be wrong to leap to the conclusion that because *that* idea would not be possible for non-language users they cannot have *any* notion of future events. My dogs very much enjoy travelling with us by car and are always on the alert for any sign that a trip may be in the offing but the one indication that they apparently (and rightly) regard as incontrovertible evidence that they are to be included is my putting into the car the container that provides them with drinking water en route.

---

[50] Wittgenstein 1953: P 11 i

When, as is often the case, I do this the night before the trip, the dogs' behaviour seems to indicate that although they do not expect to go *now* (because other necessary conditions — such as the house being shut up — are missing) they *do* believe (or perhaps *hope*) that we will go tomorrow, and the following morning when first let out of the house they will not run into the field as usual but will make straight for the parked car. Young children can certainly look forward to hoped-for events long before they can cope with the notion of 'the day after tomorrow': 'tomorrow' is more easily grasped as 'when you get up in the morning'. Those who live with dogs know that adult dogs with extensive experience of human behaviour make a similar connection for themselves.

The ability to look forward to a pleasant experience may itself be one of the pleasures of life, but the lives of animals, like the lives of humans, can be made miserable by anticipation of unpleasant experiences. The signs of an impending journey — so eagerly anticipated by our dogs, who hope to accompany us — may have very different implications for dogs who expect to be either left at home alone or sent to a boarding kennel. For them, the sight of luggage being stowed in the car can be enough to cause acute mental distress as a result of their 'expectation of events in the future'. Those who would dismiss these examples as anecdotal need only turn to the well-documented laboratory tests in which pigeons have learned to peck discs in various sequences to obtain food and, more remarkably, rats have learned to avoid foods which have previously made them ill, for ample evidence of a memory (conscious or unconscious) of 'the order of events in the past' and 'an expectation of an order of events in the future', without which such learning would be impossible.

Hampshire's claim is insupportable. My examples have shown that its two elements, that

(a) memory and anticipation of an order of events are dependent on a concept of order, and

(b) animals do not have a concept of order

cannot *both* be true. Rather it must be true *either* that a concept of order is *not* a necessary requirement for memory and anticipation *or* that animals *do* have such a concept. Hampshire's reference to 'animals, lacking the means either of expressing or entertaining even an elementary thought about their own future...' is based on a mistaken theory and Leahy's acceptance of it, coupled with a lack of relevant experience of animals, has flawed his reasoning too.

My examples so far have been of animals learning from experience that a given pattern of behaviour is likely to lead to a particular outcome and I have argued that they are therefore able to enjoy the anticipation of a pleasant experience or dread the occurrence of an unpleasant one. This argument will not do, however, to challenge Leahy's claim that only 'dangerous muddle-headedness' can explain 'the claim by liberationists like Harriet Schleifer that animals awaiting slaughter suffer from awareness of what approaches'.[51]

The journey to the slaughterhouse is one-way and the animals have no opportunity to learn from experience what to expect, so is Leahy right here? Well, if he is right to take 'what approaches' as meaning that the animals are aware that they are to die, then his objection may be justified, as may his attack on Stephen Clark's claim that animals might 'fear death, and flee it as the greatest of evils'.[52] This is not to concede that animals do not suffer great mental distress prior to slaughter but rather to point out that the fear of *death* is unlikely to be a factor here. But when Leahy describes Schleifer's claim as 'the rhetoric of the death camps but inappropriately applied' and 'confusing the agitation or even prostration which occurs in badly run holding yards as a result of heat, noise, overcrowding or lack of water, with the uniquely human fear of impending death' he implies that, without the specific fear of *death*, the animals do not suffer significantly. He also implies that, for humans, fear of death is paramount; a view that I will examine later. But first I want to argue that modern farm animals, unlike the happily unaware 'lambs to the slaughter' of the Bible, suffer not only physical but also mental distress and I will support my claim with several examples.

Firstly, although the animals at the slaughterhouse have no previous experience of *that* situation, they have probably had other unpleasant experiences which would result in their being extremely apprehensive of this one. Because modern intensive

[51] Leahy 1996: 203
[52] Clarke 1977: 40 quoted by Leahy 1991: 164

farming involves the maximum number of animals being reared by the smallest possible work force, direct contact between man and animal is kept to a minimum and in many cases the only handling that animals experience is that required for castration, tail docking, dipping, injecting etc., all of which are sufficiently unpleasant experiences to result in the animal regarding any human contact with fearful anticipation of pain to come. Even such individuals that have somehow been spared these experiences are unlikely to be unaffected by fear and mental stress caused by either (or both) of two further factors. One is the fear of unfamiliar situations which is vital for the survival of many wild species but which, in intensively reared domestic species, deprived of the opportunity to experience and investigate novel surroundings, can lead to panic reactions to any change in their barren environment, as is described by Singer in *Animal Liberation*:

'Confined pigs are so delicate that any disturbance can bring on the symptoms, including a strange noise, sudden bright lights, or the farmer's dog...' These symptoms of 'Porcine Stress Syndrome' are described as 'extreme stress... rigidity, blotchy skin, panting, anxiety, and often sudden death'.[53] If this degree of stress can be caused by such innocuous stimuli, one does not need to ascribe a fear of death to such animals in order to believe that they suffer very acute distress when packed into a lorry, subjected to a long road journey, and herded into a holding pen at a busy slaughterhouse.

The other way in which animals can be fearful even without previous experience of a situation is by the communication of fear by others, a phenomenon implicitly denied by Leahy in his claim that only language users can share the hopes and fears of others. It is certainly the case that *we* often depend upon language to do these things and Leahy's mention of the human tendency to worry over 'unexpected lumps that do not hurt' is just one example of how we are influenced by what we have read or have been told, but it would be wrong to assume that animals cannot be affected by the fear of others. It is not only Seyfarth's vervet monkeys that warn each other of danger: alarm signals are part of the repertoire of all social animals and birds. A new-born calf, lamb or foal will totter fearlessly up to anyone within reach, only to be called back by its mother's warning

---

[53] Singer 1976: 120 quoting a farm journal

voice, and within a few days it will react with fear at the approach of a stranger, even though it has had no direct experience of harm. If hand-reared from birth these creatures grow up without this learned fear and have to learn about dangers by the risky route of first-hand experience. The human ability to 'share the thoughts and hopes of others' may be more sophisticated, but Leahy is wrong to ignore the extent to which animals clearly do learn from others to fear things which they have not directly experienced as harmful. This ability to learn fear indirectly is typical of wild creatures but absent in those hand-reared by humans which are often thereby rendered incapable of surviving if released into the wild. The fate of the dodo is believed to have resulted from its lack of fear of humans and underlines the survival value of the ability to learn from the experience of others.

Leahy argues that fear in animals is essentially unlike fear in humans. He writes of 'the attenuated language-game of fear and other feelings that . . . we use of animals'[54] and claims that as soon as we refer to animals as 'being afraid . . . the analogy with human fear is already beginning to break down'.[55] This, according to Leahy, is because human beings are afraid for a *reason*, whereas animal fears are merely *caused*. He illustrates this by noting that 'People are argued out of their fear and anger if, to their satisfaction, it can be shown to have been groundless.'[56] By contrast, he argues; 'it is pointless to attempt to convince a dumb brute, cowering under the threatening lash, that its master is rehearsing his part in *A Midsummer Night's Dream* . . .'[57]

Again Leahy has chosen an unfortunate and confusing example, as it would be equally pointless to attempt to convince a Shakespearian scholar that the whip wielding master was 'rehearsing his part in *A Midsummer Night's Dream*' as there are no brute-beating scenes in the play. But in any case, it is not true that animals are unable to distinguish between a genuine attack and a mock one. Dogs and other animals often play-fight with one another and pet dogs, like young children, often enjoy being chased by a trusted adult pretending to be fierce. Leahy goes on to give a further example: 'we stroke a startled horse but do not

---

[54] Leahy 1991: 136
[55] Leahy 1991: 135
[56] Leahy 1991: 135
[57] Leahy 1991: 135

even consider reasoning with it . . .'.[58] But, once again, his example will not make the point he wants because he has moved from *fear* to being *startled* — two reactions which are as clearly distinct in animals as in humans. My horse and I are both likely to be startled if you creep up behind us and shout 'Boo!' but there would be no point in your trying to reason *either of us* out of our response; we are not *afraid*. When, however, my horse clearly *is* afraid, perhaps of entering an unfamiliar lorry or passing an alarming machine on the road, although I cannot *reason* with her I can clearly *demonstrate* to her that the object is not a threat after all. In the case of the lorry I can step on to the loading ramp, stamping on it so that she can judge its stability by the sound and I can encourage her to do the same, which she probably will, with obvious satisfaction, before walking up it. This does not seem to be very far removed from the human ability to be 'argued out of' a fear which 'can be shown to have been groundless'. Nor is it always the case that humans *can* be so persuaded: when offered a job as a window-cleaner on a sky-scraper a man who is afraid of heights does not lose his fear by being told that his safety harness is unbreakable or that no one has ever fallen from the building. Yet again, a close examination of Leahy's attempt to emphasise the *difference* between human and animal cases has served to reveal the similarities. Not only does he misunderstand fear in animals but in humans too.

But Leahy is determined to deny any possibility of usefully comparing human and animal cases and argues that any apparent similarity is illusory, a view which he hammers home with his example of a hunted fox. He suggests that we might be tempted to think of the fleeing fox as 'terrified and running for its life' but assures us that it is 'totally devoid of these dimensions of dread and distress. Its movements are purposeful, much as we might describe a plant that opens its leaves to catch the rain, but it is incapable of knowing it. The animal is acting in accordance with its nature; behaving instinctively'.[59]

This suggestion that to behave instinctively is incompatible with suffering mental distress is also apparent in Leahy's paragraph three:

---

[58] Leahy 1991: 138
[59] Leahy 1991: 257

> Mary Midgley maintains, for instance, that social birds and mammals are upset by solitude or by the removal of their young (1983 p. 90). This would be termed 'mental suffering' in human beings. This surely is sentimental talk when used of animals, the language misleadingly specific in recalling the human paradigm, where what we are confronted with are mere prototypical survival strategies.

In referring to 'mere prototypical survival strategies', I assume that Leahy intends to refer to the survival of the young or of the species as it is hard to see how the frantic behaviour of a cat whose kittens are removed could be described either as a strategy or as contributing to the survival of the cat. But this apart, why should instinctive behaviour *not* indicate mental distress and why should we regard the response of the hunted fox as more like the response of a plant than like that of a hunted human being? Leahy's answer is that since animals lack language and therefore self-consciousness their experiences are so far removed from those of humans that they cannot be compared. But this view fails to recognise that much human behaviour is also instinctive and might be described as 'prototypical survival strategies'. It is just such behaviour as protection of the young that involves our deepest emotions and which, when frustrated, can result in the greatest mental suffering. While it is obviously true that a human mother whose baby has been kidnapped is likely to be tormented by thoughts of the fate of her child — is he being looked after, has he been hurt, will she ever see him again? — in a way only possible for a language user, it is also true that as a language user she can be comforted by being reminded that most baby-snatchers are women who love and desperately want babies and that the child will almost certainly be well cared for, a reassurance denied the cat. That language is a two-edged sword which may allay as well as exacerbate distress is not considered by Leahy because he argues that *without* language, the distress is not there in the first place. He is at least consistent in extending to young children the alleged inability of non-language users to suffer mental distress, claiming that it is nonsense to suggest that a calf, or even a baby, can miss its mother because 'this requires the *self*-awareness of a developing language-user: a grasp of the significance of its mother, her absence and hoped- for return and so on'.[60]

But here we are back with the mistake made by Stuart Hampshire in the case of animal memory. What Leahy says is true only if 'missing mother' is defined as having propositional thoughts on the matter, but this is not the *only* definition possible. If, despite the ministrations of a nurse who provides every care and comfort, the baby screams until its mother returns, whereupon it smiles and coos, why should we not say that it was missing its mother? And what is true for the baby is true for the calf, as Leahy himself has noted. But for Leahy what is true of calf and baby is equally true for the mother cat: it is only the human mother who is caused mental distress by the loss of her offspring. Those of us who are struck by the similarity of the behaviour of the woman and cat whose babies have been taken and the evident relief upon their return are, in Leahy's view, suffering from 'dangerous muddle-headedness'.

In spite of his stated dismissal of Cartesianism, Leahy's description of animal behaviour as more properly comparable to that of plants than to humans is strikingly Cartesian:

> an animal does indeed strive instinctively to keep alive, much as it will migrate and forage (plants do also, in even more stereotypical and less mobile ways), but it is unduly anthropomorphic to praise its endeavour . . .[61]

I am not familiar with the practise of 'praising the endeavour' of animals *or* humans who 'strive instinctively to keep alive' but I am aware that the fact that the struggle is instinctive does nothing to prevent the fear and distress that can arise from it. I suggested above that it was wrong to imply that without a specific fear of death the animals awaiting slaughter could not suffer significantly. The same is surely true of the hunted fox to which Leahy refuses to attribute distress. But for Leahy, if my dog and I are attacked by a masked intruder who attempts to hurl us from a tenth floor balcony, although we both struggle furiously and both appear to be terrified as we are forced towards the edge, the fact that only I can think 'This man wants to kill me!' means that only *I* could be said to be 'fighting for my life'. My dog's attempt to cling to the balcony would be better described in terms of an

---

[60] Leahy 1991: 218
[61] Leahy 1996: 202

ivy plant clinging to a wall. Leahy's view here seems hardly distinguishable from that of the Cartesian physiologists who subjected dogs to vivisection and mocked their critics with assurances that the cries of the tormented animals were no more indicative of distress than the squeaking of clockwork.[62] Despite his denials, Leahy seems to be in the grip of something very like Cartesianism — an impression that is deepened by his reference to 'my central contention that animals are *primitive beings*, far removed from ourselves despite some apparent behaviour to the contrary'.[63]

The term 'apparent behaviour' suggests that even to speak of animals *behaving* is as anthropomorphic as it would be if the term were applied to plants or machines, surely a Cartesian rather than — as Leahy claims — a Wittgensteinian notion. Leahy's aim here is to persuade us that the differences between humans and animals are of greater significance than the similarities. He interprets Wittgenstein as meaning that '. . . our everyday ways of attributing psychological concepts like hope, fear, belief, understanding and so on'[64] are based on the human case and that when we apply these terms to animals we do so in a way which is 'parasitic upon the human paradigm, and to that extent attenuated'[65] and that a failure to recognise this will lead us to 'over- emphasize the similarities to human beings at the expense of the differences'.[66]

But this interpretation of Wittgenstein is not the only one, as is argued powerfully by the Wittgensteinian philosopher, Richard Beardsmore, in his paper entitled 'If a Lion Could Talk' (1996), which I discuss in detail later. Like Beardsmore, Leahy quotes both the 'talking lion' and 'the strange country' passage that precedes it, but his interpretation of Wittgenstein is that 'even when we wish to say that animal states *are* transparent to us, what we see is a primaeval *distortion* of what we see in other humans'.[67]

Beardsmore believes that writers of Leahy's persuasion overestimate Wittgenstein's view of the limitations that lack of language entails and comments:

---

[62] Quoted by Singer 1976: 220
[63] Leahy 1996: 254
[64] Leahy 1996: 140
[65] Leahy 1996: 150
[66] Leahy 1996: 150
[67] Leahy 1996: 139

> [T]o claim that an animal, say a dog, lacks language, is not to say that a dog's life becomes different in every respect from the life of a human being — that a dog's fear or anger or thought is different from the fear, anger or thought of a human being.

But Leahy's view is precisely that a dog's fear or anger or thought is so 'far removed' from that of humans that to use the same words to describe them is to run the risk of 'dangerous muddle-headedness', unless we constantly remind ourselves that when we apply such words to animals we do so only in an 'attenuated' sense. This view is typical of the writers criticised by Beardsmore who writes

> I can see no reason whatsoever to suppose that our application of such concepts to animals occurs by a sort of half-hearted extension of their application to human beings, a view which will soon lead you to see anthropomorphism at every juncture.[68]

And a tendency to 'see anthropomorphism at every juncture' is certainly a feature of Michael Leahy's writing, much of which is based on an interpretation of Wittgenstein which Beardsmore believes to be not only unfounded but 'diametrically opposed' to Wittgenstein's own view.

It is my contention that, in his determination to emphasise the differences between human and animal experience, Leahy has often misrepresented not only the nature of animal experience but of the human as well. His rejection of the views of both Clark and Schliefer, mentioned above, seems to imply that fear of death is of paramount significance in the human case, but I do not believe that this view is any more justified than the suggestion that, without such a fear, animal suffering is insignificant. I want to suggest that in the 'fear of death' case, as in so many other cases, it is just not possible to draw a sharp line between all humans and all animals in the way that Leahy tries to. Firstly, Leahy's argument that animals, lacking language, cannot be self-conscious, must also apply to pre-linguistic children, so that when he claims that *our* possession of these capacities 'guarantees that we are prone to a range and intensity of suffering light-years from that of brute beasts' he cannot avoid including young children with the 'brute beasts' as having a very limited capacity

---

[68] Beardsmore 1996: 56

for suffering. It seems unlikely that a child of less than three or four years would have sufficient language to meet Leahy's criterion of self-consciousness but we do not conclude from this that when a toddler wakes screaming from a nightmare he is not really distressed. Nor do we dismiss his terror of the dark on the grounds that he has no 'self-conscious grasp of death'.[69]

Secondly, even among adult humans who do have a 'grasp of death', attitudes to it are many and varied and it is by no means obvious that it is universally regarded as 'the greatest of evils'. In some cultures the fear of dishonour or humiliation is much greater than the fear of death and many religious believers would argue that death is neither final nor necessarily evil. If death were the greatest human fear suicide would be inexplicable in rational terms, yet so complex are our attitudes that we might not be surprised to learn that a man contemplating suicide was among the first to flee a burning building. This would seem to indicate that the terrified reaction to a life-threatening situation is less intellectual and more basic — and closer to that of animals — than Leahy would have us believe. Nor do religious beliefs automatically confer immunity to terror in the face of danger. But the fact that professed confidence in eternal bliss does not allay fear seems to suggest that for many human beings it is not the prospect of death that terrifies so much as the fear of dying. After all, none of us has experienced death but we have all experienced the distress of being ill or injured and this is obviously something that animals share with us, as I have argued above. I believe that Clark was wrong to talk of animals fleeing 'death as the greatest of evils', not because it is unlikely that they have a 'self-conscious grasp of death', but because their greatest fears, like ours, are likely to be of things of which they have had at least some experience. This is not to deny that fear of the unknown can be just as deeply felt as fear of the specific, and since it certainly occurs in humans why should we accept that animals cannot be *really* afraid if they do not know what they are afraid *of*. Instinct, too, may play a part, especially in the case of the very young, whether human children or other dependent mammals and birds, for whom the greatest danger, and therefore, for evolutionary reasons, the greatest terror, is the loss of their parents, especially the mother. That the infant is unable to

---

[69] Leahy 1996: 164

grasp the fact that its own death is the most likely consequence of the loss of its mother does nothing to reduce its terror at being parted from her. Nor is it fear of *death* that makes the life of a frail old person miserable when he worries about being mugged, burgled or suffering a fall. He is probably much more fearful of losing his independence, having to give up his home or losing touch with family and friends and when he says that he would rather die than go into a nursing home he probably means it.

If death is not necessarily the 'greatest of evils' for human beings, then the argument that animal fear is greatly limited by the absence of fear of death loses its force. Clark's claim that animals 'fear death, and flee it as the greatest of evils' seems unnecessary and, in fact, he follows it immediately with the argument that although animals do not understand death, neither do human beings 'emotionally at least, have much understanding of death: my absence from the world is strictly unimaginable to me. I am not therefore unafraid of death and moderately anxious lest I die before my time'.[70]

So far the discussion as to whether an animal can have a fear of death has centred on fear of its own death, but I now want to consider whether animals might fear the deaths of others. Many humans are much less concerned with fear of their own deaths than those of their children or partners: children are often terrified by the thought that a parent might die, long before they consider their own mortality. In line with my suggestion that other-awareness precedes self-awareness, I want to suggest that even if lack of self-consciousness may preclude an animal's fearing its own death, perhaps a case can be made for some being capable of fearing the deaths of others. There are a number of reports of African elephants reacting in a disturbed manner when coming across elephant remains in the bush and showing something very like grief at the loss of a companion. As a highly social animal, living in a group for perhaps fifty years or more, an individual elephant will certainly have witnessed the deaths of a number of her kin, perhaps including some of her own children. Since we know that elephants learn from experience, I do not think it impossible that a mature animal, seeing the increasing frailty of an older relative, might recognise the signs of impending death, or that, having lost calves to disease or injury in the

---

[70] Clark 1977: 40

past, she should fear the loss of a new baby that shows signs of weakness. What we cannot be sure of here, of course, is whether the mother is distressed by the possible *death* of her baby or by its suffering. It is certainly the case that most animals respond much more actively to an injured, sick or terrified companion, especially a baby, than to a dead one, which is hardly surprising, since the dead show no signs of distress. But humans may also be expected to show more concern for the suffering than for the dead and in some cases the death of a loved one may be easier to bear than his suffering. A cat, cow or bitch is greatly disturbed by the *distress* of her baby, but, should it die, shows decreasing interest in its lifeless body and after a while stops licking, nuzzling or calling to it. Does she 'know that it is dead'? Well, not if that involves her being able to *say* so but she certainly differentiates between a living infant and a dead one. And if she is aware that the dead one no longer needs feeding, washing, keeping warm or protecting can we deny that she has a 'grasp of death'?

But if animals develop this sort of 'grasp of death' through witnessing the deaths of others can we really be sure that an individual animal cannot make the connection that what happens to others may also happen to him? We know that animals do learn from the experiences of others and Marian Stamp Dawkins,[71] describing the work of Bennet Galef of MacMaster University, reports 'What Galef showed is that rats use each other as "testers" for what might be safe or poisonous foods for themselves'. Experiments demonstrated that by monitoring the behaviour, health and smell of their companions, rats make connections between the type of food eaten (from its smell) and the effect it has on the eater (ranging from contentment to discomfort and eventual death) and make their own selection from the available menu accordingly. Dawkins does not report whether rats were more concerned by the *death* of the 'guinea-pig' rat or by its suffering: it would be interesting to know whether a companion dropping dead without any obvious suffering would cause more or less alarm than one that obviously suffered greatly but recovered. If it could be shown that rats do indeed distinguish between non-fatal acute suffering and non-suffering death, then we would be able to say whether they fear death or suffering or both.

---

[71] Stamp Dawkins 1998: 48

Even if such evidence were available, however, it would not convince Leahy who argues that 'lacking language transforms the *content* of what they can properly be said to fear or be distressed at' and follows this by challenging Clark's assertion that a lack of language does not prevent a chicken from being distressed when it is kept in conditions which prevent it from stretching its wings. Leahy claims:

> If I am right then to say 'the chicken is distressed by its close confinement' is a dual acknowledgement of sympathy at the presence of behavioural prototypes similar to those of distressed people and a strong veterinary hint of a possible cure; but no more. Were the chicken a 5-year-old child cramped in a tiny cupboard, our judgement would carry implications of a different order, for the child would be capable of knowing, under normal circumstances, *that* she was distressed and *why*.'[72]

Leahy's frequent warnings against allowing ourselves to be misled by 'the presence of behavioural prototypes similar to those of distressed people' are by now all too familiar. His reference to 'a strong veterinary hint of a possible cure' is mystifying, and I can only suggest that he means that a dose of Prozac would solve the problem, if only by removing the behaviour which misleads the gullible into believing that the chicken is distressed. But if the Prozac worked it would be hard for Leahy to maintain his argument that the chicken's case is 'light-years' removed from the human. (Although medical researchers testing analgesics on laboratory animals have been known to defend the infliction of pain on their subjects by denying that the animals suffer pain as we do — an implausible defence of a practice which would be rendered pointless if this were true.) The point of the comparison with the child is, however, clear enough: in Leahy's view the chicken is not *really* distressed because it does not know (cannot say) *that* it is and does not know (cannot say) *why* it is. But suppose that the *child* were not capable of this either? Suppose she was not five, but two years old. Would her plight then be of no moral concern and would we be foolish to allow her 'behavioural prototypes' to arouse feelings of outrage? Or let us suppose that the five-year-old has been kept in the cupboard since infancy and, as a result, is not only speechless but, like the battery chicken, unaware that

---

[72] Leahy 1991: 164

other ways of life exist. Leahy warns that when we see birds in cages and unable to fly we must resist '[t]he temptation to anthropomorphise their plight, to compare them with human beings in similar situations . . . who would almost certainly be distressed at the opportunities that they were foregoing and make protest.'[73]

But the natural conclusion to this argument would be that a human being *unaware* of the missed opportunities and *unable* to protest need not concern us either. I do not find this any more convincing than the argument that the non-linguistic, non-self-conscious chicken is not really distressed, but it does raise the interesting question of the morality of the 'what you don't have you don't miss' argument, which Leahy appears to espouse. Leahy is quite wrong to imply that the bird's inability to know what it is missing is the inevitable result of its lack of language and self-consciousness. Animals whose lives are *not* spent behind bars or in battery cages are obviously aware of — and distressed by — missed opportunities. If we were to pack the car with beach-bag, drinking water etc., and then drive off without the dogs, how would Leahy account for their obviously disappointed response? Similarly, a normal toddler would certainly know what he was missing if he was shut in a cupboard. Like the battery-reared chicken, the unfortunate five-year-old reared in a cupboard would not, but this will not convince many of us that the latter case is acceptable while the former is not.

I have argued that Leahy's claims about the nature of animal experience are insupportable, but even if the picture he presents were right, it would be by no means obvious that their capacity for suffering would be reduced. Bernard Rollin has argued that if it were true that animals have no sense of past or future their suffering would be greater rather than less than ours and they would have a stronger, rather than a weaker, claim on our moral concern. Rollin writes:

> In terms of countering the pernicious moral power of the claim that animals can't anticipate and remember pain and that therefore their pain is insignificant, the most relevant point has little to do with the presence or absence of concepts. It comes rather from the following insight: that if animals are indeed as the above argument suggests, inextricably locked

---

[73] Leahy 1996: 201

into what is happening in the here and now, we are all the more obliged to try to relieve their suffering, since they themselves cannot look forward to or anticipate its cessation, or even remember, however dimly, its absence.[74]

Although Leahy and Carruthers approach the animals issue from rather different angles, their theses have some important points in common. Most prominent among these is the view that animals, lacking language, also lack anything approaching self-consciousness and that, as a result, their experiences and their capacity for suffering are so far removed from our own that their moral status is either (in Carruther's view) nil or at least (in Leahy's view) insignificant in comparison with our own. On these grounds both writers oppose the aims of the modern movement to give increased protection to animals. Carruthers concludes *The Animals Issue* by stating that:

> The most important practical conclusion of this book is that there is no basis for extending moral protection to animals beyond that which is already provided. In particular, there are no good moral grounds for forbidding hunting, factory farming or laboratory testing on animals.

In condemning those who challenge the morality of the status quo, Leahy seems also to damn those historic figures without whom slavery, racial persecution and the abuse of children would have continued unchallenged. He writes:

> Like so many moral reformers of the past, convinced that the tested laws and practices of their society would be much better supplanted by their own wishful thinking, the animal liberationists need to be marginalised.[75]

I have challenged the claims of both these writers and I believe that neither of them offers an adequate justification for his conclusions. Their own closing words, quoted above, identify them as followers of a long tradition of opposition to moral reform. But it is the names of Wilberforce, Elizabeth Fry and Abraham Lincoln that live on, while the names of those who ridiculed them are largely forgotten.

---

[74] Rollin 1989: 144
[75] Leahy 1996: 204

## V

As we have seen, those who argue that animals are sentient, sensitive creatures whose interests cannot ethically be ignored are frequently accused of anthropomorphism, especially by opponents who subscribe to a version of Cartesianism. Such writers generally define anthropomorphism as 'the misattribution of human qualities, in particular mental states, to animals', so that to anthropomorphise is, by definition, to make a mistake.

But this use of the term is far removed from the meaning given in the OED as 'the ascription of human attributes to the Deity'. The use of the term to refer to our view of animals seems, then, to suggest that similar problems apply to the two cases. But the claim, which many have made, that the nature of God is essentially unknowable, has a plausibility which is not to be found in the similar claims made about animals. Anthropomorphism is not, therefore, the best term to describe the mistakes that we can and do make in our thought about animals.

Modern believers may regard Old Testament references to God as having eyes, ears and a voice as quaintly anthropomorphic but they nevertheless cling to the notion of his seeing, hearing and even speaking to them. *This* is anthropomorphism in the OED sense, even if the attribution of human senses and emotions to God is understood to be metaphorical. But when I speak of *animals* as seeing, hearing, thinking and feeling, I am not using metaphors: the cases are not analogous. Nor, I believe, is there a comparison to be made between recognising that humans and animals are sentient and recognising the existence of God. Stephen Clark would not accept my view on this. He writes: 'Seeing the world as god-filled is like seeing one's human or non-human friend as sentient: it requires a movement of the heart as well as of the head'.[76] I am not sure what Clark means by 'god-filled' (when I asked my husband he wasn't sure either but remarked — while picking his way carefully between the several shaggy bodies draped around the kitchen — that he certainly knew what it was for the world to be dog-filled) but if he doesn't mean that the world is filled with God in the way that our house is filled with dogs, then I can only assume that he regards everything in the world to be the *work* of God. But seeing *this* is not at all like seeing that the earth heaps on the lawn are the work of moles, and to

---

[76] Clark 1994: 97

compare it with seeing that my friends — of whatever species — are sentient, suggests that I see God *behaving*, which seems to be an incoherent notion. If seeing the world as god-filled and seeing one's friends as sentient both require 'a movement of the heart', then the phrase is being used in two different ways. To see the world as god-filled requires an act of faith: to see my friends as other than sentient is an impossibility as John Searle notes when he addresses 'the possibility that other people might be unconscious zombies, and the dog might be, as Descartes thought, a cleverly constructed machine . . .' and answers 'I am ignoring . . . these possibilities. They are out of the question. I do not take any of them seriously.'[77]

For Searle, as for me, the interesting question is 'why have so many thinkers denied what would appear to be obvious points, that many species of animals other than our own have consciousness, intentionality and thought processes?'[78] Given Clark's parallel between recognising the sentience of one's friends and recognising the divine presence, it is interesting that Searle regards theology as the source of the denial that animals have minds. He identifies two strands of theological thought, both leading to the same conclusion: on the one hand the theological implications of Descartes' mental/physical divide and on the other the problem of animal suffering. Searle describes the first as entailing 'that if animals have consciousness, then it follows immediately that they have immortal souls, and the afterlife will, to put it mildly, be very over-populated',[79] and the second, that the suffering of animals cannot be justified 'given that they do not have original sin and presumably do not have free will', which has the unfortunate result that '[t]he arguments that were used to reconcile the existence of an omnipotent and beneficent God with a suffering human population do not seem to work for animals'.[80] The solution to both problems was to deny that animals have minds at all, with the convenient result that they could be believed incapable of suffering. I want to suggest that there is a parallel here with those modern philosophers whose convenient denial that animals have minds/feelings/ moral status is

---

[77] Searle 1998: 48–9
[78] Searle 1998: 38
[79] Searle 1998: 38
[80] Searle 1998: 39

motivated more by commitment to their theories than by a seeking after truth.

Describing these lines of thought as — to us — 'completely implausible' and ' ridiculous', Searle comments, however, that '[i]n the seventeenth and eighteenth centuries, in response to the Cartesian revolution, it made sense both philosophically and theologically to wonder whether animals have minds'.[81] I am sceptical of the idea that it might ever have 'made sense' to question the existence of animal minds. In any case, it does not make sense now, and it is difficult to take seriously the claims of writers such as Leahy and Carruthers whose theories, in spite of their protestations to the contrary, show the far-reaching influence of Descartes.

I have argued that, whereas talk of God as feeling and thinking may be metaphorical, such talk of animals is certainly not. Some writers, however, believe that descriptions of animals as thinking and feeling are useful as an heuristic device as long as we don't forget that we are using the intentionalistic terms in a 'metaphorical sense', while others argue that the danger of *forgetting* that we are speaking metaphorically is so great and its consequences so far reaching that such talk must be avoided. Prominent among this group is the scientist J.S. Kennedy, who argues that metaphor and analogy can safely be used to explain the workings of *in*animate systems because there is no danger that they will be taken literally but that 'anthropomorphic analogies for animal behaviour are the exception; they readily generate misunderstanding'.[82] I would agree that anthropomorphic analogies can lead to misunderstanding of animal behaviour but my reason for saying this is very different from Kennedy's, as I hope will become clear.

Kennedy adopts Asquith's definition of anthropomorphism as 'the ascription of human mental experiences to animals' and claims that references to animals as feeling and thinking are 'by definition examples of unwarranted anthropomorphism', which is obviously true if feeling and thinking are exclusively *human* abilities as Kennedy implies, so that, in spite of his assertion that his 'primary aim . . . was not to demonstrate that animals are unconscious but rather to bring out the danger of unthinkingly

---

[81] Searle 1998: 38
[82] Kennedy 1992: 159

assuming that they are conscious',[83] he is begging the question here. From his denial that it is his *primary* aim to demonstrate that animals are unconscious, it seems not unreasonable to infer that this may well be at least a secondary aim. Kennedy constantly refers to anthropomorphism not only as a danger, but as a 'disease' and something from which we must 'liberate' ourselves and warns that the great danger of anthropomorphic talk is that it comes so naturally to us:

> It is dinned into us culturally from earliest childhood. It has presumably also been 'pre-programmed' into our hereditary make-up by natural selection, perhaps because it proved to be useful for predicting and controlling the behaviour of animals.[84]

For Kennedy, the effectiveness of the attribution of thoughts and feelings to animals as a means of predicting and controlling their behaviour is the result of a useful but misleading coincidence. But I want to argue that it is because animals really do *have* thoughts and feelings that human beings who treat them accordingly are better able to understand them than those who treat them as if they were machines, plants or mysterious aliens (it is significant that Kennedy assumes our interest to be in 'predicting and controlling'). It is not a *coincidence* that treating my car as if it has thoughts and feelings is of no help at all in predicting or controlling its behaviour; it just is the case that my car does not have thoughts and feelings and is better understood by a mechanic than by a psychologist. A car which 'greets' its approaching owner (or, more accurately, its approaching key-fob) by flashing its lights and 'vocalising' does not seduce us into attributing thoughts and feelings to it because we know that it *has* none and not because the inverted commas that I have placed around 'greets' and 'vocalising' warn us against an ever-present danger of allowing the car's 'behaviour' (inverted commas again) to persuade us to greet it as we do the dog who welcomes us (no inverted commas here!) with obvious delight. And when I say 'obvious delight' I mean exactly that. So where is the 'danger' that Kennedy warns us against? If I assume my car to be conscious my mistake will soon become apparent. If I assume my dog to be conscious and am not rapidly made aware that I am

---

[83] Kennedy 1992: 157
[84] Kennedy 1992: 5

mistaken, the obvious conclusion would seem to be that no mistake has been made and that the dog really is conscious. But, for Kennedy, this conclusion would be to make the terrible mistake of being deceived by appearances. He warns

> We are doubly tempted into anthropomorphism because we for our part are predisposed to think that animals have minds like ours and they for their part seem to confirm this by 'acting as if they have minds' — thanks to the optimizing effect of natural selection on behaviour.[85]

The slide here from 'minds like ours' to 'minds' is a significant parallel to the God case, in which objections to thoughts of God as having a human form turn out to be something of a red herring since God has no form at all. Kennedy's slide suggests that his objection is not only to the thought of animals as having minds like *ours,* but any minds at all. The quotation above seems to suggest that my dog's appearing to have thoughts and feelings is the behavioural equivalent of the physical 'mimicry' that results in a certain insect looking like a leaf of the tree on which it lives. But if I *do* mistake the insect for a real leaf — say by taking it as a cutting and planting it in the hope of producing a seedling tree — my mistake will be made apparent by the 'cutting's' failure to *respond* as a leaf. The crucial difference here is that the evolutionary advantage to the insect is gained from looking like a leaf and from 'behaving' (that is by mimicking the stance and movement) like a leaf, need not involve thoughts or feelings. But it cannot be true that dogs would gain an evolutionary advantage by 'acting as if they have minds' if they have not. What, for example, would be the evolutionary advantage of our dogs 'acting as if' they had a desire to go to the beach and 'acting as if' they believed that the way to get to the beach was to persuade us to take them in the car if they did not really *have* that desire and belief?

My own view is that our thinking of dogs as having minds and *treating them accordingly* does indeed result in their responding in a way which confirms our supposition, but this is no illusion. The same is true of human beings; our inclination to treat babies as if they have minds is a vital factor in the development of those minds. If a baby were reared by beings that ignored his mind-developing potential he would be unlikely to fulfil that potential. In the United States Harry Harlow's experiments on infant mon-

---

[85] Kennedy 1992: 158

keys showed (as any normal person might have predicted) that maternal and social deprivation results in 'severe and persistent psychopathological behaviour of a depressive nature' such that 'even nine months after release the monkeys would sit clasping their arms around their bodies instead of moving around as normal monkeys do'.[86] In other words, lack of social interaction had resulted in the monkeys' psychological potential failing to develop properly: if monkeys didn't *have* psychological potential they would not have been affected in this way. If the leaf-mimicking insect was subjected to similar deprivation without any observable behavioural disturbance we might reasonably conclude that its psychological potential, if any, was very far removed from that of either a human or a monkey. But anti-anthropomorphists (and some of their opponents, too) usually make the mistake of lumping all animals together on one side of the imagined gulf that is supposed to separate human beings from all the rest of the natural world, failing to notice that the gulf between insect and dog or caterpillar and chimpanzee is infinitely greater than any divide between chimpanzee, dog and human.

For Kennedy, anthropomorphism is a disease to be 'brought under control, even if it cannot be cured completely' but ordinary language, which is 'suffused with anthropomorphism' is a constant source of reinfection which would be best replaced by the sterile language of science or at least disinfected by the replacement of subjective with objective terms.

> We can very well describe an animal as 'balked' instead of 'frustrated' or 'thwarted' or as 'scanning' its environment instead of 'searching' or as making an 'incipient movement' instead of an 'intention-movement'. In each case the replacement term has the advantage of directing one's attention to the actual behaviour.[87]

But the effect of these objective terms is not to direct our attention to the *behaviour* of the animal, but to its *movements*. Far from being neutral, this language presents the animal as a robot which 'behaves' only in inverted commas. Kennedy's belief that getting rid of intentional language will somehow reveal to us 'how things really are' is reminiscent of the eliminativist view which

---

[86] Quoted by Singer 1976: 45
[87] Kennedy 1992: 162

dismisses as 'folk psychology' the attribution of thoughts, beliefs, and intentions to humans beings. Although Kennedy makes no mention of this, the final paragraph of his diatribe against anthropomorphism suggests that the elimination of *this* mistake is just a first step towards an ideal world in which talk of minds will have no place. After urging us to rid ourselves of the assumption that animals have minds he writes:

> If the age-old mind-body problem comes to be considered as an exclusively human one, instead of indefinitely extended through the animal kingdom, then that problem too will have been brought nearer to a solution.[88]

This sounds like Cartesianism and I am reminded of John Searle's assertion that if we abandon dualism we will see that the 'mind–body problem' does not exist.[89]

I have argued that the term 'anthropomorphism', originally used to describe the mistake of attributing human form or behaviour to God, is neither appropriate nor useful when applied to our talk of animals. I do not deny that we sometimes make the mistake of attributing to animals thoughts, feelings, or motives that they do not or cannot have, but I have tried to show that this is not the only or even the most serious way in which we can be mistaken about the mental states of animals. It is important to remember that we also make mistakes about the mental states of other human beings. That we are not always the best judges even of our own feelings is an important part of my view that, rather than learning about others by analogy from our own case, we learn about ourselves as we learn about others, and that 'others' here does not refer only to human beings. Searle comments, 'I do not infer that my dog is conscious, any more than, when I came into this room, I inferred that the people present are conscious. I simply respond to them as is appropriate to respond to conscious beings.'[90]

Tom Regan's claim that mature mammals are 'individuals who, like us, have beliefs and desires'[91] is dismissed by Michael Leahy as an example of 'anthropomorphism; wishful thinking in the face of recalcitrant data for which alternative theories are

---

[88] Kennedy 1992: 168
[89] Searle 1998: 39, 48
[90] Searle 1998: 49
[91] Regan 1983: 78

available'.[92] Surely this is an extraordinary claim when one considers how very much more convenient it would often be to believe that animals are *not* like us in this way. This section would not have taken so long to write if I could have ignored the dogs' obvious desire to go for a walk and the horses' desire for their supper. The need to oust the rats which occasionally invade the stables would cause much less heartsearching if I could *deny* that they are intelligent and highly social creatures with long memories and the ability to learn not only from their own experiences but those of their fellows too.[93] How much more comfortable I would feel if I could think of them as automata, devoid of fear, curiosity, pleasure or pain, but in the face of the evidence, that really *would* be wishful thinking.

The claim of Leahy, Frey and others, that only humans can have beliefs and desires, is based on their assumption that these are dependent upon language, a view rejected by John Searle who says

> it seems to me obvious that infants and many animals that do not in any ordinary sense have a language or perform speech acts nonetheless have intentional states. Only someone in the grip of a philosophical theory would deny that small babies can literally be said to want milk and that dogs want to be let out or believe that their master is at the door.[94]

## Conclusion

Given the theories of Frey, Leahy and others, it is not surprising that they denigrate as anthropomorphic any suggestion that animals and humans have many emotions, responses and attitudes in common. What *is* surprising is that some apparently normal human beings need to be convinced that, for example, being chased and killed by a pack of hounds is not a pleasant experience for a deer. Perhaps 'wishful thinking' is involved here, too. When the National Trust decided to ban stag-hunting on its land,

---

[92] Leahy 1996: 195
[93] My general policy is to leave in peace all uninvited guests unless they pose a real and serious threat to residents. The stables provide shelter and nesting sites not only for sparrows, owls and swallows, but also for colonies of bees and wasps, which cause no problem if undisturbed. Action against rats became necessary when they chewed through electricity cables causing a serious fire hazard.
[94] Searle 1983: 5

the most interesting part of the statement issued was that the Bateson report had concluded that deer hunting had been 'shown (*quite unexpectedly*) to inflict extreme and unjustifiable suffering' (my italics).

That this conclusion should be 'unexpected' is evidence of a number of interconnected misconceptions about animals, adding up to a general belief that they are 'not like us' — a view which is often defended by the assertion that to deny it would be anthropomorphic. I want to say that the notion of anthropomorphism is itself a symptom of anthropocentricism which should be rejected in favour of a realisation that Homo sapiens is just one among a vast range of species, many of which have much in common so that, rather than think of them as like us we might think of ourselves as like them, or, better still, as all of us being alike in important ways.

In the next chapter I will examine the non-linguistic means by which different species, including our own, can and do understand one another.

# Chapter Five

# *Creatures Like Us*

I have argued that language is not a necessary or even a sufficient condition for mutual understanding between human and non-human animals. It is important to recognise the difference between *mutual* understanding, which is essential to the development of the sort of close relationships and partnerships that I have been talking about, and the ability of one individual to understand another's behaviour as showing particular emotions, intentions and so on. My suggestion that we cannot form satisfactory relationships with chimpanzees, for example, was certainly not intended to imply that we are not able to *understand* them as well as we understand dogs. My point was rather that we understand only too well their feelings, their requests and their despair at our failure to respond as they wish. The difference might be described as that of having an understanding *with* another as against having an understanding *of* another. Many philosophers argue that without language the first is impossible and some go so far as to deny the possibility even of the second.

In this chapter, I will look at the way in which these prejudices are themselves a greater barrier to understanding than the absence of language and explore the ways by which understanding is achieved. In section one I will examine the ways in which we gain an understanding of animals and in sections two and three I will go on to explain my claim that at least some animals are able to understand us and have an understanding *with* us. The philosophers to whose views my previous chapters have been devoted would be sceptical about my claims here but my examination of their theories suggests that they do not offer a more plausible interpretation of the behaviour I describe.

Wittgenstein's comment that 'if a lion could talk we could not understand him'[1] is often quoted as evidence that he believed that animals, unlike human beings, are essentially an enigma to us. I believe that this interpretation is mistaken and that Wittgenstein's remark could be taken as supporting my point about the language-project great apes — that even if they *do* use language we do not share with them the sort of understanding that we have not only with our human friends but with non-language-using dogs, cats and horses. Wittgenstein's much debated phrase 'form of life' might aptly describe what we share with partner animals and it is significant, I think, that Wittgenstein's example is of a lion, and not a dog.

In a paper which takes Wittgenstein's comment as its title, Richard Beardsmore argues that in the fierce debate as to the relative significance of the differences and similarities between animals and humans 'many writers who would certainly number Wittgenstein among their greatest influences, nevertheless adopt on this issue a view which seems diametrically opposed to his own'.[2] Beardsmore argues that those writers who claim Wittgenstein in support of their view that a gulf exists between humans and animals have misinterpreted the very passages that they quote as evidence. (Michael Leahy, discussed earlier, is a typical example of such writers). The famous passage from which Beardsmore takes his title is a prime example, since it is frequently quoted out of context, thus losing its point, which is to illustrate the inadequacy of words to communicate with a stranger from an alien background. Beardsmore claims that Wittgenstein's intention was not to point to an especial difficulty in communication between man and animal but to illustrate the problems which arise *between humans* from very different backgrounds and he explains

> it was precisely to draw this analogy between communication between human beings of different groups and any hypothetical communication between humans and animals that Wittgenstein earlier in the same passage remarked 'we say of some people that they are transparent to us. It is, how-

---

[1] Wittgenstein 1953: 223
[2] Beardsmore 1996: 43

ever, important as regards this observation that one human being can be a complete enigma to another. We learn this when we come into a strange land with entirely strange traditions, and what is more, even given a mastery of the country's language. We do not *understand* the people'.[3]

In Beardsmore's view, the 'If a Lion . . .' comment, when read in this context, does not provide any evidence that Wittgenstein saw humans and animals as being essentially divided by their differences: on the contrary, he sees similarities in the difficulties of communicating with others, whether human or animal, who do not share our culture.

Beardsmore supports his case by pointing out that Wittgenstein elsewhere refers to humans and animals as thinking and acting in similar ways, as in this quotation. 'Imagine a human being, or one of Kohler's monkeys, who wants to get a banana from the ceiling, but can't reach it, and thinking about ways and means finally puts two sticks together etc.'[4] On which Beardsmore comments:

> Indeed, if there is a contrast to be made here, it is not one between the behaviour of animals and humans, but rather between one animal and another (or perhaps between one human being and another). Wittgenstein goes on 'So one might distinguish between two chimpanzees with respect to the way in which they work, and say of the one that he is thinking and of the other that he is not.'[5]

There is no suggestion here of humans and animals being separated by an unbridgeable gulf, but rather a recognition that animals, like humans, vary not only according to species but also as individuals. Of course, Wittgenstein writes of the importance of language for human thought, but the quotation above is certainly evidence of his acceptance of animals as *thinking*.

Apart from the 'lion' passage, the remark of Wittgenstein which is perhaps most widely quoted and highly influential in the animals debate is that in which he observes that 'Only of a living human being and what resembles (behaves like) a living

---

[3] Beardsmore 1996: 42 (Wittgenstein's italics omitted by Beardsmore)
[4] Wittgenstein 1980: § 224
[5] Beardsmore op cit.

human being, can one say: it has sensations; it sees; is blind; is deaf; is conscious or unconscious.'[6]

But what did he mean? Norman Malcolm, who was a pupil of Wittgenstein, gives his own interpretation:

> The application of these terms has its roots in the paradigm of a living human being. It is only in the expressive human face and eyes, in the gestures, posture and actions of a human being, in human speech, that we can perceive in their fullest form, consciousness and thought, desire, decision, fear and anger. We apply some of these psychological terms to animals — but the further we go down the animal scale, the greater the distance from the human paradigm, the more difficult it is to find a foothold for these terms.[7]

But Malcolm has taken the text to refer to a significant difference between the way we think of humans and the way we think of animals, whereas Wittgenstein makes no mention of animals here at all and indeed the paragraphs following the above make it clear (well, they do to me) that his point is not to contrast human with animal but animate with *in*animate. For Wittgenstein continues 'Only of what behaves like a human being can one say that it *has* pains,' and goes on

> Look at a stone and imagine it having sensations — One says to oneself: How could one so much as get the idea of ascribing a *sensation* to a *thing*? One might as well ascribe it to a number! — And now look at a wriggling fly and at once the difficulties vanish and pain seems to get a foothold here, where before everything was, so to speak, too smooth for it.[8]

No mention here of 'the distance from the human paradigm' or of 'going down the animal scale'. Indeed, in seeing the fly's wriggling as suggestive of pain, Wittgenstein is conceding more than even many members of the pro-animal lobby are prepared to do. Yet Malcolm's interpretation is widely accepted and some anti-animal philosophers have called Wittgenstein as chief expert witness for the defence of their claim that animals are either no more than the automata that Descartes believed them to be or are, at best, so far removed from human beings that any claim that their feelings should be of concern to us is anthropomorphic.

---

[6] Wittgenstein 1953: 1. 281
[7] Malcolm 1986: 184
[8] Wittgenstein 1953: 1. 281

It might be objected that my reading of Wittgenstein is rendered invalid by the words 'only of what behaves like a human being...' but Richard Beardsmore comments:

> I think that the passage that Malcolm quotes should be read: 'Only of a living human being and what behaves, in the sense that a human being behaves...' and not 'Only of a living human being and what behaves in a similar manner to a human being' (i.e. goes to the pictures, writes autobiographies etc)...
>
> But whatever Wittgenstein may have meant by this remark, it is difficult to believe that he meant that when we apply these predicates to animals, we do so in some attenuated or analogical sense, whereas when we apply them to human beings we do so in the full, paradigmatic sense. For if there were a temptation to say this in the case of 'is conscious', a temptation it would no doubt be best to resist, there ought certainly to be no such temptation in the case of 'is deaf' or 'is blind'.

Malcolm's interpretation is only possible because of his very selective reading of Wittgenstein, ignoring the significance of the grouping together of physical states such as blindness and mental states such as consciousness. Beardsmore's point is that a more plausible case can be made for interpreting Wittgenstein as meaning that the attribution of *any* of these states depends upon the presence of *behaviour* and not on the similarity of the *particular* behaviour to a supposed 'human paradigm'. When we speak of a dog as 'blind' we do not use the term in a somehow attenuated sense on the grounds that the dog's failure to behave as a blind human might do (by reading Braille, or using a white stick, perhaps) disqualifies it from being considered blind 'in the fullest form'. What matters is that it *behaves*, which a stone does not, and Wittgenstein's argument demands that if there is a gulf between human and stone, then the dog is firmly on the human side of the divide.

I want to suggest that to deny that many animals, like us, have beliefs and feelings, indicates a way of thinking which has its roots in the Cartesian position that knowledge starts from an introspective awareness of one's own mental states and that mental states of others can only be inferred by analogy. Having first observed that *my* mental state x is accompanied by behaviour y, my observation of behaviour y in another is taken as an indication that he is experiencing mental state x. A number of writers who hotly deny any Cartesian influence, nonetheless apply an extension of this principle to the animal case and presume that our attribution of mental states to animals can only be by analogy from the human case and that its validity will therefore be in proportion to the degree of similarity between the behaviour of the animal and the behaviour of humans. This view is exemplified by Malcolm's widely accepted — and I have argued, quite unjustified — interpretation of Wittgenstein, mentioned earlier, in which the human form and human behaviour, including language, provide the paradigm case for the attribution of mental states ranging from consciousness and thought to fear and anger. I want to challenge the validity of the argument from analogy, not only in the animal case, but in the human too. Since Malcolm is well-known for his attacks on the argument from analogy in the human case, his use of it in the animal case reinforces the impression that he views animals as a totally separate issue.

I see no reason to believe that I first learn to recognise my own mental states and only then infer that other people who behave as I do have them too. Children do not learn in that way and it seems much more likely that a child comes to recognise his own anger *after* learning that Daddy is cross and indeed that Tiddles and Fido are cross too. And if this is so, why should we think that either *my* case or the *human* case is paradigmatic? To do so is to be in the absurd situation — as Leahy is — of thinking that because *my* anger is manifest in my writing an indignant letter to the Independent, a man or dog who relieves his feelings by punching a policeman or biting the cat is not *really* angry, or because *my* pain behaviour is to go to bed with an aspirin and a hot water bottle, that the rickshaw man or the cart-horse who struggle on between the shafts are not *really* in pain.

If the paradigm account were true, the Cheshire Cat's argument would not be funny.

> 'To begin with', said the Cat, 'a dog's not mad. You grant that?' 'I suppose so', said Alice. 'Well, then', the Cat went on, 'you see a dog growls when it's angry and wags its tail when it's pleased. Now I growl when I'm pleased, and wag my tail when I'm angry. Therefore I'm mad.'
>
> 'I call it purring, not growling', said Alice. 'Call it what you like', said the Cat.

The story makes us laugh precisely because the similarity of behaviour *doesn't* cause us any difficulty in identifying the contrasting mental states. It is obvious that analogy plays no part in our understanding here because not only does the tail wagging behaviour indicate different mental states in the different species but because human behaviour can offer no analogy at all, due to limitations of the human form. It is not just that a *human* paradigm will not do but that no paradigm will do at all. If we are to have a paradigm, we could equally well choose the dog case and then the human lack of a tail would force us to say that the dancing, hand-clapping child on her way to the party is not *really* happy.

Interestingly, the philosophical idea of a human paradigm of psychological states and a sliding scale of their applicability to non-humans is challenged by everyday similes such as 'The child fled like a frightened rabbit', 'The guard charged up like an angry bull' and 'He was as pleased as a dog with two tails' or 'As cross as a bear with a sore head' which describe human behaviour by analogy with non-human rather than vice versa. That I have never heard anyone say 'The rabbit fled like a frightened child' or 'The bull charged up like an angry guard' seems to suggest that we often find the emotional states of animals more transparent than those of humans.

The notion of a paradigm for the attribution of mental states is itself a mistake which indicates a failure to recognise that our concepts of pain, anger, fear etc. are as broadly based as those of beauty, goodness or love. To insist that our recognition of 'fear' is a question of our measuring every case against a paradigm of fear behaviour — human or otherwise — is as bizarre as insisting that our recognition of beauty depends upon our measuring each case against a paradigm of beauty, so that the landscape of the English Lake District, for example, might only qualify as beautiful by virtue of some resemblance to the Mona Lisa.

Rather than accept Malcolm's talk of paradigms and sliding scales I would take the advice of Wittgenstein himself when he suggests 'In such a difficulty always ask yourself: How did we *learn* the meaning of this word ("good" for instance)? From what sort of examples?'[9]

---

[9] Wittgenstein 1953: 1. 77

I have argued that we learn the meaning of many words, including those which refer to mental states, by applying them to many different beings, including humans. Beardsmore writes

> Do we talk to small children only or primarily of the pain of humans? Is it only in connection with human beings that children learn to use the term 'pain'? 'What is wrong with the cat, mummy?' 'Oh, it's in pain dear.' I can see no reason whatever to suppose that our application of such concepts to animals occurs by a sort of half-hearted extension of their application to human beings, a view which will soon lead you to see anthropomorphism at every juncture. Children learn to pity many things. They learn to pity their friends, when they graze their knees, and their mothers when, faced by the strain of bringing up three children, they burst into tears, and the cat when it is sick, and the gerbil when it is unexpectedly dying. And this is not a sort of sliding scale which finally peters out with e.g. plants or coal on the fire.[10]

It might reasonably be argued, then, that a child who thinks of pain as an exclusively human affliction has not learned the meaning of the word. Significantly, however, this is more often the failing of philosophers than of children, who are more inclined to attribute pains not only to people, dogs and cats but to dolls and teddies too, until they come to recognise, like Wittgenstein, that it is not *looking* like a living being that matters, but *behaving* like one. But that there is more to understanding the meaning of pain than being able to use the word correctly is crucial to Wittgenstein's thinking. David Cockburn — like Beardsmore, a Wittgensteinian — writes:

> In so far as someone's words 'It is in pain' are not a mere mouthing they will be connected in some way with her attitude towards that of which she is speaking. The connection with, for example, pity or, less attractively, sadistic pleasure is at least part of what enables us to say that she is using the word 'pain' as we do: and so is part of what enables us to say that she is having the thought 'That animal is in pain'.[11]

I want to add that not only may the ability to say 'it is in pain' not be a sufficient condition for showing an understanding of pain, it may not be a necessary condition either. Thus the dog who licks

---

[10] Beardsmore 1996: 56
[11] Cockburn 1994: 144

my injured hand — or her puppy's sore nose — and generally behaves in a sympathetic manner, might be said to have a better grasp of pain than a human who does not respond at all.

Having dismissed the anthropocentric 'human paradigm theory' as to how — if at all — we can attribute mental states to animals, I want to return to the Cheshire Cat who proved an invaluable ally in that case but offered no alternative explanation as to how we *do* recognise similar psychological states in remarkably dissimilar behaviour. In a typically cryptic manner the Cat provides the answers to its own riddle, so I will try to tease out the tangle by separating the strands.

The Cat's description of animal emotion and behaviour is much too simple. A dog *may* 'growl when it's angry and wag its tail when it's pleased', just as a man *may* scowl when he's angry and smile when he's pleased, but this is not to say that growling or tail-wagging is either a necessary or a sufficient condition for our seeing that the dog is angry or pleased, any more than scowling or smiling is either a necessary or a sufficient condition for our seeing that a man is angry or pleased. Neither a smile nor a tail wag, a growl or a scowl is adequate on its own to convince us: it is just part of the larger picture that we place it in to make sense of the situation.

Wittgenstein's suggestion that we ask ourselves 'how did we *learn* the meaning of this word? ("Good", for instance?). From what sort of examples?' reminds us that we do not learn the meaning of 'good' — or of 'pleased' — from a single instance, much less from a single movement or gesture. Importantly, too, we learn them in a *context*. Baby Jane is offered a spoonful of 'Baby Delight' and Daddy says enthusiastically 'Yum, yum, this is *good*', tasting a bit himself and smacking his lips appreciatively. If Jane eats it all up she is a *good* girl and Mummy will be very *pleased*. If she doesn't eat it all up perhaps Fido will finish it and be a very *good* dog, and Daddy will be *pleased* with Fido. And Fido, of course, will be *pleased* too. Jane learns that 'good' and 'pleased' belong with other words such as 'nice', 'happy', 'smile' and 'fun' in that all of them are associated not only with pleasant feelings and desirable situations but with cheerful voices, gestures and facial expressions. 'Naughty', 'bad', 'nasty', 'cross' and 'cry', on the other hand, go with unpleasant voices and threatening or dismissive gestures and facial expressions. Ice cream and trips to the beach belong in the first category, spinach and the dentist in the second. That Fido shares her views on this is something she takes for granted; the word 'beach' is enough to send both of them racing to the car, perhaps shouting, barking and jumping up and down as they go. Fido is clearly 'pleased' and Jane doesn't need to check that his tail is wagging in order to make sure, any more than Fido needs to check that Jane is smiling. But Jane also learns that there are differences of opinion as to what is 'good' or 'bad'; Fido doesn't like Coca-Cola and *she* doesn't like Bonios, but Mummy, it seems, really *does* like spinach. Jane learns that Fido doesn't like Coca-Cola by noticing that whereas he begs for Bonios, ice-cream and cake, he never begs for Coca-Cola. When she offers him some he turns away and when she tries to pour it down his throat he wriggles away and hides under a chair. It is to be hoped that Mummy will intervene at this stage with phrases such as 'Poor Fido', 'He's upset', 'He doesn't like it' and Jane will have made a good start in learning many important and essentially interconnected lessons about 'good', 'pleased', 'bad' etc. If Jane tries the Coca-Cola on Tiddles, Tiddles' response is likely to be much the same as Fido's and her 'wagging' tail is hardly going to make even Jane doubt her feelings, any more than her 'growling' as she sits on Mummy's lap by the fire is going to count against the picture of contentment she presents. Alice's final comment '*I* call it purring, not growling', is crucial here; we give a similar sound or movement a different name in recognition of its different significance. The recognition of the emotion must precede the naming of its manifestation.

The Cheshire Cat was not wrong to *start* from the assumption that a tail-wagging dog is a happy dog; its mistake was to *end* there. The general assumption that a smiling human is a happy human is equally valid as long as we don't allow it to blind us to contradictory signs. Smiles (of humans) and wagging tails (of dogs) are equally valid manifestations of being 'pleased'; 'smiles' (of chimpanzees) and 'wagging' tails (of cats) are not. The *emotions* may apply across species; the particular movement or gesture does not. The canine tail wag and the human smile are, in spite of their very different forms, remarkably similar in meaning. Just as we do not really understand smiles until we know that they are not always happy but can be sad, nervous, apologetic — or indeed, false — so we do not really understand tail-wags until we know that they can also be sad, nervous or apologetic — though at least a dog does not 'put on' a tail wag.

Not only are the physical differences no barrier to my seeing the similarities, they may actually be a help. The chimpanzee's physical resemblance to humans has sometimes resulted in serious misunderstandings, as when early students of chimpanzee behaviour assumed the chimpanzee grin to be equivalent to a human smile of pleasure. Only with much greater experience of chimpanzee life did they come to realise that the 'smile' was more closely connected with fear and distress — although, as I have argued above, even a *real* smile comes in many moods.

The response of the sick dog who answers my sympathetic murmur and gentle pat with a feeble but appreciative tail wag strikes me as so very much like the response of a sick or sad human who gives a feeble but appreciative smile in answer to sympathy, that I am not conscious of the discrepancies of physical form. What strikes me is the similarity, not the difference and the ability of both to evoke the same response in me. I am tempted to say that the similarity in this case is a very complex affair of interactive responses of a kind only possible in a situation where mutual understanding already exists, but David Cockburn reports seeing a television programme 'in which a giant squid was under threat from some other creature' and 'responded in a way which struck me immediately and powerfully as one of fear'.[12] And Cockburn was particularly intrigued by the realisation that, in spite of the 'radical differences' in the physical forms of squids and human beings, 'what struck me about the giant squid might be expressed in the words "It behaved like a frightened human being"'.[13]

What interests me in Cockburn's experience is not that he should perceive as 'human-like' the behaviour of a creature of such *un*human appearance, but that he should be struck by the similarity in a creature of a kind of which he had no previous experience. If Cockburn could see in the squid's behaviour 'an emotion which was so unambiguously and specifically one of fear',[14] then my suggestion that we *learn* to understand the feelings and emotions of others — of whatever species — by involvement with them would seem to be superfluous. But might not an

---

[12] Cockburn 1994: 135
[13] Cockburn 1994: 142
[14] Cockburn 1994: 135

observer, seeing a pack of baying, slavering hounds pursuing a running man, see in their behaviour 'an emotion which was unambiguously and specifically' one of homicidal rage and yet be wrong? Importantly, he would realise his mistake if he saw that when the hounds reached their 'quarry' he turned to pat their heads as they licked his face. But what further behaviour on the part of the squid might prove or disprove Cockburn's understanding of its emotion? When the cat 'flees in fear' from the firework display and takes refuge under the bed, we can coax her out, reassure her with soothing voices and stroking and perhaps cheer her up with something tasty from the fridge. And when she finally settles purring on the hearth rug we know that she has 'got over' her fright. Not only do I not know how to comfort a frightened squid, I do not know how I might tell that it had got over its fright. None of this is to suggest that the squid was *not* afraid, but I am sceptical about the possibility of 'seeing' that it is without the support of knowledge of squid behaviour in general or of this squid's behaviour in particular.

'Fleeing' may be one form of fear-behaviour but it is neither a necessary nor a sufficient condition of our seeing that a creature is afraid. The 'fight' response is just as valid as the 'flight' and we do not deny that a desperate small creature which flies out at a larger attacker is afraid — perhaps, just as afraid as the large one which flees from the smaller. But even an animal being pursued at speed by another may well be enjoying a game. Young dogs, chimpanzees and humans all enjoy games of chase but what about squids? When my horses suddenly race together across the field I might wonder — from a distance — whether they are really frightened, merely startled, or perhaps just indulging in high spirits or *joie de vivre*. If I want to *know* I can go over and take a closer look, both at their behaviour and the situation: but could I do this with a squid? And if I could not, then should I be sure that what I saw was fear? Is it *fear* that makes a snail withdraw into its shell, a hedgehog curl into a ball, or a possum 'play dead'? I don't know enough about any of these animals to be able to say: I need a context in which to place what I see, a wide picture of behaviour and response to various situations. The only context that Cockburn gives is to describe the squid as 'under threat' but that is surely to beg the question. In telling us that the 'threat' is 'no doubt a human being with a video camera', Cockburn shares with us his knowledge that it is not really a threat at all, for we all know that wildlife photographers are not inclined to attack the creatures they film. So why is this a threat? It can only be that Cockburn assumes that the squid will perceive it as such, but this begs the question, for any movement away from the threat will count as 'fleeing in fear'.

I argued earlier against the view that human behaviour provides a paradigm case of pain, fear etc., against which the behaviour — and thus the pain or fear — of other creatures can be measured. This is not to deny, however, that there are some central cases — such as the cat fleeing the firework display — in which we apply the word 'afraid' with complete confidence, whereas in others — such as the tightly-curled hedgehog — our description of it as 'afraid' might be more hesitant. Neither is this to say that there is no answer to the question 'Is the hedgehog really afraid?'. But I have suggested that it is a question that can only be answered in the context of a much wider picture of hedgehog behaviour than that provided by a single instance of curling up. Our response to the sceptic who doubts whether the cat is 'really afraid' of the fireworks might be to question whether he really understands the word 'afraid'. But we might have similar doubts about someone who insists that the retracting snail really *is* afraid. The case of the hedgehog lies between these poles.

In challenging Singer's view that we respond with concern to those creatures whose behaviour is sufficiently similar to human behaviour for us to ascribe to them pain, fear, etc., Cockburn argues that this is the reverse of the real situation.

> That we can see these similarities between the behaviour of flies and squids and that of human beings is a *reflection* of, not a condition of, our ability to ascribe the pain and fear.[15]

This being so, writes Cockburn,

> [i]t might be closer to the truth to say: our concern for creatures of a certain kind creates the possibility of our ascribing fear, pain, and so on to them; and that, in turn, creates the possibility of our observing a similarity between their behaviour and that of human beings.[16]

---

[15] Cockburn 1994: 148
[16] Cockburn 1994: 150

If Cockburn is right, we are only able to ascribe pain, fear etc., to creatures for which we are already concerned, so that Cockburn's ability to see the squid as in a state of fear was dependent upon his concern for squids, whereas anyone without such a concern would simply not be able to see it and our pointing to the behaviour would not help. But 'having a concern' cannot be either a necessary or a sufficient condition for 'ascribing fear, pain and so on,' as is obvious from the following cases.

Firstly, a lack of concern for animals (or people) does not necessarily entail a denial that they feel pain. Peter Carruthers allows that animals feel pain but argues that their pain should not concern us. Similarly, few slave-owners or Nazis denied that slaves or concentration camp inmates were capable of feeling pain and fear; it was just that their pains were not a cause for concern. Secondly, our concern for animals is not limited to those to which we attribute pain, fear etc. It is not a reluctance to cause fear or pain that prevents me from disturbing the webs of the numerous spiders that share our house. The revulsion that many people feel at the collecting and killing of butterflies may have nothing to do with any idea as to whether or not they feel pain or fear. I am not even convinced that 'the possibility of our ascribing fear, pain and so on' to creatures is a necessary condition for 'the possibility of our observing a similarity between their behaviour and that of human beings'. Watching a colony of ants coming and going from their underground nest, I was struck by just such a similarity when one ant found a scrap of cardboard which it attempted to carry back to the nest. As it struggled with its awkward load it met other ants on their outward journey, several of which stopped to examine the cardboard before taking a corner and helping to carry it for a little before abandoning it and continuing on their way. When the first ant eventually got home with its prize it tried in vain to carry it into the nest but it was too big to go through the entrance and was left outside. The temptation to see in the actions of the ants a parallel to the behaviour of human beings was irresistible, but I do not believe that it was dependent on my believing the ants to have a capacity for feeling pain, fear, etc.

Cockburn suggests that our seeing animal behaviour as similar to that of humans depends upon our being able to attribute pain, fear etc. to the animal, which in turn depends upon our first having a concern for it. Conversely, Singer argues that we first see a similarity of behaviour, then ascribe pain etc. to the animal, then develop a concern for it. I have argued that the situation is more complex than either allows and that we can have concern without attributing feelings of pain or fear, we can attribute pain and fear without being concerned and we can see similarities to human behaviour without either.

I have discussed several aspects of the human tendency to see animal behaviour as similar to that of humans and a range of theories about the significance of our inclination to do so. I now want to suggest an explanation which is simpler than any of those discussed, but which indicates that our ability to understand animal behaviour is more complex than suggested by the writers mentioned. I believe that we have a natural inclination to try to make sense of the unfamiliar or puzzling by comparing it with something familiar and understood. Naturally it is the familiar that is taken as the standard with which the new can be compared. Students learning a foreign language seize upon any words, idioms or rules that the new language has in common with their mother tongue, in order to gain a foothold on alien territory. It is not surprising, then, that people unfamiliar with animals, those who have not had the advantage of growing up with Tiddles and Fido, should try to understand animal behaviour by comparing it with that of humans. Equally, those who spend a lot of time in the company of animals may well see the comparison the other way around, being struck by the impression that the playing children are 'just like puppies', or that the chatting mothers and scampering toddlers at the playgroup are just like the ewes grazing together while their lambs chase about in a lively gang. Whichever situation is most familiar to us is the one which we take as the benchmark and I want to say that it is familiarity — preferably *involved* familiarity — that leads to understanding, which is why I am hesitant about accepting Cockburn's assurance that he could see in a brief glimpse of the behaviour of such an unfamiliar creature as a squid 'an emotion which was so unambiguously and specifically one of fear'.

I have argued that even so basic an emotion as fear can take many forms, of which 'fleeing' is only one, and that the correct recognition of it depends upon a wider knowledge of the context and of the behaviour of at least the species and preferably the individual. The more extensive the behavioural repertoire of the species, the more idiosyncratic the behaviour of the individual is likely to be and the more important it is for the observer to have a wide understanding of both in order to be able to make sense of any particular behaviour. What would an extra-terrestrial visitor make, for instance, of the habit of some humans (usually men, I think), of drumming the fingers of one hand on a hard surface? Is it comparable to the drumming of woodpeckers on tree-trunks? Or of rabbits when they thump the hind feet on the ground? It would take a very wide understanding of human behaviour for the alien to come to the conclusion that it usually denotes irritation and frustration in particular circumstances, but even then the observer would be wrong to apply this interpretation to all cases. It took me a long time to realise that my husband's finger tapping when apparently happy and relaxed is in fact the tapping out of a piece of music — apparently a common habit amongst musicians but disconcerting for others who take it as an indication of annoyance. Because most of us grow up surrounded by other people we are not aware that we are constantly learning to understand the behaviour of others. Because we know that human behaviour is very complex we are alert to the smallest nuances which would pass unnoticed by an alien who believed humans to be very simple creatures. We make a serious mistake if we prejudge unfamiliar animals to be simple creatures and thereby blind ourselves to the complexity of their behaviour. I want to say that those who live with animals learn as we all learn about human beings — by sharing our lives with them.

That we need to *learn* to read the behaviour of others is obvious from the fact that even the ubiquitous dog can be a mystery to those who have somehow managed to avoid becoming familiar with dogs. Thus the approach of a boisterously friendly animal may be perceived as a threat or the unhappy one being over-enthusiastically hugged by a visiting child may be described as 'loving children' because he is wagging his tail, even though an experienced dog-reader can see this as the anxiety of a creature too good-natured to defend itself. It is not only humans who misunderstand the behaviour of species with which they are not familiar; the ways of dogs are equally likely to be misunderstood by a *dog* brought up without canine company, as some pet dogs unfortunately are. That philosophers who have little first hand experience of animals should dismiss as 'anthropomorphic' the understanding of those who have lived their lives in the company of other species is as foolish as it would be for the stay-at-home Martian to dismiss as ' unscientific' or 'biased' the knowledge of human beings gained by his earth-visiting compatriots who have lived with them.

If our alien visitors were totally unlike us, of course, they might find us incomprehensible in spite of long and careful observation (and Harris's belief that *we* could recognise *them* as 'persons' is implausible), but the notion that all other species are somehow alien to us is one that I have been at pains to challenge.[17] In discussing anthropomorphism I argued that a term which was originally applied to our talk of an essentially unknowable being — God — is inappropriate when applied to our talk of animals. Animals are not aliens; all of them have some things in common with human beings — or, as I would prefer to say, all animals , including human beings, have some things in common — and some have a great deal in common. Dogs, horses and humans, for example, are all social mammals and as such have evolved to live socially, which means that not only do they thrive in company but that they also form relationships with other individuals and distinguish between them as friends, kin, rivals, neighbours and so on. They all devote a large part of their time and energy to caring for their young and maintain strong life-long ties with their offspring if not prevented from doing so. In spite of marked differences in behaviour, these common features may facilitate the development of what Stephen Clark calls 'empathetic understanding', whereas a creature such as a frog, which is neither social nor mammal and which has no contact with its offspring, is less easily comparable. This is not to say, however, that humans, dogs and horses have nothing in common with frogs; we all see, hear, feel, flee from danger and seek food and physical comfort. That frogs do not care about their offspring is not a reason for me not to care about frogs; even if I can be convinced that frogs do not feel pain, I shall not feel entitled to interfere with them. Their being 'less like us' than our fellow mammals is significant to the possibility of our forming relationships with them, but not to our duty not to harm them.

It is becoming apparent that the question 'are they like us?' can only be answered when we know its purpose. Otherwise we might amuse ourselves for hours dividing the whole of creation

---

[17] I examine Harris's view of extraterrestrial 'persons' in the Epilogue.

into various categories of 'like us' according to whatever feature we choose to specify; 'walking upright on two feet' for example, would perhaps result in penguins being the species judged 'most like us'. All too often the question is raised with a view to justifying the exploitation of animals on the grounds that they are *not* like us in some particular and the most perfidious of all is perhaps the research scientist who decides that an animal is sufficiently 'like us' to be a useful 'model' for experimentation while denying that it is sufficiently 'like us' for this to be wrong.

I have challenged Singer's claim that the language-project great apes offered an exciting new opportunity for human/animal relationships of a kind never before possible. I argued that it is not language but an ability to have an understanding with us that makes some animals special to us. Singer, having previously been 'not especially "interested" in animals'[18] saw these language-using apes as uniquely 'like us', and therefore worthy of his interest as 'persons' rather than only as objects of his impartial moral concern. I have tried to show that many animals share various types of behaviour, capacities and emotions with human beings, but that the tendency to view this as 'being like us' rather than as seeing ourselves as 'like them', or as 'all of us being similar' is anthropocentric. This pervasive anthropocentricity is comparable to racism and sexism in that one who grudgingly accepts that members of other races are perhaps in some ways 'people like us' or that women are in some ways 'like men' is still prejudiced in taking his own species, race or sex as the yardstick against which others are to be measured. One sometimes has the impression that the Victorians regarded all other races as failed Englishmen so that the best one could say about them was that it wasn't *their* fault that they didn't make the grade; they would certainly have been English gentlemen if they could. The impression that some philosophers regard all other species as 'failed humans' is one which recurs with depressing frequency and which seems to be confirmed by the attitude to the language-project great apes as being the first non-humans to 'make the grade'.

Sadly this anthropocentric view tends to blind its adherents to the many varied and distinctly non-human abilities and

---

[18] Singer 1976: viii

capacities demonstrated by animals in their daily lives. The primatologist Emil W. Menzel writes:

> Is it not chauvinistic for those who make their specialist living by talking, writing, and solving arbitrary puzzles, to assume that only living beings that can match or beat them at their own game have any intelligence worth talking about?[19]

Menzel reminds us that 'natural selection implies specialisation of adaptations' and that 'what chimpanzees do might or might not be similar to what humans do but that should not be our main concern in studying them'.

It is significant that those involved in, and those most excited by, the great ape language project, were psychologists, cognitive scientists and philosophers rather than people for whom animals were a primary interest. Those who have had long experience of living with animals, who have working partnerships with them, or are involved in training dogs, horses, elephants etc. do not share the enthusiasm for, or even see the point of, such work. Such people have been sharing their lives, their work and their interests with animals since prehistoric times without regarding lack of language as a problem.

Perhaps it is because philosophers are so much involved with *written* language themselves that they are inclined to overlook the importance of non-linguistic signals in the normal interactions of most people and all animals. Yet even our ability to make sense of a printed page depends to a great extent on the non-verbal aids of punctuation, spacing, italics and so on which take the place of the intonation and pauses without which speech would be almost unintelligible. A professional interpreter, giving a simultaneous verbal translation from one language to another, is acutely aware of the importance of intonation, gesture, context and so on, as indicators of a speaker's meaning. An interpreter who simply gave a literal translation of the *words* spoken would hardly be doing an adequate job. Any dog owner knows that dogs can recognise and respond appropriately to words, but, like the human interpreter, the dog relies on a variety of non-verbal clues to support his recognition of the spoken word. Perhaps the growth of information technology, E-mail and web sites has reduced our opportunity to develop our innate capacity to read non-verbal indications of the moods, thought

---

[19] Menzel 1990: 215

and intentions of others, although the growing popularity of video-conferencing suggests that being able to see a speaker is still considered to be an advantage over voice-only or written communication, which suggests that even in the business world we want to know more than words alone can convey. In our personal relationships the feelings of others are often more important to us than their words and when what is said and what is done give different messages we are more inclined to believe the deed than the word. Terrence Deacon — the neuroscientist and evolutionary anthropologist — remarks

> although language may play a role in communicating about one's emotional state, it is far less effective as a means of conveying emotion than the numerous non-verbal forms of communication that evolved for precisely this purpose. Tone of voice, posture, facial expression, and such specialised vocalizations as laughter and crying are incomparably more powerful conveyors of emotional state. This sort of communication is at least as well developed in other species as in ourselves, and as many commentators have observed, we humans are often less in touch with the emotional states of others than are other species such as our pets.[20]

Daniel Dennett also cautions us against underestimating the abilities of non-language-using animals; 'we tend to forget that *our* ways of thinking about the world are not the only ways, and in particular are not prerequisites for engaging the world successfully'.[21] Since, for our companion animals at least, an ability to 'engage the world successfully' includes an ability to engage successfully with human beings and, I have argued, to form relationships with them, I now want to explore how this is achieved by non-linguistic means.

In this section, I have argued that our understanding of others — whether human or non-human — is not dependent on either analogy or paradigm cases. In learning to use words such as 'happy', 'sad', 'hurt', 'pleased' and 'angry' we do not apply them first to ourselves, then to other humans and lastly — in an attenuated sense — to animals. Secondly, I have argued that it is through experience, not theory, that we learn to read the behaviour of other individuals and theory-driven philosophers are in

---

[20] Deacon 1997: 428
[21] Dennett 1996: 146

no position to dismiss the understanding that others have gained through experience. As Mary Midgley writes:

> I want to point out how odd it would be if those who, over many centuries, have depended on working with animals, turned out to have been relying on a sentimental and pointless error in doing so, an error which could be corrected at a stroke by metaphysicians who may never have encountered those animals at all.[22]

In the following sections I will explore the way in which some animals learn to understand us.

## II

Although few philosophers now subscribe to the Cartesian view of animals as automata, there seems to be a widespread assumption that, as far as animals are concerned, human beings might as well be automata, so that any 'relationship' between human and animal is going to be a distinctly one-sided affair. Why should so many philosophers ignore something that is obvious to every dog owner? The long shadow of Descartes seems to be responsible for the assumption that an awareness of others as 'selves' is only possible for an individual who is already *self*-conscious, so that research into animal awareness of other selves has been largely restricted to those animals believed to be capable of self-consciousness. The view that this is dependent on language has therefore limited investigation to those primates and cetaceans believed to have at least the potential for language use and much of the excitement at the great ape language projects has come from philosophers such as Singer who believe that the projects provide 'dramatic evidence' of self-consciousness, which, he claims, qualifies the apes for 'personhood' and so should elevate them to equal moral status with human beings. I have argued that this is neither as obvious nor as relevant as Singer implies. I rejected his essentially introspective definition of self consciousness and his view of the individual as a self-contained unit, suggesting instead that a consciousness of self might better be described as a consciousness of oneself as one among other selves. Writing of humans, David Cockburn suggests, and I would agree with him, that 'the Cartesian philosophical tradition — that which takes my recognition of *others* as persons to be

---

[22] Midgley 1983: 115

what is fundamentally problematic — gets things precisely the wrong way round' and that perhaps 'a central part of the task of coming to see myself as one among others is coming to see *myself* as a person'.[23] I see no reason why this should not also be the case in animals and I want to suggest that if we are to describe some animals as 'persons', then Cockburn's use of the term as describing a socially integrated being is much more appropriate than Singer's individualistic definition. As Cockburn writes 'there is no obvious absurdity in the view that the notion of a person has its primary home within the context of a personal relationship'.[24]

Stephen Clark also takes the ability to form personal relationships as crucial to the notion of personhood and criticises moralists who restrict the notion to human beings. On the subject of 'sacrificing' animal lives to save those of humans, where the sacrifice of an unconsenting human would be unthinkable, Clark writes:

> I myself see no important difference between the cases, and do not consider myself or anyone else obliged to save any human being by causing pain, distress or death to an unconsenting 'person' — where 'person' is defined as a creature with whom one can have at least as much of a personal relationship as one can with an infant, a brain-damaged adolescent or a senile old man.[25]

Clark's 'at least' is important, since I want to argue that the relationships that we can have with our partner animals can go far beyond what is possible with a severely brain-damaged or senile human who may not recognise us or even respond to our moods and emotions. The Utilitarian Jeremy Bentham was of the opinion that 'a full grown horse or dog is beyond comparison a more rational, as well as a more conversable animal, than an infant . . .'[26] It is interesting that Singer quotes the passage in which this line appears, while apparently rejecting Bentham's assertion that lack of language is no bar to 'conversation'. I have suggested that Bentham's 'conversability' is a matter not of language or of introspective self-consciousness, but of an ability to communicate that is not dependent on language.

---

[23] Cockburn 1990: 197
[24] Cockburn 1990: 198
[25] Clark 1997: 11
[26] Bentham 1789: ch. 17

In Chapter Three I quoted, and accepted, Stephen Clark's account of the evolutionary advantages to social animals of an ability to recognise their fellows as other selves. I now want to explore the evolutionary path which might have led the horse and dog to become 'conversable' with other species and in particular with man.

It is likely that interaction between early man and the horse was as hunter and hunted, so that close encounters were brief and bloody affairs offering little opportunity for social exchange. For the horse, man was a predator to be avoided, but a simple flight response to the sight of any predator would be a waste of energy and precious grazing time. Large herbivores which depend upon speed for escape need to be able to distinguish between a predator which offers a threat and one which is merely passing by or is perhaps safely occupied with other matters. On the plains of Africa, zebra, wildebeest and antelope will continue to graze peacefully in the presence of a lion which obviously has no intention of hunting and Canadian caribou show the same ability to distinguish between wolves bent on a hunt and those otherwise engaged. If the horse had not been able to tell a hunter from a gatherer he would have wasted a great deal of time and energy in unnecessary flight. As a herbivore, the horse had only to worry about predators, but for man, who was both predator and prey, an ability to read the behaviour of other species was even more important. This fact alone should be enough to expose the 'human paradigm' theory as a myth; for early man, the ability to recognise a bear as angry would have been at least as important as recognising a fellow human as angry and without such an ability early man would never have survived to become modern man.

It might be objected that there is an important difference between the ability to interact socially with one's fellows and the ability to predict the behaviour of one's prey or predators, so that whereas a man needs to understand that another *man* is angry, all he needs to know about the bear is that it presents a threat, and that whereas a horse needs to understand that another horse is afraid, all he needs to know about a man is that he is running away and therefore not a threat. The argument might be that the bear is a threat to flee from just as a falling boulder might be, and that, for the wild horse, an approaching human is a threat to be avoided in just the same way. But this is not the case and the responses of those under threat are relevantly different. To survive in bear country one would need to understand what is likely to make bears threaten (such as approaching their cubs) and what is likely to pacify them (such as retreating quietly). What is needed, in short, is an understanding that the bear's behaviour is a response to one's own behaviour and that by modifying one's own behaviour one can modify that of the bear. Equally important is to understand that no modification of one's behaviour is going to have any effect on the falling boulder.

Just like our capacity for language-learning, our capacity to learn to interpret the behaviour of other species would remain dormant if not used, and since modern man has removed most animals from his immediate environment, it is quite possible for him to avoid other species if he chooses to do so. The only serious 'predator' for modern man is man himself and the ability to recognise the intention of a potential mugger has far greater survival value than the ability to recognise the intention of an approaching bear. For those who *do* choose to live with animals, however, modern life offers opportunities for interaction and communication free from the predator/prey relationship which dominated contact between our distant ancestors and theirs.

The domestic horse today retains an impressive ability to differentiate between an approaching human bringing a welcome bucket of oats and the same person carrying a bucket of oats plus a halter, however well concealed, as many child owners of reluctant mounts know all too well. For the horse it is not the bulge of the halter under the jacket that gives the game away but subtle differences in the child's movements that betray a difference in intention, but the perceptual skill is acute enough to convince many owners that their horses are 'mind-readers', a notion to which I will return. That the ability to 'read' non-verbal forms of communication is especially well developed in the horse is illustrated by the much-quoted story of Clever Hans, whose owner claimed that the horse could solve arithmetical problems. Clever Hans and his owner were ridiculed when it was shown that he did not have the *human* ability with which his anthropocentrically biased associates had credited him, but no one seems to have been impressed by his demonstration of the highly developed but typically *equine* skill of responding to behavioural clues imperceptible to humans.

If the ability to 'read' non-linguistic behaviour had evolved primarily for intra-specific communication, the horse's response to human behaviour would be extraordinary indeed, given the morphological differences between human and horse. There seems to be no possibility that the horse could first learn the significance of a swishing tail, laid-back ears and arching neck and then translate the movements of the tailless human body with its immobile ears and negligible neck into 'equinese'. That a horse can readily learn to respond, as did Clever Hans, to a human nod, a movement of a finger or a slight change in facial expression, suggests that this ability, far from being an attenuated version of a principally intra-specific skill, evolved as a vital capacity in its own right.

For those species domesticated to provide meat, milk or wool, and especially those farmed intensively, opportunities for 'engaging the world' are so limited that their perceptiveness may have declined. For the horse, however, living and working with humans as partners is probably far more demanding than simply avoiding them as predators. Horses kept for the pleasure of their company are trusting and affectionate, but far from having blunted the acute powers of observation on which their survival previously depended, this relaxed and close relationship has resulted in a refinement of the ability to pick up non-verbal clues so slight as to be indiscernible to most humans. Free from fear of attack, the horse's characteristic nervous watchfulness is transformed into an intense curiosity and a desire to investigate anything novel. Safe in familiar surroundings and among friends, horses are fascinated by things which would terrify them in another context. Mine have spent hours crowding around to watch a JCB at work in their field and have shown such close interest that they have had to be removed to avoid accidents. This curiosity not only fosters a remarkable ability to learn but actually motivates learning as an enjoyable experience in itself.

For humans too, these close relationships provide an ideal environment for the development and refinement of our interpretative ability. No longer satisfied with our ability to make the simple predictions of the hunter, concerned only with a kill, we want to know whether our horses are happy, comfortable, contented and what their preferences are. The focus of our interest has moved from prediction of behaviour to involved concern which no longer regards the horse as a means to an end but as an end in itself. There is also a very practical reason why an understanding of horses is even more important to the modern horseman than to our spear-wielding ancestors; a hunter who failed to predict the reactions of his equine prey would suffer no more than an empty stomach, whereas the rider who cannot 'read' his horse risks a fatal accident. The rider cannot afford the philosopher's luxury of arm-chair theories.

It might be objected that while humans are capable of attributing mental states correctly both to other humans and to other species, animals, however acute their observational skills, do no more than predict the behaviour of others. Although inclined to feel that the onus of proof should be on the sceptic here, I now want to consider what evidence may be available to show that our 'partner' animals, at least, do not respond to us as to automata, providing food, walks and other treats as long as the right buttons are pushed.

I suggested above that the modern relationship between man and horse allows the possibility of a shift in the focus of the human partner's interest away from prediction and control of behaviour and towards a pleasure in the relationship for its own sake. Now I want to explore the possibility of a similar shift of focus on the part of the animal. For many creatures man is of interest only as a threat to be avoided: for others he also presents the possibility of food or shelter which is too valuable to be ignored even when — as in the case of rats, for example — it is enjoyed at the price of constant persecution by the unwilling host. More favoured species, such as garden birds, may be actively encouraged and rapidly learn to recognise the human behaviour that indicates the availability of food. Some of these creatures remain wary, only emerging when humans have retreated, whilst others become sufficiently bold to take food from an outstretched hand, but in neither case is there any indication that the human is regarded as more than a source of food. Some domestic species show a very similar attitude to humans, their degree of fear or boldness varying according to species and type of experience of humans. A flock of sheep which flees from the farmer in summer when grazing is plentiful soon learns to run to meet him when he brings supplementary rations in winter; but again, nothing in their behaviour suggests that they regard humans as of any interest other than as a source of food or a potential threat. Dogs, cats and horses, too, may regard humans as providers but I want to look at the evidence that they are also capable of an attitude which is both more complex than this and closer to the sort of attitude that one human has towards another.

Although the subject of human/animal relationships is becoming increasingly popular, the bulk of the published material concentrates on human attitudes to animals while the question of animal attitudes to humans remains largely ignored. The vast literature on the relationship between man and dog, for example, while covering such aspects as dogs in art and culture, working dogs, pet dogs and so on, rarely considers how the dogs feel about it all. Even when the subject under discussion is the use of dogs in psychotherapy and the benefits of such therapy for autistic children, the mentally ill, elderly and disabled, there is so little reference to the attitude of the *dog* that it is hard to see why he is more effective than a soft toy. This is an extraordinary oversight since the therapeutic value of the company of dogs comes from the animals' attitude to the people involved. In the case of Bobby and the prisoners of the Nazis it was Bobby's recognition of them as human friends that helped to preserve their sense of their own humanity in spite of the dehumanizing effect of their treatment by other people. That a visit from a friendly dog can have the same effect on psychologically damaged, emotionally fragile or institutionalised patients depends on this same feeling that their own humanity has been recognised by another creature.

My own dogs have often accompanied me into schools, hospitals, old people's homes and children's homes and the positive response of pupils, patients or residents has frequently been dramatic. Even — or perhaps especially — those who are withdrawn and uncommunicative may respond to the dog with a warmth and interest not shown to the people around them. Most tellingly, such people often express their delight with exclamations such as 'He likes me!' or 'She wants to talk to *me*.' What matters to these people is that the dog responds to them as individuals; if this were not the case then a cuddly toy would do just as well, which it clearly does not. Contrary to some of the views I have discussed, animals are neither aliens nor defectives. They are not our inferiors but our fellows and some of them are prepared to accept us as *their* fellows too.

This is not something which can be studied in a laboratory and in examining the way that partner animals relate to us, observations of animals in the wild, the zoo or the factory farm are not of relevance either. In this section my evidence will therefore be drawn mainly from my own experience of my horses and dogs which I feel to be especially interesting in that the members of both species enjoy a rich social life with their own kind so that their relationship with me is an addition to, and not a substitute for, normal intra-specific relationships.

During the summer months my horses roam freely together over a large acreage with more grass than they can eat, constant access to fresh water, shelter and a comfortable bed and no need of any additional food. Unlike the farmer's sheep, however, their attitude towards me is unchanged and they greet me as happily as they do in the winter when they are fed several times daily and are, in periods of bad weather, totally dependent upon me.

Those who insist that animals are only interested in human beings as dispensers of food are simply wrong. Partner animals frequently form relationships with humans who never offer them food at all, whereas food will not win over an animal if the human offering it is neither liked nor trusted. When food *is* involved it may play an important part but to suggest that this devalues the relationship is to forget the importance of food in the social life of human beings. Among humans the social and psychological significance of offering food or sharing a meal is universal. By contrast, the offering of food to another is comparatively rare amongst animals other than as an essential part of the rearing of young. For herbivores, such as horses, the matter never arises as their food supply normally surrounds them and is equally available to all but this does not prevent horses from forming close and lasting bonds with one another.

It is significant that very young puppies, while still having all their needs met by their mothers, and having no physical need of human support, will respond positively to human contact, wagging their tails when spoken to and cuddled, even at three weeks old when their eyes have only been open a week and they can barely toddle. Earlier in this chapter I examined the strong similarities between the human smile and the canine tail-wag; my experience suggests that, just as babies are predisposed to smile at their mothers, so are puppies predisposed to greet not only their mothers but humans too. Particularly remarkable is the puppy's inclination to respond by wagging, wriggling excitedly and licking, to exactly the same cuddling and baby-talk that babies respond to with smiles, kicking and gurgles of delight. By contrast , a litter of orphan fox-cubs that I bottle-fed from the time they were a few days old and blind, seemed predisposed to respond to my attentions with snarling and spitting. Before the puppies are ready for solid food they are greeting me with great enthusiasm, tail-wagging and attempts to climb into my lap and when, at about four weeks, I start to bring them regular meals, my difficulty is to persuade them to concentrate on the food before them rather than on greeting me and demanding my attention. The seeking of human attention is a major concern for them even though they have not only the company of their siblings but the attention of their mother, grandmother and assorted aunts. The fox-cubs, on the other hand, were only interested in the food and wanted nothing to do with me.

I have already criticised the theory, popular with animal psychologists, that satisfactory human/animal relationships depend upon the human taking on the dominant role of pack or herd leader. I suggested that this view is based on two common mistakes, the first being a misconception of social animals as living in fiercely competitive groups whose members are bullied into submission by one dominant individual and the second being an assumption that animals are only able to respond to us in those ways in which they would otherwise respond to their conspecifics. Taken together, these two mistakes are responsible for the 'cowboy' approach to training animals, regarding them as savage brutes which must be forced to submit to man, their natural master. My own experience of living with family groups of dogs and horses has taught me that their interaction with one another is based, not on domination or even confrontation, but on cooperation and approval-seeking. Their extreme sensitivity to the feelings of their fellows and their readiness to modify their own behaviour accordingly is the basis on which their relationships with humans are also built.

Marthe Kiley-Worthington's study[27] supports my own finding that the social skills learned as a young horse grows up in its natural family group are vitally important in its interaction with human beings. Her research shows that foals which are weaned

---

[27]   Kylie-Worthington 1997

and removed from their mothers (which is normal practice with most domestic horses) are much less easy to train than those which remain in a family group in which they learn not only to respect their elders but also to care for their younger siblings. It should hardly need adding that it is not only the ability to respond appropriately to humans that is impaired in a horse which has been socially deprived: its ability to form relationships with its own kind will be equally diminished. But my concern at the moment is not to consider the case of unfortunately maladjusted individuals but to show how the interaction of a well-adjusted horse with a human being differs from its interaction with another horse. I have argued that, in their dealings with humans, our partner animals are able to adapt and extend their basic repertoire of behaviour to cope with demands which never arise in intra-specific interactions and my own experience is that what might be described as the 'behavioural building blocks' used in the varied intra-specific relationships of each of my dogs and horses are rearranged in their interaction with me, so that the range of behaviour used by any individual animal in its relationship with me does not correspond to that used with any of its conspecifics. The horses provide the clearest examples of this, since, although they and the dogs each form a multi-generation family group, the social structure of the horse group is much more obvious.

Established thirty years ago, my horse family has always been led by the oldest mare — a position achieved not, it seems, by bullying or aggression but simply by virtue of her seniority and her being either mother or grandmother to all the others. The present leader is a twenty-five year old mare whose authority is unchallenged. All the other horses treat her with respect, follow her lead and come to her call. Does the fact that she always complies with my requests or commands without any sign of resistance or resentment suggest that she regards me as a super-leader of the herd? Well, if that were the case, I would hardly expect her to greet me, as she invariably does, with a show of what I can only describe as affection. If she regarded me as her family members regard her, she would move respectfully away as I approach and would certainly not come up with a friendly snicker to nuzzle my shoulder. Even less compatible with a view of me as super-leader is her protective manner and apparent recognition of my physical vulnerability, which is demonstrated by her putting herself between me and any boisterous youngsters and by standing guard over me if I sit or lie on the ground. This protective behaviour is typically shown by mares towards foals and since I am about the size of a young foal it is perhaps not surprising that a mare should react in this way; but it is interesting that the response as to a foal is limited to regard for my physical vulnerability and is certainly not carried over into social interaction. Foals may be protected but their persuasive powers are very limited.

Nor do the younger horses treat me as they do the matriarch. Although they don't approach *her* uninvited they come confidently up to me for attention and often respond to my grooming by reciprocating as they would with their peers, but to take this as an indication that they regard me as one of themselves would be to ignore the way they vie for my attention, come to me for protection if they are bullied and happily accompany me away from the herd, seeming to prefer my company to that of their family members. This apparent preference surely springs from the fact that I do *not* treat them as they treat one another. Most remarkable of all is the willingness with which each accepts my teaching her to move precisely according to my commands, to respond to bit and bridle as well as spoken signals and eventually to carry me on her back away from the security of the herd and beyond the safety of familiar territory.

A willingness to accept control may be part of equine nature, but to progress from the simple response to the demands of the herd leader — to move away, to follow, or to come — to the complex, precise and demanding requirements of the human trainer and rider, not in fear or through domination but with an obvious pleasure in a secure partnership, is to make a leap beyond the ability of most species. Kiley-Worthington cites an interesting experiment in which she reared a young male red deer in order to compare its aptitude for training with that of the domestic horse. She found that although the deer quickly learned the lessons taught to young horses and would sometimes go through his routine as required, he could never be relied upon and would suddenly take flight, not only resisting restraint but dragging with him the trainer who attempted to hold him. As Kiley-Worthington points out, the deer was only about 20% of the weight of a young horse and

> [t]his brought home to me very forcibly how cooperative our domestic horse is. There is no reason why he has to put up with our demands. Even a yearling has a great deal more strength than we have and, if he so wishes, could move off dragging us with him.[28]

Although it may not be a *reason* for putting up with our demands, it surely is the case that a relationship with a sympathetic human offers great benefits for the horse, quite beyond those offered by other equines. Food may play an important part, as may physical comfort, but my own study suggests that my horses respond to my *attitude* as well as to the material benefits that I provide. One example is their extreme sensitivity to voice and their positive response to an approving or affectionate tone while showing obvious distress at an angry — or even a merely disapproving one. All horses seem upset by angry voices and will react with uneasiness even when they have no reason to connect human anger with any physical threat to themselves. Interestingly, I find that an angry voice distresses them *more* than the physical discomfort unavoidably caused by my treating injuries which are obviously painful. A soothing voice and gentle manner can outweigh the physical discomfort. Their reaction seems remarkably similar to my own when somebody I care about is angry, even when the anger is not directed at me; my uneasiness has nothing to do with a fear that the anger might result in an attack on me.

The two important points here are that not only is the ability to sense the emotions of others independent of language use or a 'theory of mind', but that our emotions *matter* to our partner animals in a way that is not limited to the animal's concern about possible consequences for itself. David Cockburn suggests (*Other Human Beings*) that our concern with the attitudes that other people have to us is characteristic of most of our human relationships. I want to suggest that the same type of concern is a defining characteristic of the relationships that partner animals have with us and one which contrasts sharply with the 'grab the peanuts and run' attitude to humans demonstrated by most wild animals and birds.

The possibility of animals being emotionally hurt by human attitudes does not seem to occur to Peter Singer, who equates

---

[28] Kiley-Worthington 1997: 10

suffering with physical pain and deprivation. Given Singer's general disregard for personal relationships this is perhaps unsurprising, for it is in the context of personal relationships that we speak of being hurt in this way. 'It was a hurtful thing to say'; 'She was hurt by his attitude'; 'They'll be hurt if we don't invite them' are all familiar ways of speaking about relationships. Enemy action in time of war may cause great suffering but we will not be 'hurt' by it in this sense.

Singer offers an example of the 'same amount of pain' felt by animals and by humans:

> If I give a horse a hard slap across the rump with my open hand, the horse may start but it presumably feels little pain. Its skin is thick enough to protect it against a mere slap. If I slap a baby in the same way, however, the baby will cry and presumably does feel pain for its skin is more sensitive. So it is worse to slap a baby than a horse, if both slaps are administered with equal force.[29]

I don't know whether Singer has carried out this experiment: I cannot say that I have ever slapped either a baby or a horse myself, but I would suggest that the *degree of physical pain* would not concern either horse or baby (although the age of the baby, which Singer does not specify, might be significant) as much as the attitude of, and the relationship with, the smacker, so that the degree of *suffering* caused cannot be equated with the pain alone. Similarly, if you tread on my foot, the degree of *pain* I feel may not depend on my perception of your action as deliberate or accidental but whether or not I am *much hurt* will certainly depend upon your attitude. There is, incidentally, an unintended irony in Singer's description of the horse as thick-skinned: horses, like humans, can be very 'thin-skinned' in the metaphorical sense of being easily hurt by the attitudes of others.

I noted above the toleration of pain shown by horses when treated in a reassuring manner by a trusted human and it might be worth looking at this more closely as I believe it to offer firm evidence of a complex relationship far beyond any equation of advantages and disadvantages for the horse. It might reasonably be expected that a horse which has built up a good relationship with a human might not have its positive attitude towards him too much shaken by occasional painful experiences such as the

---

[29] Singer 1976: 17

cleaning of a wound might involve. One can also easily accept that a relationship might be enhanced by simple cases where the human is able to offer instant relief for a painful condition, as by the removal of a foreign body from foot, eye or mouth. But severe injuries may require intensive, painful and lengthy treatment, such as frequent dressing of wounds. I have had to deal with several cases which involved so much attention that almost all of my contact time with the horse was taken up with painful treatment. The end result, fortunately, has been complete recovery but this can hardly have been foreseen by the horse, whose experience was that every time I appeared I caused it pain, sometimes for a period of weeks. What does the 'reassuring manner', mentioned above, amount to if it cannot be a reassurance that 'this won't hurt'? It can surely only be a reassurance that no hurt is *intended*, that there is concern for, not antagonism towards, the sufferer. Their being reassured implies a recognition of *intention* and that the human/horse relationship survives such experiences undamaged is not best characterised in terms of 'pain vs. gain'.

There is also scientific evidence which suggests that the relationship of trust between horse and human can actually result in a reduction of pain. Patrick Wall, the specialist in pain relief, writes of the importance of attitude and expectation in relation to suffering and explains: 'If you have strong reason to expect a pain to disappear, it may disappear. This is called a placebo response'.[30] Wall sets out to prove wrong the widely-held belief that a placebo response is evidence that the pain was not real, that the placebo is 'the same as no treatment'[31] or that 'only weak-minded suggestible people in minor pain respond'.[32] He describes an experiment at a London dental hospital, where patients suffering from the effects of wisdom-tooth extraction were treated by massage with an ultra-sound machine. When, in a double-blind experiment, some patients were treated with a machine which was switched off, unknown to both patient and doctor, it was found that not only was the *pain* reduced, but that 'the swelling of the face was markedly reduced and the ability to open the mouth was improved'.[33] Wall comments : 'The reason for choosing this example from many is that the effect was not

---

[30] Wall 1999: 151
[31] Wall 1999: 153
[32] Wall 1999: 153
[33] Wall 1999: 154

only on the pain, which unthinking dualists would say is 'only mental', but also on the swelling and on the muscle spasm'.[34] Wall believes that the pervasive effect of dualism leads to a reluctance to believe that the psychological consequences of the trust in the doctor and his treatment could have a real effect on the physical symptoms. He argues that it is quite wrong to think of pain as a 'message' from body to mind, and he suggests that: 'Pain is not just a sensation, but, like hunger and thirst, is an awareness of an action plan to be rid of it'.[35] The placebo effect is therefore explained in that:

> If the person's experience has taught them that a particular action is followed by relief, then they respond if they believe the action has occurred. In this scheme of thinking, the placebo effect is not a stimulus but an appropriate action. As such the placebo terminates and cancels the sense expressed in terms of possible action. Pain is then best seen as a need state, like hunger and thirst, which are terminated by a consummatory act.

This may not explain those cases where, as I have described, I have had to continue painful treatment of horses for some time, but it does offer a very plausible explanation of a phenomenon which I have very frequently observed in my dogs and always found rather puzzling. On our daily walks in the forest the dogs often pick up small thorns in their feet. When this first happens with a puppy, she will limp, hold up the foot and perhaps attempt to remove the thorn with her teeth, until I offer to help and quickly pull it out. The puppy trots off and after the experience has been repeated a couple of times, she learns to come to me unprompted, holding up the foot for my inspection. Occasionally, however, a careful examination either fails to reveal the cause or shows it to be a cut or other injury for which I have no immediate solution. The remarkable thing about these cases is that when I have completed my examination and put down the untreated foot, the 'sufferer' will very often trot off as if the problem has been solved. Wall's explanation is that my 'as if' is superfluous — the dog's confidence in my healing power really *has* solved the problem. I imagine that cases like this are commonplace among pet dogs but that their owners often misinterpret

---

[34] Wall 1999: 154
[35] Wall 1999: 210

them as evidence that the dog was not really hurt in the first place, merely 'putting it on' to gain sympathy.

Wall's experiments on animals have also shown that the placebo effect — or more often, its converse, the 'nocebo effect' — are not unique to human beings. Rats which have been made to feel ill by being injected with a nausea-inducing substance showed the same symptoms when, months later, they were injected with a harmless substance in circumstances which, otherwise, were similar.

Wall's work confirms my belief that writers on the animals issue frequently misunderstand and oversimplify the significance of pain in the suffering of animals (and of humans, too). It is clear that what we describe as pain cannot be considered as separable from a complex range of factors amongst which attitudes and relationships are of particular importance. For the pet or partner animal, pain and suffering can be significantly reduced by the attention of a trusted human. For the unfortunate occupants of the laboratory cage or factory farm however, it is the nocebo effect that is more likely to have been learned. Once the animals have come to associate human attention with pain, the expectation will magnify their suffering. In a fear-inducing environment this will snowball, since, as Wall comments: 'Fear generates anxiety and anxiety focuses the attention. The more attention is locked, the worse is the pain. There is therefore a marked correlation between pain and anxiety'.[36] If the fear can be allayed and the attention distracted, the pain can be significantly reduced, but again it is the companion animal who is likely to benefit from secure and interesting surroundings while the laboratory beagle or breeding-crate sow have their suffering compounded not only by fear but by the barren environment in which there is nothing for them to attend to but their own pain. It is not a coincidence that Wall, whose animal experiments were limited to laboratory subjects, gives examples of the nocebo rather than the placebo, effect.

I am claiming that partner animals recognise our intentionality, but it might be objected that none of the above supports this, since the placebo effects I have described could just as well have resulted from the sort of conditioned response shown by Pavlov's dogs in their reaction to a bell. I have two answers to

---

[36] Wall 1999: 185

this objection. Firstly, Wall argues that the idea that Pavlovian conditioned responses are 'entirely mechanical processes' has been seriously challenged by 'very careful repeated investigations in humans [which] have never shown that conditioned responses are free of cognitive awareness'[37] so that, not only would it be 'wrong to assume that there is no cognitive component'[38] in the placebo effect but that 'pari passu, it is wrong to assume with Descartes that animals are simply automata reacting second by second. Animals, too, have expectations of reward and punishment, as any pet owner knows'.[39] My second defence is that the case of companion animals, such as my dogs described above, parallels that of children as described by Wall. Wall notes that 'young children have not had time to learn that people in white coats with horrible-tasting medicine and needles bring relief. Therefore they do not respond to placebos in an adult fashion even though they have learned that "Mummy will kiss it better"'.[40]

The child's fear of the doctor and confidence in the omnipotence of Mummy is paralleled by the dog's fear of the vet and confidence in his owner. The sceptic who might deny that personal relationships are crucial here, arguing that an analgesic-dispensing robot would work just as well, would have to claim that this would be true not only of the dog, but of the child as well.

The above discussion is relevant to John Harris's claim, quoted in Chapter One, that 'since animals cannot consent to pain or distress, the infliction of these upon them is always a case of torture . . .'[41] While it is obviously true that an animal cannot verbally give its consent, it can willingly accept — or even seek — treatment which causes it pain. The word 'torture' is not applicable. This is not to deny, of course, that there is a world of difference between an animal freely accepting painful treatment for its own benefit and having pain inflicted upon it by others for their own ends.

---

[37] Wall 1999: 167
[38] Wall 1999: 167
[39] Wall 1999: 168
[40] Wall 1999: 161
[41] Harris 1985: 219

## III

I have described how a puppy can learn — by experiences such as having thorns removed from a foot — that his human friend can relieve pain. At the same time, he will also be making other discoveries about human capabilities; that his friend can open doors, provide food etc. The process seems no different from that by which a human baby makes the same kind of discoveries. At first the baby — or puppy — simply cries when he is cold, hungry and so on, and depends upon his mother to interpret his cry and satisfy his need. He does not *learn* to cry when he is distressed but as he grows he does learn from experience that his cries are answered and he responds by refining his behaviour to achieve the desired result, so that the baby learns to ask for his bottle by reaching out and gurgling and the puppy learns to ask to go out by scratching at the door and whining. Presumably this basic learning could take place without human contact: if the puppy's actions activated an automatic door opener, for example, or if the baby's actions resulted in a feeding bottle being automatically presented to him. But in normal circumstances, as baby and puppy gain experience and awareness, they constantly refine their behaviour in response to the people in their lives, and for the growing dog, as for the growing child, this entails a gradual development of the awareness that these people have intentions, emotions, feelings and preferences.

As I noted previously, it is not just that our dogs do not treat us as automata, but that they do not treat us as they treat each other either. The methods of communication and persuasion that they use with us are much closer to those that we use with them than to those which they use with each other. With our own dogs this is most obvious when they decide that an outing in the car would be nice. It often happens that I am working quietly at my desk when I become aware of the presence of a dog at my side. Looking down, my eyes meet the intense gaze and my attention will be rewarded by a wag of the tail. If I turn back to my book a gentle nudge might be used, or a loud sigh, and again, any positive response on my part is reinforced by tail wagging and an encouraging lick. So the persuasion goes on, with each desired response being enthusiastically rewarded and encouraged with licks, tail wags etc. If I stand up I am shepherded towards the door, then out of the house, then alternately led and shepherded down the garden path to the car. (Although most of their plans involve the car, the dogs never waste any effort in trying to persuade *it* to take them out — although one did once help to push it when it wouldn't start.) The similarity between the dog's method and *my* method of training a puppy to do what I want is undeniable: first gain the attention, then praise: next work in easy stages, extravagantly praising and encouraging any move in the right direction — even the slowest learner will respond in time!

Also of significance is the ability of the experienced dog to generalise from its knowledge of the capabilities of particular humans to humans in general so that a 'street-wise' dog may ask a stranger to open a door, or a well-socialised companion dog will invite a stranger to play ball. A more interesting form of generalisation is shown by my own dogs who, having gained from experience and observation a fair idea of my capabilities, will ask for my help in a completely novel situation such as occurred recently when the eldest, Branwen, suffered a stroke during the night. Two of her daughters came upstairs to fetch me and led me to her, standing by anxiously as I attended to her. When I had settled their mother back in her bed before the fire their relief was obvious. No less obvious, to me, was the 'thank you' of their licks and tail wags as I went back to bed and it is hard to imagine what more plausible interpretation of their behaviour the sceptic might offer. This particular example raises a number of questions, including that of the concern of mature animals for the well-being of a very old mother, but their coming to fetch me to help in a situation which is new to them is a regular occurrence and an important indication that their expectations of me are not limited to stock responses or familiar situations.

It is significant that the tendency of dogs to seek out human help with problems they cannot settle for themselves is not limited to satisfying purely selfish desires for food or outings. The case mentioned above of seeking aid for another member of the group is an interesting but not unusual example of concern for another. My dogs will also take it upon themselves to draw my attention to situations which they feel I should know about such as the arrival of a visitor or the misbehaviour of a puppy. That this is a widespread inclination in dogs is apparent from the ease with which it can be fostered to provide dogs to assist deaf people by alerting them to specific situations. Of particular relevance to my case is that the spontaneous occurrence of this behaviour in my own dogs provides evidence of a type of partnership which not only makes our mixed-species household a true social community but also suggests a sense of social responsibility. Because it is therefore a very significant kind of behaviour, it deserves closer attention.

A dog which barks when somebody knocks at the door may indeed alert his owner to the presence of the caller but he does not necessarily do so intentionally; dogs have a natural tendency to challenge intruders. It is the conflict between this tendency and my disapproval of dogs barking at callers which has given rise to the dogs' own solution of coming to fetch me. This ability to work out a compromise to accommodate conflicting demands is a crucial element in social partnerships. In our own household the compromise and cooperation which are essential to communal life are sometimes so subtle that it is difficult to distinguish between them. Certainly there appear to be 'house rules', observed by all, but it is by no means clear that the code of conduct is always contrived by the humans and imposed on the dogs. Old Branwen, mentioned above, in addition to coming to fetch me when young dogs were doing something of which *I* would disapprove, would also behave in a way which is most naturally described as enlisting my help to censure behaviour of which *she* disapproved, such as unaccompanied dogs going into the stable yard.

Other aspects of the dogs' behaviour suggest something very like cultural transmission. My present dogs are part of a dynasty covering many generations since I first acquired their ancestors more than forty years ago and puppy-rearing has always been a communal affair, shared by dogs and humans alike. Puppies learn not only that different individuals have to be treated differently but also that there is an accepted 'code of behaviour' to which they are expected to conform, and interestingly, this learning takes place without any formal teaching. The basic rules that I taught to my original dogs a dozen generations ago seem to have been passed down from generation to generation ever since. Two simple examples are the rules that dogs must not bark in the house or car and dogs must not help themselves to food that has not been given them. Although never having been directly taught to the present dogs, these rules are strictly observed even in our absence, as when tempting food is left unattended within easy reach. Rules which *have* been taught seem to be regarded as more flexible. When we moved to our present home the dogs were told that they were not to go upstairs and this is generally observed unless unusual circumstances prevail. When a night-time emergency, such as Branwen's illness, requires them to come upstairs to fetch me, they do so with none of the anxiety that normally accompanies disobedience, but the emergency action is not taken as a precedent to sanction further infringements.

In Chapter Three I quoted Hearne's remark that chimpanzees brought up in human families seem not to learn 'as much about not biting and toilet training as the family dog.' My experience with my dynasty of dogs is that 'not biting and toilet training' never need to be taught at all, being understood by all without ever being mentioned. That they apparently *do* need to be taught to many family dogs may support my view that an upbringing in a stable extended family is as advantageous in the raising of well-adjusted dogs as it is for well-adjusted humans.

In Chapter Two I suggested that the demands of close social relationships change all those involved and that cross-species relationships are likely to require greater change than those with conspecifics. When humans and animals live and work together, both parties develop understanding and communication skills of a type that they would not otherwise have and the communication skills of those individuals whose social contacts have been restricted to their conspecifics should not be taken as indicative of the limits of the whole species. Nor should we limit our expectations of the psychological or intellectual capacities of our non-human companions to what they show in their dealings with one another. In Chapter Three I argued that our companion animals are able to adapt to living socially with humans in a way that the great apes are not. I also want to say that the benefits of living with us provide our companions with the motivation to communicate in ways which life with conspecifics alone would not. The dog is perhaps the best example of this because the family dog, almost uniquely among non-humans, lives its entire life in a situation not unlike that of a young human in one particularly significant way. Young humans are dependent on the care of their parents for a long time, much of which is spent in learning not only to communicate their desires but to persuade others to satisfy them. Species in which the young are not dependent have no need of such skills. The family dog, although maturing much earlier, lives in a situation in which it has opportunities to acquire sophisticated desires — such as car rides and trips to the seaside — which it cannot satisfy for itself. It therefore has both the motivation and the opportunity to develop an understanding of humans and an ability to communicate with them which is either unavailable or unnecessary to other species. Thus, although I share Tim Ingold's scepticism about the claims made for language-using apes, I believe that he is wrong to argue that we should not expect animals in contact with humans to develop communication skills beyond those needed in their own social groups. Ingold writes:

> Animals that converse with humans ought to be able to converse among themselves, so why do they not do so? . . As George Steiner has suggested, it is in the intimacy of the small group and not in the demands of communication with strangers and aliens, that language acquires its primary force and motivation.[42]

But what may be true of the development of linguistic skills in human beings is not necessarily true of non-linguistic communication skills in non-humans. It is also important to realise that, for the family dog, the human family does not comprise 'strangers and aliens' but does provide exactly the 'intimacy of the small group' which Ingold — rightly, I believe — takes to be crucial. For companion dogs, the demands — and the benefits — of living with humans do provide just the motivation needed to extend their communication skills beyond those required in a dogs-only society. In this respect it is significant that dogs are generally willing partners, whereas the language-project apes are not and cannot be said to benefit from living with humans, as became clear in Chapter Three. Certainly they are motivated to ask for food and treats which they cannot obtain for themselves but, since they are physically confined, there is nothing to suggest that, given the choice between captivity and independence, they would choose the former. By contrast, many dogs, including my own, *do* have the choice, and opt for our society. My dogs, for example, although free to come and go as they please and with no physical barriers to prevent them from roaming, do not choose to go far from the house unless I go with them, even on our own land. It would be a mistake, however, to think that the

---

[42] Ingold 1988: 91–2

lack of physical restraint means that they are free in all senses, for all social animals, including dogs and humans, are bound not only by bonds of affection but by the conventions of social life. It would also be a mistake to think that all the dogs regard me as a parent figure — the older ones often give the impression that I am the one who needs looking after. Certainly they come to me for reassurance when they are frightened by a thunderstorm, but they also run back to fetch me if, when offered an outing in the car, they find that I am lagging behind. The sense in which they cannot go without me does not seem to be significantly different from the sense in which I cannot abandon them. That dogs, like humans, are thus psychologically constrained although physically free is crucial to my case that they are true partners whereas Washoe and her fellows have to be physically restrained because they lack the psychological restraint to respect the demands of living socially with humans.

Those who believe that all animal behaviour can be adequately explained in mechanistic terms will dismiss the above as anthropomorphic nonsense but I believe that the ethical implications of the behaviour I have described are far-reaching. If, as I have suggested, the language-less and unself-conscious (at least in the linguistically defined sense) dog is capable of social responsibility which seems to be beyond the allegedly language-using and self-conscious chimpanzee, then neither language nor self-consciousness are as essential to the roots of moral behaviour as is generally believed.

Carruthers claims that 'no animals appear capable of conceptualising (let alone acting under) general socially agreed rules',[43] but I want to suggest that this over-intellectualises the behaviour of social mammals, including ourselves. Hearne's 'not biting and toilet training' are just two examples of 'socially agreed rules' that do not require any conceptualising and are certainly vital to many species. That *some* human behaviour — like driving on the left hand side of the road in Britain, for example — is explicable by reference to a formal rule, does not mean that acting in accordance with a rule is only possible for those able to conceptualise it. No one growing up in Britain needs to be told, when he takes his first driving lesson, that he must drive on the left; he knows that that is how things are done. What matters is that the new

---

[43] Carruthers 1992: 145

driver conforms, not that he conceptualises the rule. Living together without conflict depends upon this ability to conform and there is plenty of evidence to suggest that humans are not more successful at harmonious living than other species.

Much of what I have said here about dogs is also true of horses and my own horses, like my dogs, live in an extended family group in which the rearing of foals is a shared responsibility which both depends upon, and re-inforces, the cohesion of the group. For practical reasons, however, the horse is rarely integrated into a human family in the way that the dog is and close relationships between horse and human are more often in a one-to-one partnership than in a family setting. The closeness of these partnerships nonetheless often results in the development of communication between human and horse which is no less remarkable than that between human and dog. I mentioned earlier the belief sometimes expressed by horse owners that their animals are able to read minds and I suggested that it is in fact the horse's remarkable ability to read *bodies* that enables it to predict human behaviour so accurately. My suggestion that some aspects of equine behaviour are more easily explained in terms of a recognition of the intention of another indicates that there is no such distinction to be made. Oskar Pfungst was surely right in his explanation of *how* Clever Hans managed to 'answer' the questions put to him. (He had been taught to tap his foot when asked a question and he learned to continue tapping until a signal — probably an unintentional change of posture by his owner — told him to stop.) But Pfungst offered no theory as to *why*. If Hans's only interest was in predicting his owner's behaviour what behaviour was he predicting which would warrant such intense concentration in the difficult situation of repeated public performances? An occasional titbit? Punishment for a mistake? A simple stimulus/response theory would say so, but, as I have pointed out above, horses which have a good relationship with a human partner will respond willingly to his wishes without the need for either carrot or stick. Could it not be that Clever Hans's motivation was a desire to do as his owner wanted, and that his reward was the approval of his human partner? This possibility is certainly supported by my earlier observation that horses and other partner animals care about our attitudes to them, but is there an important distinction to be made between attitudes, intentions and knowing what another wants as opposed to being able to make the right response to the stimulus? Terrence Deacon believes that there is and raises the question of 'whether animals know that there is some*one* behind their perceptual experience of others' and answers that they do not, since 'The lack of symbolic referential abilities in non-human species limits them to representation of associations between stimuli, including the behaviours of others.'[44]

Leaving aside the claim that non-humans 'lack symbolic referential abilities',[45] Deacon's question is itself question-begging in assuming that there *is* 'some*one* behind their perceptual experience of others' — that the someone who has the intentions, desires and attitudes is not to be seen in the body that produces the behaviour. Is there not a suggestion of Cartesian dualism here and might it not be argued that the failure to see the intention, desire or attitude *in* the behaviour is due, not to their being essentially unobservable but to the observer not being observant enough? Before Pfungst solved the Clever Hans mystery, the case had been investigated by a commission which included among its members an impressive array of academics, animal trainers, zoologists, a researcher into animal behaviour, and the directors of both the Psychological Institute and the Physiological Institute of Berlin University, all of whom, at the conclusion of their investigation, signed a document declaring themselves to be convinced of the truth of the claims made for Clever Hans' mathematical ability.[46] Hans's owner, Herr von Osten, appears to have believed in the ability claimed for his horse. The behaviour on his part which Hans took as a signal to stop tapping was not intended as such: indeed von Osten cannot be said to have *intended* that Hans should stop tapping when the right answer was reached, but he probably *wanted* him to do so. The commission observers were not observant enough to notice von Osten's behaviour, so they could not have seen the want — the desire — that it expressed but that does not mean that it was essentially unobservable. Hans was certainly observant enough to see the behaviour and it is possible that it acted as the stimulus to trigger a response learned as a result of carrot and stick training, but it is also possible, as I have argued, that Hans's motivation was the

---

[44] Deacon 1997: 426
[45] For an interesting discussion of symbol use by animals, see Midgley 1979, especially pages 310–17.
[46] Candland 1993

desire to please his master, a desire which could be achieved by doing what von Osten wanted. And if Hans was observant enough to see what von Osten wanted, could it not be said that in reading his owner's body-language he was also reading his mind?

It might be objected that, even though the animals are unaware of their dependence on us for their home and all the comforts they enjoy, their interest in us is none the less as providers in that we are a source of reassurance in times of alarm, amusement in times of boredom, and perhaps of more considerate companionship than their fellows provide, and that any protective behaviour towards us is either 'instinctive' or an attempt to preserve useful resources. I can only answer by observing that those who wish to interpret the evidence in this way could do the same with our close human relationships. The case for scepticism about animal attachments is no stronger than in the human case.

I do not believe that my horses or dogs have 'a theory of mind' or even that they have an opinion on this matter or any other, since the having of either theories or opinions seems to be language-dependent. But Wittgenstein's words '[m]y attitude towards him is an attitude towards a soul. I am not of the *opinion* that he has a soul', not only describe, to an important extent, my attitude towards them but also, I suggest, their attitude towards me.

I have noted elsewhere that because man's over-population of the earth threatens the existence of many species, those which can live with us as friends and partners may have the best chance of long-term survival. Man is a feature of the environment to which other species must adapt if they are to have any chance of a future. Just as language development in Homo sapiens played a crucial role in his survival at the expense of other species, so may the evolving ability of our dogs, cats and horses to communicate with us prove to be the key to their survival. This ability to communicate with us, rather than simply predict our behaviour, is one important difference between these animals and others and it seems likely that interaction with sensitive humans, able to interpret attempted communication, encourages the animal to extend its 'vocabulary' and thereby its intellectual capacity. In this way *our* language use may influence the intellectual development of other species.

I have also noted that the philosophical perception of animals as 'lacking' language is not shared by those who include animals among their friends and family, many of whom consider absence of language to be one of the more attractive qualities of animal companions. If they ever learned to answer back, I suspect that they would soon join the tiger and the chimpanzee on the endangered species list — a view clearly shared by Saki, whose short story 'Tobermory' tells of a domestic cat who learns to speak with the result that his previously fond owners are driven to plot his demise. The idea of a talking cat may be fanciful, but Saki's view relates to my observation in Chapter Two that we are happy to allow our cats an intimate view of our lives which we would not want our human neighbours, or even our children, to share. Singer regards animals as unworthy companions because they 'lack' language; others may find that this makes possible a particularly comfortable type of relationship with them.

## Conclusion

Man's language use may make him unique but it does not isolate him from other creatures. That animals are not themselves language users is not a barrier to our understanding of them, nor does it prevent our having an understanding *with* them. A preconception that it *must* be a barrier is, however, a serious problem. We should not be characterised only by our language use and the particular type of introspective self-consciousness that goes with it but also by our sociability and need for close relationships. We are social mammals and these similarities with other social mammals explain our empathetic understanding of them. Normal human beings learn about pain, fear, delight and so on, by their application to many creatures, not only to themselves or their own species. There is no single paradigm.

Those whose main interest in animals is to discover which, if any, are self-conscious, overlook the evidence that many animals respond to *others* as thinking, feeling beings and that our 'partner' animals respond to us in this way. Personal relationships not only depend upon this ability, they also foster it. 'Other-awareness' is of no less significance than self-awareness. A concentration on what distinguishes us from other animals is not only a barrier to the understanding of other animals; it is a barrier to the understanding of ourselves.

# Epilogue

# *Dogs, Frogs and Extraterrestrials*

> *For they are not regarded as strange alien beings from another world, but as participants in the same world to which the people also belong.* (Tim Ingold. From Trust to Domination)
>
> *If you prick us, do we not bleed? if you tickle us, do we not laugh? if you poison us, do we not die?* (Merchant of Venice Act 3. sc. I)
>
> *Man is not a god, nor in any imminent danger of becoming one. He is not a celestial star-babe dropped down among mundane matters for a time and endowed with wing possibilities and the anatomy of a deity.* (J.Howard Moore. The Universal Kinship.)

Throughout this book I have challenged the apparently widespread view that the particular capacities of Homo sapiens make our species superior to others. Further, I have argued that the perception of man as being set apart from other animals by his special abilities is mistaken. Not only are differing capacities unproblematic in many personal relationships but they often play an important role in the formation of mutually beneficial partnerships. Having argued strongly for the importance of relationships, I suggest that the introspective self-consciousness regarded by many philosophers as man's most important feature, is not necessarily more valuable than an ability to live in harmony with one another and the rest of the world. Indeed, it may well be that self-consciousness can itself be an obstacle to this harmony, since only a self-conscious species could have invented the myths about its own importance that have always been so popular among humans.

Uniquely among species, man is able to consider what sort of being he wants to be and all too often the answer has been that he hungers for an importance, a significance, a value, denied to any other species. This special status is often claimed through myths that portray man as not really belonging to — or with — the other species but as having some special essence which can somehow be detached from the natural world. The most obvious version of this view is the myth of an immortal soul. Although this is not put forward as such by any of the philosophers that I have discussed here, an element of it — the notion of man as an essentially cerebral being in contrast to other animals which are seen as merely bodies — seems to linger in the 'personhood' theory, discussed in Chapter One. In this final section I will therefore return briefly to the views of John Harris to examine some of their implications in the light of the arguments I have put forward in the intervening chapters.

John Harris wants to be able to identify which beings might be 'persons' in order that he should know how to treat them. It is important to him that the criteria be 'species neutral'[1], so as not to exclude the possibility of non-human 'persons'. The likelihood of non-human animals qualifying as persons, however, is, for Harris, remote, since language use is an essential component of the sort of introspective self-consciousness he requires and Washoe is the only non-human candidate he mentions. This by no means limits Harris's class of possible non-human persons to one, though, since he entertains the possibility of a much more promising source:

> ... the question of whether there are people on other planets is a real one. If there are, we need not expect them to be human people. ... nor need we expect them to look or sound or smell (or anything else) like us. They might not even be organic, but might perhaps reproduce by mechanical construction rather than by genetic reproduction ...[2]

---

[1]   Harris 1985: 18
[2]   Harris 1985: 9

Nonetheless, says Harris, if we can identify them as *persons* '[w]e will be deciding whether an appropriate response to them would be to have them for dinner in one sense or the other.'[3]

The most extraordinary thing about this claim is Harris's confidence that the presence or absence of self-consciousness is the deciding factor that makes a being either suitable as a dinner guest or of no more moral significance than a potato. Yet, although there are many questions that one might consider in drawing up the guest list for a dinner party, the matter of self-consciousness is not likely to be among them. We want our guests to get on well together, to enjoy each other's company and the meal that we can provide. We must consider whether it would be tactless to invite Jane as well as her ex-lover and whether Tom will be happy with a vegetarian meal. If Fido can be trusted not to cadge titbits there is no reason why he should not be included — at least he won't bore us with shaggy dog stories or talk with his mouth full.

But what about Harris's extraterrestrial guests? If, as Harris suggests, they are 'mechanical constructions', they won't need feeding, but that is just the beginning of our difficulties with them. It is not only that, as we tuck into our meal they will be oiling their joints or plugging into the mains to recharge their batteries, but that we won't be able to make anything of them at all. If, as Harris also suggests, they do not reproduce as we do, they will presumably be devoid of the desires, emotions and attachments that human sexuality and child bearing entail. Perhaps they won't age either; perhaps their mechanical construction will be indestructible. But if this is so, it is not just their suitability as dinner guests that is in question. How will we apply Harris's injunction that our duty to persons is to protect their welfare and wishes, especially their wish to go on living? If they are indestructible, impervious to disease or damage, do not know pain or fear, love or anger, how can we respond to them at all? And of more immediate concern, perhaps — how will they respond to us?

Harris expresses the hope that his extraterrestrial dinner guests will be persuaded '... that we are also people, not just like them maybe, but enough like them to be valuable, and to warrant being accorded the same concern, respect and protection as they

---

[3]   Harris 1985: 10

would show to each other.'[4] But the 'concern, respect and protection' they show to each other is not going to be much help to us. Harris has not explained how, if *they* are indestructible, devoid of our emotions and human attachments, if pain and distress are unknown to them, they could know — or come to care — that these considerations are not just *important* to us but that our existence depends upon them, or even, I might say, that they *are* our existence.

Harris assumes that there will be some way in which we can communicate with these beings but this seems over optimistic. They qualify as 'persons' simply by virtue of their being capable of introspection, but introspection is of no use at all here. The possibility of our being able to detect their introspective ability and so identify them as 'persons' seems remote. The possibility of their identifying us as 'persons' before they have inadvertently — or even advertently — destroyed us, seems remoter still.

Even if we put aside these objections, how could we possibly communicate with them? Even if they had a language, there would be no possibility of our learning it and using it to express to them the things that matter to us, since their language would have no place for human hopes, fears, joys or pains.

We are not brains in vats but flesh and blood social mammals. Like all others of our kind we are vulnerable both physically and psychologically and social living depends on all parties recognising the others' vulnerability. The ability to recognise vulnerability and respond appropriately to it cannot be less important than the ability to introspect or to recognise introspection in others. Nor is it either an exclusively human ability or an exclusively intra-specific one.

Harris dismisses as 'soggy sentimentality' the human protective response 'classically evoked by proximity to dependent sentient creatures ...'. Presumably he would be glad to find no such response amongst his extraterrestrial friends. Beings which 're-produce by mechanical construction' will not start out as helpless infants, stagger about as toddlers, agonise over their acne as teenagers or decline into the tottering frailty of old age. If the vulnerability of our infants and others did not evoke a protective response in us they would not survive, but it would be a mistake

---

[4]   Harris 1985: 10

to argue that this is a *reason* for our protectiveness, any more than it is for all the other animals who respond to the vulnerability of *their* infants in the same way. Caring for one another, and responding to one anther's vulnerability is not so much what we *do* as what we *are* — and by 'we' I mean all those creatures that share this characteristic. Nor are human beings the only creatures to extend these protective responses to the vulnerable of other species. Whenever I have shared a stable with a horse for the night my anxiety has been, not that I might be trodden on as I slept, but that the horse would be deprived of a proper night's sleep by her insistence on standing guard over me as if I were a foal. Harris might dismiss the animal's behaviour as 'soggy sentimentality'; I offer it as just one example of the ability of other animals to recognise humans as 'creatures like them' in one of the most important ways of all.

Kant's observation that 'we love animals for we see how great is their care of their young' is much more plausible than the personhood theory which entails that we show persons 'concern, respect and protection' because they introspect. And I would add that we love best those which, unburdened with the prejudices of philosophers, extend their care and affection to us.

Clearly it is the other social mammals which are best suited to be our companions and friends. Within this group — our own group — are those who can live with us, work with us, eat, play and sleep with us: who can be trusted not only with our lives but those of our children, too. What matters here is not whether they can *reflect* on their births, lives and inevitable deaths but that they, like us, *are* born, grow up, grow old and eventually die and all this as part of a community. Creatures which do not live socially or rear their young lack the capacities most important for the development of relationships and although they may become tame and live contentedly alongside us they cannot relate to us as social mammals can and do. This does not, however, make them alien to us. Even frogs and turtles are, if not born, at least spawned or hatched, grow to maturity, find mates, breed, become old and die. They too, as Shylock said of his people, are 'warmed and cooled by the same winter and summer' as we are. What matters is that we have all evolved to live and die on earth as part of one essentially inter-connected whole.

The philosophers whose work I have challenged, although representing a very broad spectrum of often opposing views, are united by a common belief that there is one feature that identifies 'us' as special and superior to 'them'. The choice of key features ranges from language and self-consciousness to membership of the human species but not one of these philosophers has seriously questioned the assumption that 'we' are at the top of a hierarchy in which all other beings are closer or further below us 'in proportion to the resemblance between them and ourselves' as Singer puts it.

Whilst not denying that language use and the intellectual abilities which go with it do indeed make Homo sapiens a very remarkable animal, I have challenged the view that these qualities make him a superior animal in any objective sense or that they entitle him to regard the lives of others as being at his disposal. I would rather say that his special abilities entail not special privileges but special responsibilities and that if persons have a unique awareness of the consequences of their actions, then persons have a unique responsibility for their actions.

So what of the question 'are they like us?', which, at the beginning of Chapter One, I identified as a common theme running through the views I set out to challenge? The answer, of course, is that it all depends on how we define ourselves. Those who define 'us' by our ability to introspect give a distorted view of what is important to and about human beings and ignore the fact that many creatures are like us in more significant ways in that we all share the vulnerability, the pains, the fears and the joys that are the life of social animals.

# References

Beardsmore, R.W. (1996), 'If a Lion could Talk' in *Wittgenstein and the Philosophy of Culture*, ed. K.S. Johannson and T. Nordamstam. Holder-Lichler-Tempsky. Vienna.

Bentham, Jeremy (1798), *Introduction to the Principles of Morals and Legislation*.

Blixen, K. [Isak Dinesen] (1987), *Out of Africa*. Penguin. Harmondsworth.

Budiansky, Stephen (1998), *If a Lion could Talk*. Weidenfeld and Nicolson. London.

Candland, Douglas Keith (1993), *Feral Children and Clever Animals*. Oxford University Press.

Carruthers, Peter (1989), 'Brute Experience', *Journal of Philosophy* LXXXVI: 258–69.

Carruthers, Peter (1992), *The Animals Issue*. Cambridge University Press.

Clark, Stephen (1977), *The Moral Status of Animals*. Oxford University Press.

Clark, Stephen (1994), 'Companions on the Way. Critical Notice', *Philosophical Quarterly* 44 (174): 90–100.

Clark, Stephen (1997), *Animals and their Moral Standing*. Routledge. London.

Cockburn, David (1990), *Other Human Beings*. Macmillan. London.

Cockburn, David (1994), 'Human Beings and Giant Squids', *Philosophy* 69: 135–50.

Dawkins, Richard (1986), *The Blind Watchmaker*. Longman. London.

Darwin, Charles (1872), *The Expression of Emotion in Man and Animals*.

Deacon. Terrence (1997), *The Symbolic Species*. Penguin. Harmondsworth.

DeGrazia (1991), 'The Distinction between Equality in Moral Status and Deserving Equal Consideration', *Between the Species*. Spring.

DeGrazia (1991), 'Response (to Squadrito)', *Between the Species*. Spring: 79–80.

Dennett, Daniel (1996), *Kinds of Minds*. Weidenfeld and Nicolson. London.
Finkelkraut, Alain (2000), *In the Name of Humanity*. Columbia University Press. New York.
Fox, Michael W. (1971), *Behaviour of Wolves, Dogs and Related Canids*. Harper and Row.
Fox, Michael W. (1980), *Returning to Eden; Animal Rights and Human Responsibility*. Viking. New York.
Frey, R.G. (1980), *Interests and Rights; The Case Against Animals*. Clarendon Press Oxford.
Frey, R.G. (1983), *Rights, Killing and Suffering*. Blackwell Oxford.
van Lawick, Jane [Jane Goodall] (1971, *In the Shadow of Man*. Collins. London.
Godwin, William (1793), *An Enquiry concerning Political Justice*.
Hampshire, Stuart (1959), *Thought and Action*. Chatto and Windus. London.
Hare, R.M. (1999), 'Why I am a demi-vegetarian', in *Singer and his Critics*, ed. Dale Jamieson. Blackwell Oxford.
Harris, John (1985), *The Value of Life*. Routledge and Kegan Paul. London.
Harris, John (1998), 'Four Legs Good, Two Legs Better', *Res Publica* 4.1: 51–8.
Hearne, Vicki (1987), *Adam's Task*. Heinemann London.
Hume, David (1904), *Essays*. Grant Richards. London.
Ingold, Tim ed. (1988), *What is an Animal?* Unwin, Hyman, London.
Ingold, Tim (1994), 'From Trust to Domination' in *Animals and Human Society*, ed. anning and Serpell.
Jamieson, Dale ed. (1999), *Singer and his Critics*. Blackwell. Oxford.
Johnson, Samuel (1963), *Prose and Poetry*, selected Mona Wilson. Hart-David. London.
Johnston, Bruce (1995), *Harnessing Thought: The Guide Dog*. Lennard N.J.
Kant. I (1924), 'Duties towards Animals and Spirits', *Lectures on Ethics*.
Kavanagh, J. Lee (1967), 'Behaviour of Captive White-footed Mice', *Science* 155: 1623-39.
Kennedy, J.S. (1992), *The New Anthropomorphism*. Cambridge University Press.
Kiley-Worthington, Marthe (1997), *The Behaviour of Horses*. J.A. Allen. London.
Leahy, Michael (1991), *Against Liberation*. Routledge London.
Leahy, Michael (1996), 'Brute Equivocation' in *The Liberation Debate*, ed. M. Leahy and D. Cohn-Sherbok. Routledge. London.
Leopold, Aldo (1949), *A Sand County Alamac*. Oxford University Press.
Levi, Primo (2000), *If This Is a Man*, transl. Stuart Woolf. Folio Society. London.
Levinas, Emmanuel (1990), *Difficult Freedom: Essays on Judaism*, transl Sean Hand. Johns Hopkins Baltimore.

Linden, Eugene (1986), *Silent Partners. The Legacy of the Ape-language Experiments*. Times Books. New York.
Maclean, Anne (1993), *The Elimination of Morality*. Routledge. London.
MacIntyre, Alasdair (1999), *Dependent Rational Animals*. Duckworth London.
Magee, Bryan and Milligan, Martin (1995), *On Blindness*. Oxford University Press.
Malcolm, Norman (1986), *Nothing is Hidden*. Blackwell. Oxford.
Menzel, Emil W. (1990), 'Kohler and Studies of Animal Intelligence' in *Understanding Chimpanzees*, ed. Heitner and Marquardt. Harvard University Press.
Midgley, Mary (1979), *Beast and Man*. Cornell University Press. Ithaca.
Midgley, Mary (1983), *Animals and Why They Matter*. Penguin. Harmondsworth.
Quiatt, Duane and Reynolds, Vernon (1993), *Primate Behaviour*. Cambridge University Press.
Regan, Tom (1983), *The Case for Animal Rights*. Routledge and Kegan Paul London.
Rollin, Bernard (1989), *The Unheeded Cry*. Oxford University Press.
Ryder, Richard D. (1985), 'Speciesism in the Laboratory' in *In Defence of Animals*, ed. P. Singer. Blackwell. Oxford.
Ryder, Richard D. (1975), *Victims of Science*. Davis-Poynter.London.
Searle, John (1983), *Intentionality*. Cambridge University Press.
Searle, John (1998), Animal Minds. *Etica and Animali*. 9: 37–50.
Serpell, James (1986), *In the Company of Animals*. Blackwell. Oxford.
Singer, Peter (1976), *Animal Liberation* Jonathan Cape. London.
Singer, Peter (1981), *The Expanding Circle* Oxford University Press.
Singer, Peter and Cavalieri, Paola ed. (1993), *The Great Ape Project*. Fourth Estate London.
Singer, Peter ed. (1981), *In Defence of Animals*. Blackwell. London.
Singer, Peter (1997),*Practical Ethics*, 2nd ed. Cambridge University Press.
Squadrito, Kathy (1991), 'Commentary. Interests and Equal Moral Status', *Between the Species*. Spring: 78–9.
Stamp Dawkins, Marion (1998), *Through Our Eyes Only?* Oxford University Press.
Wall, Patrick (1999), *Pain, The Science of Suffering*. Weidenfeld and Nicolson London.
Wittgenstein, L. (1953), *Philosophical Investigations*. Blackwell Oxford.
Wittgenstein, L. (1980), *Remarks on the Philosophy of Psychology*. Blackwell. Oxford.

# *Index*

animals,
  and consciousness, 81–2, 99–103 Chapter 4 *passim*
  and contractualism, 123–8
  their interests, 118–21
  their understanding us, 195–215
  our understanding them, 169–195
anthropocentrism, 3–4, Chapter 1 *passim*, 159–167, Chapter 5 *passim*,
  see also: 'like us', 'us-ism' and 'superiority of man over animals'
anthropomorphism, 159–167
apes,
  their inability to form relationships with us, Chapter 3 *passim*
  and language, 81–3, 99–108, 170

Bateson Report, The, 167
Beardsmore, R. vi, 151–2, 170–6
Bentham, Jeremy, 98, 130, 190
British Union for the Abolition of Vivisection, 16, 17, 18
Budiansky, Stephen, 95, 103–4

Carroll, Lewis, 68, 70
Carruthers, Peter, 121–9, 158, 182, 211
Cartesianism, 151, 159–67, 172–4, 189–90, 205
chickens, 34–7, 77

Clark, Stephen, vi, 2, 43, 62, 101–2, 145, 153–4, 159–60, 185, 190
Clever Hans, 212–4
Cockburn, D. vi, 176–83, 189, 200
criterion of equal consideration of interests, 52

Darwin, Charles, 100–1, 103
Dawkins, Marian Stamp, 30, 155–6
Deacon, Terrence, 188, 213
DeGrazia, R. 7 ,8, 11, 25–32, 37, 38, 47
Dennett, Daniel, 102–3, 105–6, 188
Dickens, Charles, 63
Dinensen, Isak, 97–8
dogs,
  their ability to live with us, Chapter 3 *passim*, 195–215
  see also partnership, self-consciousness, trust.
dolphins, 73, 93

elephants 73
  understanding of death 154–5

Fox, Michael W. 38–9
Frey, R. 7, 8, 27, 33–7, 38–40, 41, 76, 114–121, 166

Godwin, Fenelon and the chambermaid, 50–2, 79
Goodall, Jane, 86, 92
'Good Samaritan', 51

Hampshire, Stuart, 142-4, 150
Harlow, Harry, 164
Harris, John, 7-20, 37, 110, 205, 216-22
Hearne, Vicki, 87, 107, 209
horses 21, 25, 29, 94, 96, 191-202, 212-214, 221
House of Lords Select Committee on Animals in Scientific Procedures, 15-18
Hume, David, 38, 113

imagination used by Singer as a means of establishing differences in value, 20-5
impartiality and neighbourliness, 56-68
Ingold, Tim, 72, 210

Johnson, Samuel, 67
Johnston, Bruce, 88

Kant, Immanuel, 127, 129-32, 221
Kennedy, J.S. 161-165
Kiley-Worthington, Marthe, 197-200

La Mettrie, J.O. De, 83 , 86, 107
Language,
    and relationships, 81-3
    and the possibility of mental suffering, 142-59
Leahy, Michael, 133-58, 165, 166, 170, 174
Lecky, W.E.H. 62
Leopold, Aldo, 41-2
Levi, Primo, 111-2
Levinas, Emmanuel, 112
'like us' as a criterion of moral status, Chapter 1 *passim*
Linden, Eugene, 106-7
Locke, John, 9
Lorenz, Konrad, 85-6

MacIntyre, Alasdair, 48-50
MacLean, Ann, 14, 51-2
Magee, Bryan, 23-4
Malcolm, Norman, 172-5

mental suffering, 142-159
Menzel, Eric W. 187
Midgley, Mary vi, 2, 87, 104-5, 149, 189
Mill, J.S. 24-5
Milligan, Martin, 23-4

pain and suffering, 3, 10-19, 125-8, 133-42, 200-5
partnership with animals, 73-8, 86-7, 195-215
personhood, Chapter 1 *passim*,
    and language, 81-3, 110-1
    and non-human persons, 218-22
pets, 70-2, 76, 77
pleasure, 3

Quiatt, D. 95

rationality as a criterion of personhood, 20.
rats, 61, 66, 166
    as pets, 62
    learning from the experience of others, 155-6
Regan, T. 7, 27, 31-3, 37, 40-7, 50, 63, 165
Reynolds, V. 95
Rollin, Bernard, 35, 141-2, 157-8
Ryder, R. vi, 71

Saki, 215
self-consciousness, chapter 1 *passim*, 99-108
Searle, John, 115, 160-1 , 165-6
Serpell, James, 61, 70-2
Singer, Peter, 7, 8, 19-25, 41, 47, 55-69, 78-9, Chapter 3 *passim*, 146, 186, 190, 200-1
speciesism, 4, 7, 58-68
Squadrito, Kathy, 27, 38, 47
superiority of man over animals, 2, 3. Chapter 1 *passim*

Tinbergen, N. 115-6
'totting up' as a criterion of the value of a life, 25-33
trust, 108-10

value of life, Chapter 1 *passim*
vivisection, 37

Wall, Patrick, 202–5
Wittgenstein, L. 136, 143, 151–2, 170–6, 214

uniqueness of human beings, 16, 18
'us-ism', Chapter 1 *passim*